THE AUTOBIOGRAPHY

The Life and Crimes of

FRANK ROSTRON

From Poverty to Paradise
and Nearly Everything In Between

All rights reserved. No part of this publication may be reproduced in whole or in part, or stored in a retrieval system, or transmitted in any form or by any means, electronic, mechanical, photocopying, recording, or otherwise, without written permission of the author, except for the inclusion of brief quotations in a review.

Copyright © 2022 by Frank Rostron

For information regarding permission, please write to:
info@barringerpublishing.com
Barringer Publishing, Naples, Florida
www.barringerpublishing.com

Cover, graphics, and layout by Linda S. Duider
Cape Coral, Florida

ISBN: 978-1-954396-27-2
Library of Congress Cataloging-in-Publication Data
The Life and Crimes of Frank Rostron / Frank Rostron

Printed in U.S.A.

The Life and Crimes of FRANK ROSTRON

Many, many, times over the years after telling stories at dinner, on the beach, in a bar with friends or with strangers, they have always said you must write a book. Even this week, I met a couple at the bar in Osteria Tulia, an Italian restaurant here in Naples, who said they were from Philadelphia. We started talking; I told them that my wife was from Philadelphia. They asked how we met and how I arrived in Naples. Five minutes later, he said, "You must write a book." Only a few weeks ago, an old pal of mine who I had not spoken to for over twenty years found me on social media. The first thing he said was that I still tell that story all the time about you in Majorca. You must write a book. Hundreds of people in between have said the same, so a year ago when COVID-19 arrived, Jane said, "Now you have lots of time on your hands, why don't you write THE BOOK." I went to Best Buys and bought a laptop and here we are—THE BOOK has begun. It's my life story from poverty to paradise but with a few stories and experiences included. These will probably never happen in most people's lives, but I was fortunate, or some might say unfortunate to have them occur in my life. I think that you might find them interesting.

DEDICATION

I dedicate this book to my mother, Lena Rostron, who put this show on the road. First, giving birth to me on New Year's Day, and then giving me the material to make my first shirts. She worked sixteen hours a day to provide the best of everything she could afford, so I wouldn't feel insecure with respect to the other boys in town. This insured that I felt the same way the rest of my life.

To my sister's children Carol, Bernie, Terry, Deborah, Paddy, and my great niece, Hannah, who looked after and visited my mum every day of her life whilst I was away so much. Last, but not least, my beautiful wife, Jane, who picked up the reins after Lena passed away and has been taking care of me ever since, which, as most of my friends know, is an impossible task but she is doing a great job.

Thank you to them all.

ACKNOWLEDGEMENTS

It's been a privilege and a blessing to have so many people wanting to help and guide me throughout my life for no personal gain. To take me from the streets of a council estate in Middleton to my retirement in paradise here in Naples, Florida. Don Wilson, my schoolteacher and friend from when I was eleven years old until he passed away in 2003, at the age of 73, who taught me right from wrong. Millie Demmy, the mother of my friends and mentors, Selwyn and Harvey Demmy, who found me in John Michael Menswear as a sixteen-year-old and told everyone that one day I would "make it big." Mr. Alan Gallagher, my manager at John Michael, who trusted me and gave me that job and taught me to sell and all about the rich and successful people in Manchester that I never knew existed. Mike Summerbee who had enough confidence in me to set me up in my first business and become my partner. Paul J. Hanly Jr. who walked into my shop and into my life and changed it forever, taking me to New York, introducing me to all his friends, and the rest is history. Without Paul Hanly there is no book or paradise.

I also want to take this opportunity to apologize to the people I have hurt and abused mentally and physically, male and female, friends and enemies.

HARRY CONNICK, JR.
Singer, Pianist, Composer and Actor
"My dad was the DA for New Orleans and would not go to work unless he was wearing one of Frank's shirts."

EDWARD HAYES
Lawyer, Journalist and Actor
"No one can make an upper class English spread collar like Frank Rostron can which is amusing since he's up from the streets of Manchester."

SIR HAROLD EVANS
Journalist and Author
"What's a lad from Middleton doing in New York selling made-to-measure shirts . . . what's a lad from Newton Heath doing in New York that he can afford made-to-measure shirts."

ANTHONY SCARAMUCCI
Founder and Managing Partner of SkyBridge Capital and the former White House Director of Communications
"Frank is a brilliant shirt maker and a cunning entrepreneur. I always saw him as the James Bond of tailors. I always looked forward to him coming to New York, he has such great charisma and charm."

PAUL STEWART
Former Manchester City, Spurs, Liverpool and England Soccer Star
"When Frankie walks into a room you know he's there, funny, daft as a brush but one of the most entertaining and lovable rogues I have had the pleasure of knowing for a long time. I cannot wait to read this book."

BILLY SCHWER
Former British, Commonwealth, European and World Light Welterweight Boxing Champion

"Having known Frank for many years with all the mutual connections that we have from all around the world from all walks of life his story from poverty to paradise is a must read, the title says it all."

JIMMY SWORDS
Former Professional Boxer, Author, Alleged Gangster and Leader of The Quality Street Gang

"Frank played football for our team The New Cross Motors and what a player he was. But we could look forward on a cold, wet Sunday morning a Miss England or a model cheering him on from the touchline. Even though his day job was mixing with Lords and Ladies he mixed easily with us . . . he was one of our own."

LORD JOEL BARNETT
Former Politician and Chief Secretary to the Treasury

"Besides Frank being a gentleman's shirt maker he was also a perfect gentleman. Once when a restaurant had mixed up my reservation he gave me and Lady Barnett his booth and he waited until a table became available."

MIKE SCOTT
Former Sheriff of Lee County, Florida

"A special thanks to our friend and Honorary Lee County Deputy Frank Rostron for his unwavering commitment to this noble cause. The Frank Rostron Golf Invitational for Make-a-Wish of Southern Florida."

I decided, very early on, just to accept life unconditionally; I never expected it to do anything special for me, yet I seemed to accomplish far more than I had ever hoped. Most of the time it just happened to me without my ever seeking it.

~ Audrey Hepburn

Growing Up in Middleton

I have always felt unusual and been treated differently than most of the lads I grew up with starting on 1st January 1950, New Year's Day. I was the only baby born the whole of that day in Middleton, a town just outside Manchester, in the industrial north of England. Our council house was like most of the others—two bedrooms, one bathroom but no toilet. It was in the back yard and there were two rooms downstairs, a lounge and a kitchen. Under the stairs was a cupboard with coin operated meters to put shillings in for gas and electricity. So, often, we could be watching TV or my mum cooking and the electric or gas would go out. Then someone, usually me, had to rush with a flashlamp to put a coin in so the gas or electricity started again. Beside that special day for Lena and Fred Rostron, my parents, I will say throughout the book of all the other times, I felt that I was treated in special, different, lucky and even privileged ways from everyone else that I grew up with.

The early days were the same for everyone; we didn't know we were poor because we all lived in the same council houses.

All our parents had the same job and we didn't know anyone who was rich, so we didn't know any difference, but life was good. I was born in our council house with a mid-wife not delivering me in a hospital like most kids which was different. My mum, Lena, worked in a cotton mill like most of the people in our town weaving cotton which I will come back to later. I was born as I said on New Year's Day, 1950, at 9 Byron Road, Boarshaw, Middleton, just outside Manchester. My mum, Lena, worked at the Cromer Ring Mill from the age of fourteen and my dad, Fred, worked as a fire beater, working nights stoking furnaces up with coal to keep the factory powered.

I was named after my maternal grandad who also worked at the Cromer Ring Mill weaving cotton. I had two siblings, Maureen who was born eleven years before me and Edith, eight years later. Three years before I arrived on the scene, Edith died as a baby which was quite common in those days and my sister, Maureen, who like most girls where we came from, got pregnant at the age of sixteen and left home. I didn't really remember any siblings. I always felt like I was the only child and Lena spoilt me and bought me everything she could afford. Maureen died when she was sixty-two years old. She was an amputee like my dad, and both had poor lifestyles—diets with smoking; it was probably diabetes.

Byron Road was a cul-de-sac of sixteen houses, and everyone knew each other like family. They used to leave their doors unlocked all day so you could just walk in if you needed to borrow any milk or sugar. Our next-door neighbors, Mr.

and Mrs. Jessop, I used to call Uncle Jack and Auntie Alice. Their daughter, Winnie, was like a sister and still is to this day. She took me to my first football match when I was eight years old with her then boyfriend, Terry Kerr, and of course it was Manchester City. I can remember going on the bus with her like it was yesterday and looking out of the windows at the crowds. As we got nearer to the ground, I had never seen so many people in my life. Her husband to be, Terry, was a joiner and did the build out of my original office in Corporation St., Manchester, and then my other four retail stores over the next twenty years, plus all the carpentry at the houses I owned during that time.

As a kid, the memories are vague, but I remember at night a bell ringing and looking out of the window with excitement because that meant it was either the rag and bone man or the black pea man. To the rag and bone man, you would usually take your old clothes or any junk and he would give you in exchange a goldfish or a donkey stone so my mum could clean our front doorstep. I had many goldfish but they always died within a couple of weeks, so the cycle started again.

The black pea man used to have an urn-like barrel full of very hot black peas and you brought your own cup or mug and he would fill it up. They were great—so warming and filling on a cold Lancashire night. It was during these years that I remember other things like Whit Sunday. It was always in May and mums used to buy you new clothes. You would go to all your aunties and uncles on the street plus all your real aunties and uncles and show them your new clothes and they would give you money. It was a great day and my first memory of a good little earner.

I remember that in summer, we would go swimming in the Manchester ship canal near our house and we loved it. There might be thirty or forty kids swimming and diving in at the locks. We thought nothing of diving head-first into a dead dog or dead kittens that people used to throw in because they couldn't afford to keep them, or even a cow that was rotting at the bottom of the canal. Yet, we never seemed to be ill like kids are today.

Then later, on Whit Sunday, there would be a parade-style carnival in the town and all the churches, boy scouts, girl guides, and other local groups would be represented. It was an annual thing that I used to look forward to not necessarily because of the new clothes or the parade but the money that I would get. I never realized it but that is where the love of a few quid must have started.

One thing I hated and that was so embarrassing was that every 1st January, our local newspaper, *The Middleton Guardian,* used to put my birthday in the paper because I was the only baby born on that day, 1950. Happy Birthday, Francis William Rostron. I was known as Frank and hated Francis William but I was reminded of it every year and I dreaded it. At the Millennium, 2000, the newspaper contacted Lena to ask if she would be interviewed about me since it was exactly fifty years since I was born, using the heading 'Where Is He

Now.' She couldn't wait to tell them with pride all about her successful son even though not once did she ever tell me. We were not that kind of family; we didn't hug or kiss or say we loved each other. It was only later on in Lena's life that I did hug her and tell her that I loved her. Even then, she shrugged or moved away like she was embarrassed. So, when the reporter went to Lena's apartment in Middleton to interview her, she couldn't wait to tell them about my success. She talked all about my shirt business and my house in Majorca, my cars, my trips on business to America and she said, and I quote, "He's even had me on the Concorde twice" as if I had to drag her on it. She told him that I now live in Wilmslow, Cheshire, with my partner, Fiona, and daughter, Elle, but we spend the summer at my house in Majorca and every Christmas in Barbados. She gave him the whole story and was proud but, as I said, she never once told me how proud she was.

Another thing that happened about this time was that my dad started to have health issues. The blood circulation in his toes on one foot stopped. The doctors said it was a blood clot and he had to have one toe amputated. Then, all was good for about another year when it started again in his other toes on the same foot and he had those amputated. The same happened about a year later with the circulation in his foot so they cut his foot off at his ankle. I seemed to be going as a young kid with Lena every night on two bus rides to the Northern Hospital in Cheetham Hill, just outside Manchester, visiting my dad who was having amputations every year or so on a regular basis.

Then, it was below his knee as the blood clot moved slowly up his leg then the rest of his leg to total five amputations on one leg. Things seemed alright for a while after that. Then, a few years later, it all started again in his other foot. The doctors told him they needed to amputate his other foot and he said no way was he going through all that again and that they must take his leg off in one go.

So, they did and from one prosthetic leg now it was two but he was mainly in a wheelchair. In between all this, Fred still worked the last few years. Whilst with one leg, he worked all night as a watchman for housing developments that were being built at an alarming rate around the town and beyond. He would sit all night inside and outside of a wooden hut, with a big fire burning, guarding all the bricks, tools, machinery and appliances on site that otherwise would be stolen by local thieves, trying to get a few quid the only way that they knew how. So, after years of going to the hospital with Lena every night, now we were going to half-built housing estates, taking my dad's dinner. This was usually meat and potato pie that Lena had made in a dish with a rag cloth wrapped around it to keep it warm until we got there. It's funny but I remember this so well and years later, I had friends living in these same houses that I knew as they were being built.

I was going to school until I was eleven years old at Boarshaw Junior School—a council school near my house. It was fun. We played football in the yard every day and learned the basics of most things as a kid. I met boys on our "estate" that became my friends throughout my teenage years and longer and some are still friends today. After Boarshaw Junior School, it was to Moorclose County Secondary Modern School with the big lads.

It was here that I met my schoolteacher and hero, Don Wilson. He had played pro soccer as a junior with Manchester United and had a great fourteen-year career with Bury Football Club. He was a no-nonsense, tough tackling halfback who took no prisoners and when his career was over, he became a schoolteacher. I didn't know this until years later, but he had heard about my sporting ability and when he knew I was coming to Moorclose, he fixed it so I was in his House of York. So, I played football, basketball and athletics for him. Don used to walk around the school and playground in white short-sleeved sports shirts, white shorts and white ankle socks and he always had a suntan. So, along with his great physique, not only did all the girls like him but all the boys who played soccer did also.

He was a tough guy and I remember one day someone came up to him in the gym and said that an ex-pupil was waiting at the gates to have a word with him. The guy was now about twenty-two years old and thought he was a gangster and a hard man. His kid brother had told him that Don Wilson had been giving him a hard time at school, so he had come to threaten and straighten Don out. Don went to the gates with all of us watching from a distance. He walked straight up to this so-called tough guy and without saying a word knocked him spark out. It was unbelievable and taught us and any other ex or current pupils not to mess with Don Wilson.

Dai Bevan was his partner in crime, and also our PE teacher. Dai played professional rugby for Oldham RUFC, Wales and Great Britain, and these two were unbelievable. They joked about women and taught me everything I needed to know as an eleven to fifteen-year-old about sport and life in general. They used to hug you when you did good and beat you literally when you didn't try or played badly. These two were my heroes and friends long after I left school—even after many beatings sometimes drawing blood that today a teacher would be sacked or even jailed for. But that's how it was in those days. I had great respect for them both, particularly Don who became my friend for the rest of his life. I would take him and his wife, Flo, to every VIP opening night of every new restaurant and club that opened in Manchester that I was privileged to be invited to. I used to have my friend and mentor, millionaire bookmaker, Selwyn Demmy, send his Rolls-Royce and chauffeur to pick them up and take them to and from all these occasions.

All this time, I loved to share my success and the many privileges that I started having in my life with friends from Middleton and still do today with those friends from England and around the world who don't have homes in paradise. In later years, unfortunately, some have taken advantage of me and my generosity and I know that deep down they have been jealous, so I have had to let a few of them go.

I would see Don all the time until he passed away at seventy-three. I was with him at his house a few weeks before he died and he looked bad with the chemo for his cancer. He said to me, "Rossi, this is the only bad card he's ever dealt me. I have had a great life and I have no complaints." What a man. I still today have photos of Don and me in my house. Over 500 people went to his funeral which speaks volumes for what a man he was. Don was my math and PE teacher. Needless-to-say, I was good at both because he was teaching me and if he had taught me history and geography, I would have excelled at those also.

Lena was still working at the mill five days a week and Saturday mornings. She would work all the hours they would let her because she needed the money. She would then come home, cook dinner for me and my dad, do all the shopping, clean the house, wash the dishes and wash and iron our clothes. In the morning, she would wash and dress my dad then get me ready for the nursery. Then she would go to work and start all over again. She bought our clothes but made her own and she didn't stop for one minute. Her life was me, my dad and working. It's unbelievable to even contemplate what she went through. I didn't realize or appreciate until I grew up what a superhuman being she was. I just took her and everything she did for granted, but later on, I did everything I could to make it up to her—impossible but I tried.

Two or three nights a week, she would push my dad in his wheelchair half a mile to the Cotton Tree Inn, the pub he used to go to, drop him off, and go back for him at the end of the night. She used to pick him up and push him home. Sometimes, she would bring me a bag of "crisps," or potato chips and I would have them on bread and butter. It was a real treat like the black peas. During the day, my dad would sit in his wheelchair at our front door talking to anyone who was passing by. He must have been so lonely at home all day. He had nothing to do and no one to speak with. We didn't have a telephone or television at this time, only a radio. Many times, I would arrive home from school and my dad would have Jehovah's Witnesses or Mormons in the house, sitting on the sofa with a cup of tea in their hand. They were thinking they could convert him and his family not knowing he was having them keep him company until we got home.

By this time, after going to my first football match with Winnie Jessop, I got the football bug. It completely took over my life and I was only eight years old. We played every night until it was dark and even later under the streetlamps. That was until my mum shouted for me to come in for bed and even then, I didn't always do it until I was threatened with the brush handle or slipper—then I knew she was serious.

Our local newsagent was owned by an ex-soccer player who played in the FA Cup finals of 1951 and 1952 for Newcastle United. His name was Tommy Walker. I would be in his shop all the time talking to him about his career and playing at grounds like Manchester United, Manchester City, Liverpool, and, of course, Wembley Stadium. It was then I knew I was going to be a professional football player—not want to be but I was going to be and why not? I was a better player than any of my pals and most people in our town. I played for Middleton Boys that consisted of the best players from each school in Middleton, representing our town. I played for Middleton Boys for two years when everyone else played for only one year which was their limit. That's how much better I was than the others. So that was it. I was going to be rich and famous and girls never came into it. I just wanted to be a footballer. I was going to buy a house for my mum and that is all I wanted, so we could live together forever.

When Lena died, in her box where she used to keep all her private papers, along with my first driving license and my expired passport, she had a letter that I wrote. It was in pencil, and I must have been eight or nine-years old when I wrote it. It's very faded but it was an essay we had to write at school titled, "When I Grow Up." It says, "When I grow up, I am going to be a footballer, I am going to play for Manchester City and I want to be a goalkeeper; when I grow up, I am not going to get married, I am going to buy a house for me and my mum and dad to live in." I have copied this from the letter but it's so faded I cannot read the rest and so football was all that I lived for during these years.

Tommy Walker even organized a trial for me at Stoke City which then was a top professional soccer team, and the youth team coach was Alan Ball Sr., the dad of the famous World cup star, Alan Ball. Later on in life, I got to know Alan Ball Jr. very well. Alan Ball Sr. used to pick me up at our house very early Saturday mornings and drive me to Stoke as the youth teams played at 11 a.m. and the first team pros at 3 p.m. in the afternoon. I played one season for Stoke and that was it. I thought that I was on my way, only Stoke City did not retain me the following season. I thought, *do they realize what they are missing*. I was the best player on the team but obviously they didn't think the same. After Stoke City, I played Saturday and Sunday and later Wednesday all amateur and semi-pro football. However, it didn't help my career that, by this time, I was sixteen years old, had bought a scooter, and had started liking girls.

I left Moorclose Secondary Modern School at the age of fifteen. We had played our last match of the season on a Saturday. The exams to go to the next school started the following Tuesday so I never went back. I got a job on the Monday and that was it. I was working and getting paid six pounds a week at Beaverbrooks, the jewelers. As a junior, I was making tea, cleaning jewelry, polishing the brass counters, going for lunch for the staff and was the general dog's body but I loved it until I got fired six months later.

I had my scooter and a couple of times it had broken down which made me late for work or not able to go at all, so they fired me. I got another job immediately at Bensons of Bury, a menswear shop in a town a few miles from home with the same money but with commission. I parked my scooter outside the shop front door and all the girls used to stop outside and look in to see the cute mod that owned this fabulous scooter. It had chrome panels, chrome spare wheel backrest and chrome leg guards, ten chrome mirrors—the works. This scooter was special and attracted all the girls.

One of the many incidents on my scooter that definitely would not happen today occurred when I was driving at night into Manchester towards Victoria Avenue. A police car flashed his lights and stopped me for speeding. I pleaded with him, saying that I wasn't speeding but he said to go back to my house, and he would follow me—about five miles away. I drove home with the policeman following closely behind and I was scared stiff of what he was going to say to my mum but hoping that he would let me off.

We got to my house; I was so embarrassed. It was the first and only time the police had called at my home. Even though, for some of the houses in the street, it was a regular occurrence, and the police were there all the time. He knocked at my door and Lena answered asking what was wrong. We went into the house with the police officer explaining that I had been speeding but with me claiming that I wasn't and saying honestly, Mum, I wasn't—honestly. The officer said, "Mrs. Rostron, would you rather me be knocking on your door tonight telling you that Francis had been in an accident and had died or would you rather me be saying he's been speeding." Obviously, she said the latter; me still pleading my innocence but he gave me a ticket and we had to appear in court.

Being a juvenile and sixteen years old, my mum had to go to court with me. The day arrived and we were seated in the waiting room, with all the low life and scallywags from all the other council estates in Middleton. This was normal for them and their parents but not for us; it was so embarrassing. What made it worse was when it was our turn to go into court, the magistrate that presided over my case was a neighbor that lived in the next road, and she knew us well. I was still fined two pounds and got three points on my license but when we got outside, Lena pulled me to one side and said that if you ever put me through that embarrassment again, I will kill myself. I know that she meant it because it was the worst day of her life and besides that, she had to take a half day off work and lose money that she couldn't afford.

Nearly twenty years later, I was stopped and got a DUI in Manchester city center. When it was time to go to court, my lawyer said to me that there was a court reporter there that would put the story in *The Manchester Evening Newspaper*. With me being a minor celebrity in Manchester and the owner of a well-known shop that soccer players and TV stars went to, it would be newsworthy. But if I didn't want the publicity and paid him fifty pounds in cash, he wouldn't put it in the paper. I didn't mind the publicity—I never did—but I always remembered what Lena said to me outside court in Middleton that day and I didn't want her to read about it in the newspaper. So, my lawyer paid him the fifty pounds and Lena never knew that I had been stopped for driving whilst under the influence and got banned for a year. After working at Bensons of Bury for just over a year, I applied for the job that would change my life forever.

John Michael

Savile Row, London

I was sixteen years old and I applied for and got the job as junior sales assistant at John Michael, a menswear shop that had recently opened in Manchester from Savile Row, London. I went for two interviews and was interviewed by the manager, Mr. Alan Gallagher. I couldn't believe it when I received the letter saying I had been successful and got the job. The other salesman, all quite posh from middle class families, could not believe it either. This was a very expensive and exclusive shop that used to close on Saturdays at 1 p.m., the busiest day in retail. The manager said it was because our customers could afford to come anytime during the week and didn't want to mix with the Saturday shoppers in Manchester.

He didn't say the word common, but I know that's what he meant and here I was, a mod from a council house in Middleton, working in this beautiful shop. I found out later, the staff had told the manager, Mr. Gallagher, not to hire me because I would steal everything. Little did they know that before long, I would be the best salesman in the shop making more than any of them in commission. All the *crème de la crème* of Manchester used to come into the store asking for me personally because they liked me, and I gave them the best service. Most of them followed and supported me when I opened my own shirt business with many of them today, over fifty years later, still my close friends.

I learned so much at John Michael—not only about sales techniques but life in general from the clientele and my manager, Alan Gallagher. Because of him, I became a great salesman, although he said I was a natural. Every well-known and successful businessman in Manchester used to come into the shop along with celebrities and soccer stars from all over the country, including two that became my close friends, George Best and Mike Summerbee. Mike later became my business partner in Frank Rostron Shirtmakers Limited. John Michael was unbelievable and the first shop of its kind in Manchester where everything was expensive and priced in guineas, not pounds, like every other store. We had gimmicky sales that used to start at midnight and people would be lining up all day to get in to buy a cashmere sweater that was 100 guineas for only 10 guineas—this was unheard of in those days.

Mr. Gallagher used this to get publicity, because it was in the local and national newspapers all about this fancy store whose sale started at midnight, and finished at 5 or 6 a.m. We had music playing, it was packed like a nightclub, and we took in a fortune in those few hours. It was the first place I had worked where we had a lady cleaner that came in every day. Other places, the juniors, usually me, did the mopping, vacuuming, or polishing. I was still living in my council house and going out with my pals on the estate at night and telling them stories about who had been in the shop that day. Pop stars like Lulu, film stars like Ian McShane, TV stars like Lionel Blair, and singers like Cliff Richards or local businessmen in their Rolls-Royces or Bentleys. However, they were more impressed if I had been taken out for coffee or lunch with George Best and Mike Summerbee.

    I was always the last to serve anyone at the beginning as I was the junior sales assistant. One day, a lady came in and everyone was serving, so I asked if I could help. She said that she wanted shirts for her two young sons, so I presented shirts that she liked and then ties and she then said that she would take them all. Mr. Gallagher came over and said that it's all right, Mr. Rostron, I will take over this sale for Mrs. Demmy and she said, "No, I want this young man to serve me. He's been excellent." I didn't know it at the time but Mrs. Demmy was the wife of one of the most well-known, successful and prominent men in Manchester. Her husband was Gus Demmy, a famous bookmaker, and the mother of my friends for the rest of my life, Selwyn and Harvey Demmy. Since that day, Selwyn and Harvey have told everyone that their mother, Millie, had found Frank Rostron and she said to them that one day he will make it big. How could she possibly know—how could anyone know—that a kid who lives in a council house with a toilet in the back garden would do anything more than fulfill an ambition of perhaps one day being the manager of John Michael.

The next week, Mrs. Demmy phoned the store and asked to speak to 'little Frankie' as she called me. Mr. Gallagher was shocked that the lady of one of the most prominent families in Manchester was asking for me, the sixteen-year-old, junior sales assistant from Middleton. She wanted me to select clothes and bring them to their company office in Swan St., Manchester. I had their sizes from the shirts she bought, so I went around the shop like the TV show supermarket sweep and packed bags with shirts, sweaters, ties and even blazers and trousers. I then got a taxi to 58 Swan St., Manchester, the Demmy organization head office, walked up four flights of stairs to the executive floor and knocked on the door. Someone opened it and there I stood holding all these bags. That's where I first met Selwyn, Harvey and Mr. Gus Demmy.

Like a lot of things in my life, I did not realize just how important these people were, so I wasn't scared, nervous or intimidated. I was just being myself; so, I think they liked that. They tried everything on that I brought, they needed a different size in some things, asked for different colors in other things, but spent a lot of money. I had an unbelievable sale. Mr. Gallagher was impressed, and I earned what was to me a fortune in commission in those days. Selwyn passed away just a few weeks ago as I am writing this book but over the years, he mentored me, helped me, told me off, and more than once saved me from serious trouble.

Manchester Nightlife

Selwyn owned a prestigious nightclub called Blinkers. It was for members only and for girls who were models or pretty—they could get in also. Selwyn used to say that wherever the girls go the men would follow and he was right. He also had a strict dress code of dark lounge suits for men, and everyone had to obey the rules or they couldn't get in, except the late, great George Best. Everyone was wealthy or famous that went into his club but I got in because I worked at John Michael and knew Selwyn. This was another one of the many privileges that I became to expect but I still appreciated them. Even today, the privileges that I still get I don't take for granted or expect but really thinking about it, I suppose I do.

He also opened two high class restaurants, Blinkers French and Blinkers Bijou, where I was a regular. The special treatment that I used to receive I got at all the restaurants, clubs or bars. First, it was because I worked at John Michael then because of being business partners with Mike Summerbee and later being Frank Rostron who owns Frank Rostron Shirtmakers. Of course, being a good customer and always having a good-looking date also helped.

One of the first restaurants I went to was called Napoleons and it was partly owned by the Manchester City coach, Malcolm Allison, a very flamboyant personality himself. Being with Manchester City all the time, because of Summerbee, I could write a book just on Malcolm's exploits. After a match one day in the player's lounge, a friend, Jack, a wonderful older Spanish man who was the manager of Napoleons said, "Why do you never come into our restaurant?" He then insisted that I come that Saturday night. But I had only just started dining out and had absolutely no idea about food, wine or anything but Jack said just leave it to me. I turned up on that Saturday night in my Jaguar E-Type, wearing my velvet jacket with shirt collar outside my lapel, looking like an extra out of Starsky and Hutch, along with the obligatory 5'10" girl in hot pants and five-inch heels, looking like a million dollars.

The place was full of Manchester's elite. Plus, the top soccer players from both City and United who I knew said hello and smiled as Jack showed us to our table. He said, "Mr. Rostron, I have saved your usual table for you as if I went all the time. She was certainly impressed and so were all the guys in the restaurant, with my date getting THE look from their wives. Then Jack brought the menus, and I had no idea what to order and Jack said, "We have your favorite on the special menu tonight, Mr. Rostron, would you like to have it?" I said, "Of course, thank you and my girlfriend will have the same." Immediately Jack said, . . . "and your usual wine, Mr. Rostron."

I learned quickly and said, "thank you, Jack." For ten million dollars, I had no idea what food was coming or the color of wine but it was great, and she was impressed with me, the car, and the restaurant. She was even more impressed when, during the evening, a couple of the famous soccer stars came over to say goodnight as they were leaving. But they really wanted to check out hot pants again and meet her more than they wanted to speak to me. But I didn't care as I was as impressed with the evening just as much as she was.

Another restaurant I used to go to on a regular basis was Mario and Franco's, Terrazza, a hot Italian restaurant in town that Mike Summerbee and his wife first took me to. It was a busy, trendy restaurant again full of Manchester's elite and celebrities. But when I went without Summerbee, I still got the preferential treatment because he was my partner. As before, it wasn't long before I was getting my own VIP treatment because I had become a good customer and I always had a pretty girl with me. The manager at the time was Giulio Nobillo who later became the owner and who became a great friend and still is to this day over fifty years later. I could write a book on the wild stories about me in these restaurants but I will tell you a couple from each one. Some are simply not printable.

In the Terrazza, there were many and on one occasion, I called for a table and the voice on the other end said, "I'm sorry, we are full." I couldn't believe it. I said can I speak to Giullo; he asked whose speaking? I said Frank Rostron and Giullo came to the phone. I asked what's happening, the waiter said that you're full. He told me James Last was having his birthday party in the restaurant but of course he would fit me in. I thought to myself, *Of course you will, I'm Frank Rostron.*

I had become so used to this special treatment, privilege, and service that I spoke about at the beginning of the book in such a short time that it was embarrassing but I loved it, so why not. I turned up on that Saturday night with the obligatory beautiful date whom I had flown in from Holland that I had met like many of my girlfriends in Majorca. She was tall and very elegant. I had the jacket, shirt and my Jaguar at the door—although a different jacket and shirt, again a privilege of owning a shop—it's all free. When we arrived at the restaurant, it was strange because it was divided in two halves. One half was full and the other half completely empty. Our table for two was just inside the empty half until the James Last Orchestra arrived later on and filled the other half completely.

The girl couldn't believe that James Last was coming in as he was her mother's favorite entertainer. I had heard of him but had no idea just how big he was. He travels constantly around the world performing and always to sold out venues—he was unbelievable. Then Giullo comes to my table with a bottle of Dom Perignon. I asked, "Where did that come from?" and he said, "James Last asked who you were and what do you drink?" Giullo winked at me and said, "I told him only DP." I think at that time I had never tasted Dom Perignon but by this time the girl was more impressed than they usually are and more so a little later when the man himself came to our table to introduce himself.

He asked if we wanted more to drink and some of his birthday cake which was made in the style of a golf course as he was a mad golfer and was playing at Mere Golf Club the following morning. I did say that the owner, Stephen Bowler, was a great friend of mine even though I had only met Stephen a couple of times. He also said that if you ever want to come to any of my concerts just call and ask for Hansi not James as that was his real name. They would know I was a friend if I asked for Hansi. Later, after dinner and another bottle of DP, Hansi invited us back to his hotel to carry on with his party and it was there I met and talked to a stunning black girl who was a backing singer in his band. Her name was Madeline Bell.

I had been in love with Madeline Bell for years even though I had never met her. She had a number of hit songs in England with her group, Blue Mink, but during this period of undying love for her I read an article about her and her girlfriend, the famous Dusty Springfield. I was heartbroken because I was also in love with Dusty, and I had just found out that they were both lesbians. I couldn't believe it. I was devastated at the time but there were others later like Debbie Harry from the band, Blondie, and all the girls from Sister Sledge so I survived. But meeting and spending time with Madeline Bell was special and I think she was the first American women I had ever spoken to which in itself was an experience. As I said, that was one of many stories in The Terrazza, so I might return to them later if I have a few drinks and get the nerve to.

The next restaurant that I went to on a regular basis was the excellent, Isola Bella, and the owner was Evandro Barbieri, another close friend who died too soon. Evandro was a brilliant restaurateur and a perfectionist who served the finest Italian food along with the best service. After many years, he moved from his original location to a much bigger and more glamorous location near my shop. It was never the same. A mistake many restaurateurs make but it was open for quite a few years before it closed. During the buildout, he used to call into my shop and ask me to come and take a look at its development and I selected which table I would like to use when he opens. One day, he was showing me around as he was choosing the chairs for the restaurant. The choice was a plain one or a carver one with arms at the side. He asked me what I thought and I said that I preferred the carver with arms. He chose the plain ones but I said to him that I still preferred the ones with arms, so he bought 180 plain chairs and eight chairs with arms for my table. I had my own table and chairs in the most popular restaurant in Manchester. When any of my friends knew that I was in Majorca, they would call for a reservation and say that their friend, Frank Rostron, was on holiday. Can we have his table and chairs. Many years later, people used to ask if it was true that there was a restaurant in Manchester where you had your own table and chairs. I used to just smile and nod my head—so modest but again I loved it.

Besides all these great restaurants, the club scene was buzzing and we had some of the best clubs in the country—as good if not better than London. I mentioned Blinkers but I started much earlier than that in our local club in Middleton which was called the Limit. It wasn't long before I was hitting the town, first at the original Twisted Wheel on Brazzenoe St. Some people say they went to the 'wheel' but on Whitworth St.; most don't even know it began in Brazzenoe St. I was fourteen or fifteen years old and couldn't afford to go in, so I used to hang around outside with the mods and their scooters. It was cool and good enough in those days for a wannabee like me. But I wanted to be inside, especially for the all-nighters. They had massive stars from England and the States like Long John Baldry, Julie Driscol, Edwin Starr, Ike and Tina Turner, Charlie and Inez Foxx, Spencer Davis, with Stevie Winwood the lead singer, to name just a few. Rod Stewart used to sing in John Baldry's band and if they played all week at the Wheel, Rod used to work in The Cona café on Tib Lane, clearing coffee cups and plates for extra money.

So, being from the streets and doing what I have really done all my life, I thought of a move. If I could raise the five shillings to go in, I could then go to the fire escape and let other people in the back door. I spoke to a few people outside and said that I can get you in for two shillings. I think about five paid me. I had ten shillings and told them to go around the back and wait. I paid my five shillings at the door, went in, then climbed straight up the fire escape stairs at the back to let my new customers in. I was in business with another nice, little earner plus five shillings for my profit. This went on for ages.

Every Saturday night, I was stepping over bodies on the stairs that were out of their heads on the pills that everyone took then to stay awake all night.

One night, I shoved with my foot to move a couple of guys who were blocking my way on the stairs. They looked up at me and it was Eric Burdon, the lead singer of The Animals, along with Brian Auger of The Brian Auger Trinity. They were so absolutely stoned out of their minds, they couldn't talk. God knows what they were on, but it wasn't a joint they had smoked—something far more serious. The big shot Mods from the Wheel and who owned scooters sometimes used to ride over to Sheffield, just over an hour away, for the all-nighters at a club called The King Mojo. One time, I was asked if I wanted to go with them, so I jumped on the back of one the guy's bikes. He said that I could mind the scooters while they were inside which was fine with me. It wasn't long ago that I stood outside the Wheel thinking I had made it, so going to The King Mojo was massive for me. I thought *next week when some girl says we didn't see you last Saturday,* I could act cool and say no, I went over to The Mojo. Little did they know that I was outside watching the scooters for the guys, not inside, but I was still trying to impress and only fifteen years old.

One night, I was outside The Mojo sitting on one of the scooters looking like I owned it as the guys were inside dancing and listening to the music, when a young man came outside and spoke to me. He asked why I was sitting outside, and I told him I couldn't afford to get in, so I was minding the scooters for the guys. He asked my name. I told him Frankie and he said my name's Peter—I own the place. Come on in with me. He bought me a coke and showed me around. I couldn't believe it. I remember that night clearly because it was "Fat Boy" Billy Stewart from the USA on stage singing his hit song, "Summertime," and the guy, Peter, was the legend, Peter Stringfellow. Peter went on to own clubs all around the world, starting off in Leeds then Manchester and London. I was fifteen years old and even though I talk about my VIP treatment and privileges, at that age, I didn't realize it.

After The Wheel, there were many clubs: The Jungfrau, Rails, Time and Place, Explosion, Applejacks, The Connection, The Sandpiper, The Portland Lodge, Annabels, The Millionaire, Rubens, Brambles, Bavadage, Slack Alice, and the best of them all—the world famous, Hacienda. But, as I said, there were hundreds more that I went to. I knew all the owners as friends or customers and always walked straight in—no lining up or cover charge for me and my gang. Because of my love of Blues and soul music from the Wheel that came mainly from the States, I found myself as a teenager walking around Manchester, looking for clubs that played this kind of music. I would walk past a club which was usually in a basement and if the music sounded right then I would just go in.

The only problem, and it wasn't a problem at first, was that these clubs were usually only for black people. I would sometimes be the only white guy in there and perhaps one white girl with her boyfriend. It didn't bother me as I was only there for the music—a little naïve perhaps but I didn't have any fear because I didn't see the difference. Not that I was tough or anything but I thought there was nothing I could do with 200 against me, so I just went in because I loved the music. I started dancing and that was when the men were fine. They smiled and offered me a joint which I never accepted and still have not had one to this day. After a while, one or two girls would dance with me and I found them cute. I still do. But then one night, I said to one girl, "Do you want to dance?" She said, "Yes" and I asked, "Are you single," she said, "Yes." She and her boyfriend had finished, so we were dancing and got closer and closer. Then a couple of guys came over and looked like they were not very happy with me being so close to this girl. I asked, "Who are those guys? Is that your brother or something." She said, "No, it's my ex-boyfriend," so I asked, "When did you two finish?" She said, . . . "About two hours ago." Needless to say, after that, I asked a lot more questions. It was my first but not the last close shave that I had with girl's boyfriends.

One night, I was in Slack Alice which was owned by my friends, Colin Burne and George Best, and this beautiful, well-known, Manchester model and beauty queen came over to me. She said, "I see you out and about in town all the time with different girls. How come you never ask me out for dinner." Before I could open my mouth, she gave me a piece of paper with her name, address and telephone number on it. She said that I could pick her up on Wednesday at 7:00 pm.

I couldn't believe it. She was sensational and the sexiest

dancer in the club. She had long, dark hair, the greatest figure, and again a beauty queen. I had seen her in clubs and bars in Manchester all the time but even cocky, confident me never had the nerve to talk to her never mind ask her out. Anyway, I thought at the time that she was dating a club owner who was a friend of mine, but she said they had finished, so I thought, *ok, why not*. It wouldn't have mattered anyway as I was fearless and thought I ruled the world—well, Manchester at least.

One thing she didn't know or remember was that only a few years earlier, she used to come into John Michael where I worked as the junior salesman always with different boyfriends. Soccer players, businessmen and I think even once with a Spanish prince and many times I had made them coffee while they browsed and shopped. But she wouldn't have even noticed me then if I had died at her feet; she would have stepped over my body and now here she was asking me to take her out.

I was as nervous as hell like a fifteen-year-old boy going on a first date. I knocked on the front door of this pretty cottage in Alderley Edge, a very exclusive part of Cheshire, south of Manchester. When her mum opened the door and said, "Are you Frankie? Please come in," and seated me on the sofa, "she won't be long; she's just getting ready." I sat there on the sofa, hands on my knees, looking innocent so as to please her lovely mum, passing small talk until her daughter came downstairs. Then all of a sudden, she came halfway down the stairs stark naked screaming, "Mum, where have you put my fucking hairbrush. I can't find it anywhere." Then without taking a breath said, "Hi, Frank. I won't be long." Her mum saying it's in your drawer. Both issues as if they were nothing—the swearing or her being naked in front of me. I was already nervous about this date with being the kid who made her coffee when she came into the shop and could never have imagined sleeping with her never mind seeing her naked even before our first drink or dinner.

She came down fifteen minutes later, and she looked like a million dollars and I felt even more nervous. But she was great, said see you later to her lovely mum who reminded me of Lena, a sweet proper mum, and we got into my car. We hadn't gone two miles and she started rooting in her purse, got out a cigarette, some Rizla papers, cannabis, and started rolling a joint. I couldn't believe that she made it like a real pro. She lit it, took a large draw, and passed it over to me—well, she attempted to. I nearly crashed saying no thanks as I had never smoked a cigarette in my life never mind a joint. So, she smoked most of it then put the rest away in her purse.

We arrived at La Terrazza and she completely took over. I had been a few times by now, but I was not in her league socially. She was greeted like a Hollywood film star that she looked every inch of. She got kissed by Giulio on both cheeks and he led us to our table which I think was in her name. He said hello to me while she checked out the room seeing who was in and who she knew. The menus came and she ordered her favorite wine which was fine by me as I still didn't have a lot of ideas regarding wine, and we ordered dinner. After a few drinks, I started to relax and feel a little better and the Frank Rostron show was up and running but going very carefully. During dinner, we talked about my life and my shirt business but working at John Michael was never mentioned and she didn't remember me so that was good. She talked about her life and her career and general Manchester chit-chat so everything was cool and I was doing great until after dinner and she asked if I was having a Sambuca. I had no idea what she was talking about. I was twenty-three years old going on eighteen and she was twenty-nine going on thirty-five. She was a million miles in front of me when it came to life experience.

I said, "Are you having one?" she said, "Of course," so I said, "I am as well then." We waited a while then these two drinks arrived on fire. I had seen these drinks on fire before in restaurants but with me being a big shot and supposedly knowing everything, I couldn't ask what they were now that one was in front of me. I know with being a reasonably bright guy that you cannot possibly drink anything on fire. I waited for her to make the first move, I waited and waited while chatting. She then casually picked up a saucer, put it on top of the Sambuca glass for a couple of seconds and like a magician she put it out. Not to look obvious that I was copying, I waited a few minutes then put mine out—now with no fire. I can take the lead like I've had this Sambuca stuff for years. I take a sip, and not knowing that the glass would be a million degrees hot, the glass stuck to my lip. I screamed; the Sambuca spilled on the table and was on fire. The waiters rushed over and put the fire out, me with a swollen, red lip and her saying, "What the fuck are you doing? Didn't you realize the glass would be hot?" I quickly said, "Of course, but with being in deep conversation with you, I completely forgot that I had just put it out." I managed to fanny my way out of it like I have done a hundred times before and a hundred since. I got the bill and we drove back to Alderley Edge, with me sweating because of the Sambuca stunt and my lip swollen like Mike Tyson had wacked me. *All this time I am trying to impress this film star and not doing very well,* I thought to myself.

As we approached her cottage, she said, "Pull around the back," where she had a paved back garden instead of a lawn that fit one car. I did as my teacher said and as we pulled up at her back door, she jumped out and went inside leaving her kitchen door open without saying a word. I thought that it was strange that she didn't say good night but what do I know. I sat there for a few minutes. She came back saying, "Are you coming in or sitting there all night?" I got out of my car, locked it up and walked into her kitchen and waited and waited. Then five minutes later, she appeared at the top of the stairs naked and said, "Are you coming up or not." Well, sweating like a dog, my lip swollen and nervous as hell, I walked up the stairs into her bedroom. She was in her bed saying get in, so I took my clothes off. I thought I wouldn't ask for a coat hanger for my trousers and jacket with the night going as it did, so I just put them over a chair and got in.

Remember, with younger girls who are easily impressed, I

was the King but this one had been there, seen it and done it all and in her world, I just was an apprentice. As she started kissing me, all I was thinking was whether or not her mum could hear us in the next room. It was a cottage with cottage doors that had a gap at the top and bottom and I had never slept with a girl whose parents had been at home before. So, you can imagine after an hour of kissing and petting, the captain would not stand to attention. We fell asleep but like The Twisted Wheel Club and The King Mojo Club, I was just happy to be there without going inside.

I got up the next morning and was trying to sneak out so her mum wouldn't hear me and before I got to the kitchen door, she said, "Good morning, Frankie, would you like some breakfast?" I said, "No thanks, I'm late for work." Even though I had ages, I jumped in my car, embarrassed as hell, and drove into town. Later that day, I was shocked to get a call from her thanking me for a great night and asking when we were going out again. One thing she wasn't and that was shy. Also, later that day, I got a call from my club owner pal who used to date her or that's what she told me. He said, "I went around to my girl's house last night after work about 3:00 a.m. and your car was in my spot. I said quick as a flash, . . . "and it wasn't only my car that was in your spot." He was sick but it's happened to us all over the years, its only male ego. We were still great friends. Years later, I had a black model girlfriend called Francesca Assumah whom I dated for ages and really cared about. Then one night over a drink, he said to me you trained Francesca well, she was great. She stayed all weekend at my place. I was sick even though we had split up a few years earlier. It still hurt. Again, ego but *touché*—after all these years, he got me back; he hadn't forgotten my car being in his spot.

Another club we used to go to in the day was Applejacks and it was there I met the boys from Lebanon. Great guys who were in the precious stones business—diamonds, emeralds etc. and they spent money like they printed it. Later in life, going out with bank robbers and drug barons, even they didn't spend money like these boys did. The club would seal off an area with velvet ropes and have two of the security standing at each side to keep people away from these guys drinking their champagne and black label whisky. Needless to say, they saw me and my gang always with a crowd of girls and asked the manager about me and would I be good enough to join them for drinks. Obviously, I did.

We got on really well, became great friends, and after that every time they came to Manchester, they would call me. We would go drinking, then to dinner, and hit the clubs and party big style every night. The head of these guys was named Slim. They called him that because he was about 280/300 pounds but with a lovely, cute, handsome face—a quiet man and you could even say shy. The other boys made up for him, drinking heavily, pulling the girls and taking them back to their hotel or house. Slim used to pay all the bills in cash and even in those days it was thousands of pounds a night. At the end of the night, he would walk around Applejacks and give every single member of staff: door man, waiters, waitresses, chefs and even the people who wash up in the kitchen a fifty-pound note tip. He was so generous.

They would go to London and always wanted me to go with them which was alright because I could do shirt business during the day while they did their diamond business. They always stayed at The Holiday Inn at Swiss Cottage which was a fine hotel in those days and occupied the seventh floor, taking about five or six suites. At night, we usually went for dinner at one of the many fine Lebanese restaurants in London then to a club. They were not too well up on London clubs but I was, of course, so we had no problem getting in—especially when the bill for whisky and champagne ran into thousands of pounds a night. One club they always loved to go and have dinner was Stringfellows in Covent Garden owned by my friend, Peter Stringfellow. Peter was always happy that I was bringing these big spenders but nice guys into his club.

Slim never spoke to the head waiter or manager in Stringfellows or in other London restaurants but left me or one of the boys to ask the questions. He would lean over to me and ask what size the caviar jars are and I would then turn to the manager two feet away and say what size are the caviar jars. He would bring them to the table then Slim would whisper to me three of the large ones and I would turn to the manager and say three of the large ones, please. It was hilarious but he never asked the price as would anyone else. Then every few months, they would go to The Gambia and Sierra Leone on business, visit family and would always take me with them. A couple of days before we were going, Slim would say go and ask those girls if they wanted to come to Africa this weekend for a party. I would ask and obviously most of the time they said yes. I took their names, and the next day booked their flights.

They would fly coach and we always booked first class. The guys would stay in homes they owned there but the girls and I always stayed in a hotel. We had great fun during the day. The boys would come to the hotel and hang out by the pool drinking but Slim loved it when they played bingo, the winning prize being six Coca-Colas. Slim got excited if he won which is crazy as he spent thousands of pounds on booze and food, so I couldn't understand the Coca-Cola thing. I think it was just because he won. At nights, we had parties at the house. They would send a large Toyota SUV to pick me and the girls up and take us to the house, which had large gates and about six African security guards twenty-four hours a day at the gate, continually walking around the compound. As we approached them, they would open the gates manually and let us through, closing them behind us. The bar in the house they used to call Andy's bar. I don't know why, or I've forgotten but we had Andy's Bar T-shirts made for all the girls to wear then take home as a memento of their holiday along with other things.

The first time we got on the plane, we turned left into first class. It was unbelievable as I had never flown first class before, so obviously I was impressed. I have flown business and first many times since and when you get to your seat, the flight attendant comes and asks to take your jacket then hangs it on a coat hanger in the closet. Slim used to take his trousers and jacket off and have them hang them up and make the flight just in his boxer shorts and shirt. He said he was more comfortable than in his trousers. I've never tried it but I think anyone else would be thrown off. That first flight was on British Caledonian and being owned by BA had first-class and club world which was business class and economy which is now called coach class. Slim said, "We are in first-class; follow me," and he took me into the next cabin. Then he said, "This is club world; follow me," and then he took me into the economy cabin where the girls were and said, "This is third world." I've told that story many times since first-class, club world and third world. When you saw the two hundred or so seats squashed together after first-class, it really did look like the third world.

Another thing Slim always did that I copied later in a slightly different way was that he would buy every member of the flight crew—the captain, his flight crew and all the male and female flight attendants—a bottle of perfume or cologne from their duty free and it was always the most expensive and best that they had. As I said before, he was a very generous and obviously an extremely wealthy man. After that, if I was on a flight going anywhere when the flight attendant came around with the duty free and I fancied her, I would say that I want to buy some perfume for a girlfriend. I would ask which one is your favorite and buy that. I would put a small slit down the side of the cellophane and insert my card and as I got off the flight, I handed the bag with the perfume to the girl. She wouldn't realize until later when she opened it and saw my card behind the cellophane wrap but every single time it worked, and the girl would call me.

So usually, after The Gambia, the girls would fly back to Manchester and we would fly down to Sierra Leone where the boys had relatives. It was a strange place to be as we used to stay in a 5-star hotel called Mama Yoko Hotel but with no phone service. There wasn't any phone service anywhere in Freetown—no one had a phone. If you wanted to make a call you went into town to the town hall where you would wait your turn, sometimes an hour or longer, to make a call. It was unbelievable. During the day, whilst the boys were with family or working, Slim would take me to the beach. Miles of beautiful beach with nobody in sight except a couple of uniformed police and a few local boys, hanging around to beg tourists for money.

The country was corrupt and the money worthless. Slim shouted to the cops, "Hey, you two, come here," like they worked for him. He said, "Stand by my friend's lounge bed until I come back later today." He gave the cops some bank notes and left. The poor guys stood at attention by my sun bed, in full uniform, all day, in weather of over 90 degrees. When I walked the fifty yards or so to the sea, they walked with me. I was there for three or four hours. Then all of a sudden, there was a great roar and Slim and the boys came tearing up the beach on three-wheeler sand bikes but there were massive signs all over saying "NO MOTOR BIKES" on the beach. The cops didn't move away from my side, until Slim arrived and gave them some more money and said, "You can go now." They thanked him and left.

That night, we went to the casino and the boys won so much money they had to send out for more notes. We left carrying plastic shopping bags full of brand-new printed bank notes. When we got back to the hotel, there were piles and piles of money. It looked like millions, but Slim said it was worthless—probably about a few hundred pounds which he would use for tips. Like all good things, it came to an end and the boys stopped coming to Manchester. The fun ended but I am still in touch today with one of them called Adnan who lives with his beautiful family in Beirut, and he keeps me up to date on the other guys.

Everywhere I went—to clubs, restaurants and on holiday—I met people who molded my life, educated me, became customers and friends for life, and nowhere more so than Majorca, Spain.

Majorca

I was nearly twenty-one years old and had never been on an airplane and a friend suggested we go to Spain and again I had no idea. I was so naïve. My friend was Michael Morris whose sister was engaged to my best pal at the time, ex-Manchester City player, Bobby McAlinden. Michael went on to become a successful soccer agent who, as I write this book, has been having serious health issues and we keep him in our prayers. There are two Michael Morrises in my book, both good friends: one the soccer agent and the other Michael is a very successful businessman from London, with whom later on in life I used to spend my Christmases in Barbados. He booked Majorca for Christmas and New Year with another pal called Paul Fredericks. Even though I had never heard of Majorca, Michael said he saw the brochure and it had beautiful beaches packed with girls and sunshine. Now, after spending most of my adult life in Majorca, I now know that in winter, it is colder, with chances of rain—nothing like the summer. We arrived and it was raining with no one around and most of the bars and clubs were closed and definitely no girls. It was awful. The representative wasn't due at our hotel for three days and when she came, we told her we wanted to go home to which she replied, "You can't for two weeks." I said, "We don't want a refund; we just want to go. We don't like it here." Again, she said that it was impossible. I picked up a bar stool and threw it against the wall. It disintegrated into a pile of firewood as it slid down the wall. I cannot tell you how close I was to throwing it against the bar like a cowboy film, smashing all the bottles and glasses but at the last minute, threw it against the wall. Michael stood there in shock but not as shocked as the rep who said, "I will try my best," to which I said to her, "Believe me, we want to go home." She obviously had no idea about my temper or my determination. The next day, she said that you are on the flight on Saturday, exactly a week after we arrived.

It was now coming up to Easter and Michael was planning another holiday in Spain and I said I am in but make sure it's not the same place as last time. Also, there must be sun and girls this time around and he promised there would be. We flew in the evening and arrived at The Hotel Barbados late at night and it was dark. We went to our room and looked out of the windows but it was pitch black. We couldn't see anything, so we drew the heavy, blackout, lined curtains and went to bed. I was the first to wake because we didn't close the curtains completely and a beam of sunlight was hitting me in the face. I jumped up and opened the curtains and there it was—Magaluf beach in all its glory.

I shouted to the guys as I was running out of the door,

and they chased after me down the four flights of stairs. I didn't wait for the lift. I ran through the reception, past the hotel swimming pool, onto the beach and dived into the blue Mediterranean Sea. I had only ever been in the sea at Blackpool so you can imagine how excited I was. It was the best day ever. I got red not brown but that's ok. I felt great and it wasn't until later that day that I found out we were back in Majorca where we went at Christmas. Even Michael didn't know—that's how naïve we were. We stayed on the beach all day that had lots of bars, places to eat and drink and lots and lots of pretty girls of all nationalities.

That's where we met two girls from Connecticut, USA, named Carla Argosy and Liz Ing. We took them out that night and spent most of the time with them until they left a few days later when we swapped telephone numbers and addresses—no cell phones in those days. They said that you must come to visit us in America but we had only just gone to Majorca, so going to the States was like inviting us to the moon. We finished the holiday, and it was the best time of my life. I had fallen in love with Majorca and couldn't wait to go back. I had no idea geography-wise where it was or even that it was an island. I just knew it was Spain.

We booked our summer holidays and there was only one place for me and that was Majorca. We stayed in a different hotel a couple of miles away in Palma Nova. Stupid me, I thought Magaluf was Majorca and that was all there was to see but Palma Nova was brilliant and with even more girls. By now, I was seeing customers in Birmingham and two guys who bought shirts said that they went to Majorca. Their names were Johnny Hart and Lenny Smith. One day, we were walking down Son Matius beach and started talking to girls who were from Birmingham, I said, "Do you know Johnny Hart and Lenny Smith?" Today, people ask where do I come from and you say England and they say do you know Tom, he's English. So stupid but people still do it all the time. They said, "Yes, we do; they are at the La Baraka—the beach club in Palma Nova. I looked for two days and couldn't find this La Baraka place and then bumped into the girls again who asked if I had found them. I told them I couldn't find the bar and they said follow us and just a minute away was this trendy, French, beach restaurant.

There were people playing backgammon, dancing to music, having lunch, drinking wine and champagne, and water skiing. I couldn't believe it and it was certainly way out of my league at the time. I saw Johnny and Lenny who were big shots on this beach and surrounded by girls with their friends like Radar Haddad from Lancaster, Pennsylvania, and Claus from Germany. The scene was unbelievable. They introduced me to the owner, Claude Berdah, and he asked what I wanted to drink. I said, "I'm ok, thanks." There was no way I could afford this place. Within days and for the next twenty-five years, I lived at La Baraka until it closed down and fifty years later, I still go to the beautiful island of Majorca. Claude Berdah is still my good friend today who I speak to every week and who visits us in Naples on a regular basis with his partner, Sally.

As you can imagine, spending the summers in Majorca for over twenty-five years, there are hundreds and hundreds of stories and even more girls—far too many of both to mention. I will tell you about some of the funny ones and some not so funny that I think you will enjoy.

Most days would consist of everyone getting to La Baraka about 10-11 a.m., depending on what time we got home the night before. Then we would plan the day either staying there all day or going out on someone's boat for lunch at one of the many beautiful bays and ports around the island. Being from La Baraka and supposedly being the in-crowd, we got invited to all the new bar and club openings on the island and we were in all the magazines and newspapers not only on the island but around Europe also.

This was because of all the celebrities and stars that used to frequent La Baraka like George Best, John Bloom, Freddie Laker, Ingemar Johansson, Bobby and Tina Moore, Wim Suurbier, James Coburn, Doug Ellis, Susan George, Grahame Souness, Jimmy White, Paddy Crerand, Paddy McGrath and many more—again far too many to mention. Millionaires and billionaires from the UK and Europe, particularly France, used to always head for La Baraka as the restaurant was French. Claude, the owner, being French Tunisian, attracted lots of this famous and infamous clientele and, of course, the wannabee celebrity and future millionaire, Frank Rostron.

One day, I went out for lunch with two friends and their families who were also good customers of mine. Most of the people I met all over the world became customers as well as friends. These two were called John Luper from Leeds and Jack King from Canvey Island in Essex. Both had beautiful Sunseeker boats worth many millions of pounds. This day, we went to Port Andratx and moored the two boats side by side in the bay, with waiters bringing drinks and canapes from one boat to another. So, I'm standing there with John and Jack, a glass of champagne in my hand, looking across the bay, the blue sky and the turquoise Mediterranean sea and thinking to myself, *What's a kid from a council house in Middleton doing on these multi-million-pound boats drinking champagne; how blessed am I.* Then I came out with the classic line saying to the guys, "I wonder what the poor people are doing today," to which John replied, "You are here with us, Frank, you are here with us." He said it twice so I would realize I am the poor people compared to these two at the time. I was still relatively poor but again privileged to be on these boats as my pals from Middleton were a million miles away from this lifestyle.

After a year or so, I bought my own apartment above La Baraka, with the balcony overlooking the beach and the restaurant. I would wake up every morning, walk out onto my terrace and see what the new day had brought us. Girls from Sweden and other Scandinavian countries or friends from last year had arrived for two weeks holiday, while we were there for three-four-five or even six weeks holiday.

One time, a famous, Scottish, International soccer player called me and said three of his friends were coming to Majorca and he had sent them to La Baraka and said to ask for me. He asked if I would show them around. So that night, after dinner, we went to a few bars and then ended up in Alexander's night club in Magaluf. These three brothers were giants, the shortest one being about 6'3" and cocky. After about fifteen minutes, this very pretty girl walked past. He said, "Who's that, wee man?" to which I replied her name is Suzy and I know her. Let me have a word with her (Suzie happened to be a guy). She was very pretty, had terrific legs, with lovely blonde hair and great breasts which she flaunted by always having her blouse open to her naval.

I have done this stunt many times to friends who fancy themselves with the ladies, so I thought, *why not with this guy.* I went over to Suzy gave her 5000 pesetas and said come over in five minutes and take this guy for a walk meaning for sex. Five minutes later she comes over and says, "Hi, Frankie," gives me a kiss on both cheeks and I introduce her to the boys. I said to the one, go with Suzy; she will take care of you. She gets hold of his hand and walks away with him. Fifteen minutes later, he came back with a big smile on his face saying to his brothers, you won't believe what just happened. She took me to the ladies' toilets into a cubicle and gave me the best blow job I have ever had.

I said what do you mean SHE gave you the best blow job. He said, "Suzy did," and I said, "You mean HE gave you the best blow job," with a smile on my face. He looked at me and said, "You had better be joking, wee man," so I called over a waiter and said, "Tell my pal about Suzy," to which he replied, "You mean Suzy, the guy." The giant Scotsman didn't find it funny and was obviously embarrassed in front of his brothers and went to grab my throat. I ducked and ran with him chasing me, out of the club and through Magaluf. Obviously not catching me, as I was the fastest 100-yard sprinter in Middleton and had the medals to prove it. I would probably have been the fastest 200 yard and half-mile runner, as well, if I always had someone chasing me who was trying to kill me. The next day, Claude called me and said, "What the fuck have you done now? The Scottish brothers are here wanting to kill you." I said, "Sort it out, Claude"—like he usually does. I think it was three days I had to stay away from La Baraka until they had left and then it was business as usual. One time, I rented an apartment of mine to a couple of English guys that were on the run from the police in England. They had done a robbery and fled to Majorca with their haul until it was safe to go back. So, they were in Majorca for a year or so. One of them was a taller, good-looking guy and a player with the girls but his partner in crime, the nicer of the two, was shorter, a little chubby, shy and not as good-looking. One weekend in winter, I went to Majorca and visited a local restaurant for dinner and who was sitting at a table for two, having dinner, holding hands, all very romantic was the shorter of the two robbers with Suzie. I said, "Hello," but couldn't believe it. I was sure he knew that Suzie was a guy. The next day, I went to the apartment and asked, "What were you thinking, taking Suzie out for dinner?" He said that you know, I'm not very good with the girls and she's beautiful and it's winter and I get lonely with no one around and she gives a great blow job so I thought why not. He looked so innocent and helpless, so I thought bless him and why not.

Another day, I am on the beach with a couple of pals and some girls and a soccer ball flies over and lands on the lounge. A minute later, a young Norwegian boy came over, asking for it back. I threw it to him saying soccer is not allowed on the beach. For this exact reason, people are relaxing and don't want to be hit with soccer balls but about ten minutes later the ball comes back with the boy a minute behind, asking for it back. I said no more but again ten minutes later the same happened, so I picked up the ball and gave it one of my best volleys way out into the sea. The boy cried and ran away; minutes later, he returned with his mother screaming and shouting. I told her where to go in my best English. She replied that she could bring her husband later to which I replied bring him plus a few more swear words thrown in. A couple of hours later, it was like the sun went in and the beach went dark when these two, giant, Norwegian guys come around the corner with the women pointing to me and the guys wanting to kill me. I said as if I was tough and wasn't scared, "Come back tomorrow at 1:00 p.m. when my pal arrives, and we will fight you in the hotel car park." They left and the day carried on.

The next day, my pal, John Moroney, arrived from Birmingham. I met him about the same time as Johnny Hart and Lenny Smith but we had become great pals with John helping me out many times in fights in the clubs and bars of Birmingham, Manchester and Majorca. John was tough and could have a row and when he arrived on the beach the next morning, Claude told him you are early, Frank has a fight for you at one o'clock, so don't go far. John tells the story to this day. He says I hadn't even unpacked my case or had a drink and Rostron already had a fight waiting for me. The Norwegians didn't show up that day but we had about twenty of the lads ready just in case.

Another time, there used to be some French gangsters—big spenders that came to La Baraka. As I said, with Claude being French, a lot of French people came there on holiday. They spent their days eating and drinking at the restaurant, going on their boat, and chasing the girls. One day, I was walking past their table and one said, "Sell me your chain." I used to wear a heavy, hand-made gold chain around my neck to which I said, "It's not for sale," to which he said, "Why not; it's only shit." Without a pause or thinking, I grabbed his chain and swung it around his neck saying this is only shit also.

The Frenchman and his pals jumped up to grab me and again I was off; 100 miles an hour down the beach, leaving them in my wake. I called Claude from a bar down the beach and asked what was all that about. Claude telling me that on his chain was his Magen David, his religious Star of David, and you insulted him by calling it shit. But everyone who knows me is aware, I would never do that with many of my friends being Jewish, including Claude himself. It happened in seconds.

I didn't even know there was anything on his chain. I think that time I only had to stay away from the beach for two days until they left for home and Claude had sorted it all out.

Claude assured me that if they had caught me, I would have been found in the gutter or washed up on the beach the next day dead. A few years later, the same gang was arrested and jailed for kidnapping Baron Edouard-Jean Empain in Paris at gunpoint and holding him for ransom. They wanted 80m Francs about 45 million pounds, cutting his finger off, and sending it with the ransom note. Funny, many years later, I bumped into one of them at The Fontainebleau Hotel in Miami Beach with his wife and passed pleasantries. He asked about Claude and everyone on the beach but there was no mention of the chain incident or the Baron.

On the beach, we had many characters and friends none more so than an elderly couple from London who had retired to Majorca called Wally and Betty Gordon. They loved watching all the action and the fun and games that we used to get up to—the girls, and the arguments that used to happen daily. They didn't drink alcohol, only pots of tea and played scrabble and cards with their friends. One day, Wally said to me, "Frank, last night at our ex-pats club we had a lad sing and he was fantastic; you would have loved it. His name was Billy Idol." I said, "Wally, Billy Idol would not be singing in your club. He lives in LA, takes heroin, crashes motor bikes and is a wild man. He certainly wouldn't be in your club"—to which Wally replied, "Well, he said his name was Billy Idol."

That night after dinner and a few bars, we walk into Alexander's night club in Magaluf and who is standing at the bar with a pal—bloody Billy Idol. The white hair, white T-shirt, black leather jacket, blue jeans, boots—the lot unbelievable. Apparently, he comes from a very wealthy family not from the streets like he would want you to believe, and his parents had a villa, lived in Majorca, and he was visiting them from LA. The next morning, I was reading the local English paper, *The Majorca Bulletin,* and on the front-page headlines: "Billy Idol rock star visiting the island." So, apologies to Wally were in order later that day for not believing him.

Lots of soccer players came to the island for end of season relaxation with their clubs or with friends on holiday and always headed to La Baraka. One year, the Wolverhampton Wanderers team came and their goalkeeper was an unbelievable character called John Burridge, nicknamed Budgie. He was a wild man that everyone loved and was full of fun. Well, one night, we are out on the town and about 2:00 a.m., we ended up in a club called Bananas and they were just about to start 'The Mr. Bananas' contest. This is where ten young men on holiday would show off their good looks, bodies and tans in their swim trunks for the title of Mr. Bananas and a prize of I think 100 pounds and a bottle of champagne.

As they walked down the steps one at a time onto the dance floor, holding up their number card at the back, following them walking on his hands stark naked was Budgie. I stood with another Wolves legend, Kenny Hibbitt, watching this. I looked behind me where Budgie stood a second earlier and all that was there was a pile of clothes. Budgie was the fittest guy you knew and could walk on his hands for hundreds of yards. He came down the steps onto the dance floor and everyone was laughing their heads off. With this, he did a back flip onto his feet, bowed, took all the applause and walked over to us. He got dressed as if nothing had happened. It was one of the funniest things that ever happened in Majorca and I wasn't involved for a change.

One character that I met on La Baraka was Malcolm "Mickey" Gooch from London who went on to become a close friend. He even bought the house next door to me that I built in Torre Nova. Mickey was larger than life, loud, brash, flash and didn't mind letting everyone know that he was once a bank robber and now a major drug baron. He had a large house in London. In Majorca, at the house next door, there was a Porsche 911 Turbo and a large boat that he bought from a wealthy family who were friends of mine from Liverpool. They were called Austin and June Wilson who when they sold Mickey the boat, it was called *Golden Lady* but he immediately changed its name to *Dirty Laundry*. Talk about wanting everyone know what you do for a living, but Mickey didn't care.

He had many visitors to his house in Majorca and was very generous with them. They were usually pals who had just come out of prison or that were on the run and it was usually left to me to entertain them if Mickey was busy or travelling. As I said, there were many, but one was a notorious bank robber that I liked and got on with very well called Peter Coulson. I had met his wife and daughter as they had been to Majorca as a guest of Mickey's while Peter was serving his time, so I knew them before I met Peter. He had just come out of prison after serving eleven or twelve years of a twenty-one-year sentence and Mickey had invited him to Majorca.

This was for one of the most famous bank robberies in British history—the Bank of America in Mayfair. What happened was that the inside man who was an electrician became the police informant. He was in the vault ceiling doing work, noticed and watched the bankers opening and closing the vault and saw and copied the number to the safe. They got eight million pounds in that one robbery which was a lot of money in 1976 and only 500,000 pounds was ever recovered. There were many books written about Peter, his gang, and this robbery along with their other famous heists. A movie was also made about this robbery called *A Nightingale Sings in Berkeley Square.*

Peter wasn't a big guy; probably only 5'6" tall but he had done nothing for twelve years but go to the gym every day, hit a leather punching bag and obviously was a very angry man with a lot of steam to let out. One night, I took him into a local night club called Banana disco and two Spanish guys pushed passed us which was no big deal as it happens all the time in a busy club. They were both much taller than Peter, but Peter shouted at them as they didn't say sorry or anything for bumping into him. When they turned around and, in my life, I have seen many fights but nothing like this. He hit them both—one, two, bang, bang and they both dropped to the floor, spark out, both just crumbled on top of each other. I had never seen anything like that before or since, especially two guys at once.

After a couple of holidays in Majorca, the next time I saw Peter was on the front page of the *London Evening News*. A full-page photo of Peter and a plain clothes police officer with his knee on his neck, a gun stuck in his face. Apparently, Peter and his brother had just done an armed robbery of a security van in Knightsbridge, just across the road from Harrods, outside The Scotch House. They were getting away on a motor bike with their haul when a German tourist driving a Mercedes who had seen the robbery in action drove his car into the brothers and knocking them off their bike. Peter and his brother were laying dazed on the ground until the police arrived seconds later. Most people think that British police don't carry guns but in and around the West End of London, most of them do and all in plain clothes. This is because of the Royal protection and terrorist presence. Unfortunately for Peter and his brother, they were around and with a German tourist wanting to get involved, it wasn't their lucky day.

Mickey came to Manchester regularly to see me, always with his pals who also had lots of money. Every time they came, they used to play a game in Bavadage to see who could spend the most money and have the biggest bill in one night. They thought this was all very funny and so did the girls who drank the champagne with them—they loved it. They didn't expect me to get involved in this game but my pal, Colin, who owned the club, loved that I always brought them in.

Mickey once asked me if I wanted to go to Hong Kong and Thailand with him on holiday and that he would pay. I had never been, so of course I would but being naïve and thinking that it was just a holiday, I didn't realize because of what he did for a living and the places we were going what the consequences could have been with me just being with him.

We had a great time staying at The Peninsula Hotel in Hong Kong and The Mandarin Oriental in Bangkok. We were only supposed to stay for five days in Hong Kong but ended up staying two weeks. This was because his friend, with whom he was doing business, was late and we had to wait until he arrived. I didn't mind, we were going shopping during the day and going out every night to great restaurants partying and meeting girls. When his friend arrived, they had a couple of meetings and then we all flew to Bangkok together. His name was Howard Marks, the world's biggest cannabis dealer. He had his own shipping line, carrying cannabis around the world, picking up and dropping off like any cargo ship would, only with drugs.

I spent the next three weeks becoming good friends with Howard who was the nicest person you could ever wish to meet. Hence, one of the many books written about him is called *Mr. Nice* which is well worth reading. There are also movies about him that you can watch but it certainly was another experience being away on holiday with Mickey Gooch and Howard Marks.

They knew Hong Kong and Bangkok like it was their town, going to the finest restaurants and clubs and getting VIP service everywhere. Everyone knew them in Bangkok. We went to Patpong, an entertainment district full of bars and clubs with all the girls being young and beautiful. But it was also sad seeing hookers from large, poor families who sacrificed one of their children—a girl or boy—to go out and be prostitutes to bring home money for food and pay for school for the others, hoping that they would be educated and hopefully one day become doctors or teachers. The Mandarin Oriental wouldn't allow girls in the hotel for security reasons, so the guys booked rooms at another hotel nearby, just to take the many girls that we took home every night. Then afterwards, we went back to The Oriental to sleep. Whatever time we got back to our beautiful hotel suite, which had a terrace overlooking the Chao Phraya River, there was always a member of staff, in full, white uniform, waiting outside our door saluting us and asking if there was anything we needed, like running a bath or pouring a drink. It was great service but also very sad because of the poverty there.

When we checked out of The Peninsula in Hong Kong, I was in the hotel Rolls-Royce that was ready to take us to the airport, waiting for Mickey who was getting the bill. The receptionist said to him, "Mr. Gooch, housekeeper has informed us that Mr. Rostron wishes to purchase one of our robes. Should we put it on your bill?"

"Of course, you can," he said and when he got into the

Rolls he said to me, "Have you nicked a fucking robe from the room because they just put it on the bill?" I laughed and thought what class they had putting it like that to him . . . "housekeeper has informed us that Mr. Rostron wishes to purchase one of our robes."

Back in Bangkok, we lay around the hotel pool and guys would arrive in linen suits for a meeting with Howard and Mickey and he would always say "on your toes," meaning get lost until we call you back. They would never let me stay anywhere near whilst these talks were going on and in retrospect it was probably best, in case they were being filmed. Once, they left me alone for three days whilst they went away on business. I never left the hotel, but I ate some sensational food and drank some great wine in the hotel restaurant. There was a really elegant nightclub downstairs in the hotel called Diana's. I couldn't take any of the girls back to the suite even though they were not hookers. It didn't matter unless they were registered and staying at the hotel; they were not allowed back in our rooms. Some were doctors, lawyers and business owners and we danced the night away and drank some great champagne that I charged to my suite—I mean Mickey's suite.

When they returned, I asked where they been and Mickey told me that they were deep into the countryside where Howard had a factory canning peaches and other fruits. But you can imagine, it wasn't peaches being sealed into those cans then shipped around the world on one of his ships. What a great experience it was and to become close friends with Howard who used to always call me years later when he was in the north of England on one of his lecture tours or radio or TV interviews. We had some great nights out talking about the old days but by then he had been to prison, come out, and had been retired for a long time.

One night in Majorca that I was involved in big time was in a club called BCM in Magaluf. They were having their own Miss Wet T-shirt contest and this club held over 4000 people. It was one of the biggest clubs in the world and with the manager being a friend, I was always asked to be a judge of the contest. If any of my pals were staying with me, they would also be judges with me as the main judge. The girls used to smile and flirt to hopefully get our votes and, if I was alone, the winner would usually end up with me later that night.

This particular night, I wasn't alone but with a girlfriend named Marley Marques, a beautiful, mixed-race Swedish girl whose mother was Swedish and her father was from Aruba. This girl I dated for a couple of summers. She came to Manchester and later came to New York to see me, so it was quite serious in those days. This evening, the contest was being filmed for Spanish Television and the club was packed but they had lots of giant screens around the club so everyone could see everything. Marley couldn't get near the dance floor but was watching from the back with her friends on the giant screens.

The manager announced the judges, saying that tonight we have celebrity judges from England that flew in especially for the contest in their own jet. We have multi-millionaire shirtmaker and friend of Hollywood stars, Mr. Frank Rostron. He usually went over the top, but this night went way over with me and my fellow judges. They were my pals, so I didn't care; also, this night, we had been drinking and I think even taken some illegal substances and we were flying—particularly me.

All the contestants were on holiday from Sweden and other Scandinavian countries and came out onto the dance floor one by one in their cutoff T-shirts and bikini bottoms, waving and smiling at us. All were hoping to get our votes and win the grand prize of 100 pounds and a bottle of champagne. One girl in particular was really beautiful from Switzerland of Asian origin and was buzzing as well, either drunk or had been taking stuff or both. She came out waving and blowing kisses at me and one by one they had their turn in the portable pool had water poured over themselves, showing off their breasts and bodies through their wet T-shirts.

When it was her turn after the water was poured over her, she ripped off her T-shirt along with her bikini bottom and threw them away, then came dancing over to me stark naked, gesturing for me to come with her. When I didn't, she came to my stool, took hold of my hands and danced me back to the pool where she lay backwards, legs open and pulled me by my hair between her legs. As you can imagine, all hell let loose with everyone cheering. The TV company pulled the plug on the cameras and lights.

My girlfriend, Marley, saw all this live on the giant screens; she pushed her way through the crowds, grabbed me and dragged me off the girl and out of the club, shouting and screaming in Swedish all the way back to my house. I had until the morning to find an excuse so she wouldn't be on the next plane to Sweden and with my experience in these situations, I did. She forgave me and all was good until the next day. I thought we would go out alone on my boat and have lunch somewhere and we did, arriving back at La Baraka about 4:30 p.m. As we pulled in, a crowd of about thirty to forty people were looking inside the restaurant which was very unusual. Some were standing on chairs to get a good view of whatever they were looking at. We walked up to the crowd, and I asked someone what's going on, to which this guy replied they are watching a video of the Miss Wet T-shirt contest in BCM last night. One of the judges got in the pool with one of the contestants who was naked and started having sex with her then his girlfriend came and dragged him off her. I walked in, saw Claude and said, "What's going on?" He thought it was funny that someone had brought in the tape of last night and was playing it to everyone. Marley didn't think it was so funny, so we went around the corner to Roger's bar for a drink until it was all over and the crowd disappeared.

As I said, lots of soccer players came to the island and in 1982, Scotland was playing Brazil in the World Cup in the beautiful Spanish city of Seville. A few of us, including some players, went to watch the match but I should have been back by noon, two days later, as my best friend, Cliff Brierley, was arriving on holiday to stay at my house. Our flight was delayed, and we didn't get back to Majorca until late that evening. I went straight to La Baraka looking for Cliff but Claude told me he had finished his dinner, bought drinks for everyone in the restaurant which he often did being a very generous guy and left to go on the town.

I went to several bars looking for him but with no luck. So, I went to Alexander's night club and who was at the bar, surrounded by four, beautiful, Swedish girls and the bar full of bottles of champagne, but Cliff. After he introduced me to the girls and me making my apologies for my delay, I noticed that the girls were wearing his jewelry. One, his gold Cartier watch, another, his gold Gucci necklace, another, his Cartier bracelet and the fourth, his diamond ring. I said, "OK, girls, the fun's over, give Cliff his jewelry back." To which they replied no, he's given these to us as presents to which Cliff said no, I've given them to the girls as presents. Well, even in those days, this jewelry was probably worth over fifty thousand pounds—150 today—probably more than the house they lived in and they are all saying, including Cliff, no, they are ours.

I went to get the manager who was a friend and explained what had happened and he came over saying give him his jewelry back, otherwise I will call the police and you will go to jail. They reluctantly did with Cliff drunk, still arguing, saying it's theirs, I gave it to them. I asked the manager to put it in his safe and I would pick it up the next day and then took Cliff home to sleep. The next morning when he came downstairs, I was having coffee on the terrace, and he said what a night that was and what a hangover I have, showing me bar bills for hundreds of pounds. I said that's cheap; you gave all your jewelry away as well. He couldn't believe it even though he's done stupid things in the past that had cost big money. I thought I would keep him in suspense for a couple of hours to teach him a lesson, before I told him I had his jewelry.

Another time, a guy I had met years earlier in Birmingham, with the nickname of Coventry Wally, arrived on the island. He was spending money and looking for a house to rent. By this time, I had sold my apartment above La Baraka and had a house built on the cliffs in Torre Nova, overlooking Palma Nova and Magaluf bays which had a self-contained apartment adjoining it. So, always looking to earn money, I rented Wally my house for a year with me moving into the apartment. Soon Wally bought an expensive speedboat, a BMW car and was spending on La Baraka big time.

With me as his landlord and living next door, we socialized and he confided in me what he was up to. He was running a con similar to Bernie Madoff. He advertised in *The Sunday Times,* very professionally offering big interest on investments with an accommodation address 2 Berkeley Square, Mayfair, London W1, one of the most prestigious addresses anyone could have. I cannot believe how greedy and stupid people are. The office in Mayfair sent all the mail to a PO Box in Jersey, Channel Islands, who forwarded his mail to Majorca.

I saw the checks—twenty-five, fifty, seventy-five thousand pounds. It was like Christmas Day for him every week as his mail arrived from Jersey. The investors never heard from him again. Near the end of his first year in Majorca, he told Claude that he wanted to buy some jewelry for himself and his girlfriend, perhaps a watch or bracelet. Claude was well-known and had friends in Palma, who had high class jewelry shops. We had all bought stuff from them over the years so Claude took Wally into town to look. Wally saw a few watches with diamonds and other pieces he liked but said he was undecided. Claude's friend said, "Take the stuff home, look at your leisure, bring it back tomorrow and pay for anything you like." Wally took home jewelry worth about 50,000 pounds but there was no tomorrow. Wally unbeknown to everyone had sold the boat and BMW and left the island that night even leaving a bill at La Baraka for a few hundred pounds. The jewelry was his final prize in Majorca—a little going away present for himself. We heard a few years later and it was in the newspaper that he was found dead in Amsterdam wrapped in a carpet, shot in the head.

    As I said, there were hundreds of single girls that I dated in Majorca, but it was also a magnet for married women. It's unbelievable what a blue sky, the Mediterranean Sea, and a couple of bottles of champagne can do to make their heads spin and forget their wedding vows. There was one particular crowd from Sweden that used to come three or more times a year and had homes on the island. They always spent their days when they weren't playing golf on La Baraka sunbathing and having lunch. They used to drink only the finest wines and ate great food and became good friends of everyone. They used to come with their husbands a couple of times a year but also had a girls' only trip once or twice a year.

On the girls' trips, we would see them at night in Palma at all the fashionable restaurants and clubs. We drank and danced with them and saw them on the beach the next day. They were all fantastic people but one of them, Gullbritt, became closer to me than the others, and we started an affair. This lasted many years; we even keep in touch today. She is a very special lady. She and her husband had a successful international business and travelled a lot, so she could say that she had to go to London and stay in one of London's finest hotels just to see me. We would enjoy our time together in the best restaurants and nightclubs the city had to offer, and we were both sad when she had to go home. She told me later that she had confessed to her husband of her affair with me, but they are still together to this day. Gullbritt and her husband are heavily involved in racehorses and travel the world watching their horses run. One time, she was in Dubai for The Dubai Gold Cup. At the after-dinner party for the owners and VIPs, she sat the whole evening next to Frankie Dettori who was the ruler, Mohammed bin Rashid Al Maktoum's, personal jockey. Gullbritt knew Frankie was a friend of mine and spent the evening talking about my escapades in Majorca. Frankie told her similar stories about me in Barbados. I don't know if she confided in him about me, but if she didn't, Frankie would have guessed, I'm sure.

There are lots of married women that I cannot mention

because they are still married today, and their husbands never knew about their Majorca La Baraka escapades. Some of them are wives of my very close friends. One of them was Vim Suurbier, a friend from La Baraka and a soccer legend from Holland. Vim was a great guy who came to visit me in Manchester once and we had our photo in *The Manchester Evening News,* saying he was there to sign for Manchester United—afraid not, he was only visiting me. He was handsome, rich and famous, played in two World cup finals for Holland and won three European cups for Ajax and even his wife, Mia, strayed. She fell in love with my pal from Birmingham, Johnny Hart, and after the affair was in the open, left Vim and moved to Birmingham to live with John. Johnny was a millionaire playboy so I was shocked when he settled down with Mia and was a dream catch for all the girls. He was a *cordon bleu* cook, spoke four languages fluently, water skied mono and barefoot and was a brilliant snow skier. He had beautiful homes in Majorca and Birmingham and had a new ski boat in a different color delivered to La Baraka every year. Even my personal doctor, David Herbert, who was my friend from the age of fifteen, bought a house in Majorca but with his very busy work schedule couldn't make every holiday with his wife, Astrid, who was also my close friend. Even she succumbed to the temptation and had an affair eventually leaving David and ended up living in Majorca. My accountant and friend for over thirty years, Ray Tish, and even his wife, Pat, joined the sunshine club for married women. So, not only did the young, single girls come to La Baraka looking for boyfriends but also many mature married ones also.

We spent most nights in the beautiful city of Palma even though it sounds from some of the stories that we spent most of the time in Magaluf. We didn't, we only lived there and called in on our way home to make sure we hadn't missed anything. The restaurants and clubs in Palma were far more elegant than in Magaluf. No Miss Wet T-shirt contests in Palma but beautiful streets like Plaza Gomila and Carrer de Sant Joan and bars like Abaco, Harry's Bar, and The Waikiki bar as well as clubs like Club de Mar, Sgt. Peppers, Babbles and El Rodeo. The managers of all these bars and clubs were friends and again we were VIPs in all of them. I played football for Sgt. Peppers for many years.

One particular close friend was Gabrielle, the manager from El Rodeo. One night after I had left for England, a Swedish girlfriend who I was seeing called Berit Colhead was in the club. She was telling Gabrielle how much she missed me and how much she loved me and this night he was with another friend, Miguel, who happened to be chief of police at Palma Airport. These two thought it would be funny to put her on a flight to Manchester to see me. She couldn't believe it when they asked her if she wanted to go. "Of course, I do," she said. They took her to the airport in the middle of the night. Miguel walked her through the airport security personally and put her on a plane to Manchester.

I got a call from Manchester airport immigration at 6:00 a.m., saying there was a girl called Berit at the airport who had come to see me. She had no suitcase, clothes or money and would I vouch for her. I'm not sure and can't remember if she even had her passport with her. I drove to the airport, signed some documents and drove Berit back to my house with her explaining the story and me seeing how Gabrielle and Miguel would find what they did so hilarious. They called me later that day and couldn't talk for laughing about what they had done. But it wasn't such a bad thing. I had a very beautiful Swedish girl in town for a while that I was very fond of, and we had a great time together.

Now the only problem was she had no clothes, underwear, toiletries—nothing, so we had to go shopping. In itself, it wasn't that expensive but the following Saturday, I had a black-tie charity ball at Mere Golf Resort & Spa in Cheshire, a very exclusive and prestigious annual event. Berit, being Frank Rostron's date, had to have an evening dress as good if not better than any of the other girls. And then, there was the shoes etc. which did cost a lot of money and never to be used again. But it was worth it. She looked great—a suntanned Swedish beauty on my arm with little or no makeup so that even my closest pals wanted to know where she came from. I said it's a long story; I will tell you another time and ten days later, we both flew back to Majorca. She had a wonderful time in Manchester; Gabrielle told that story to everyone for years.

One morning, I walked on the beach, looked around and about fifty yards from La Baraka, a beauty lay sunbathing. I asked a couple of the guys already on the beach if they knew her, but they didn't and that they had already tried picking her up but with no luck. I called Manolo, our waiter from La Baraka, and said take a bottle of champagne with an ice bucket and stand, put a white napkin over your arm, walk down the beach to that girl and don't speak to her. Just place the stand next to her towel, open the champagne, pour a glass and hand it to her. Again, don't speak unless she asks you where it came from. Then you can say Mr. Frank at La Baraka and walk away.

About one hour later, she starts to get up from her towel and what a vision. She was 5'10", had a Louis Vuitton beach bag, Louis Vuitton towel, long blonde hair, suntan and she was stunning. She walked over to the restaurant asking for me as any person with manners and class would, introducing herself as Dominique Notterman from Antwerp, Belgium. She asked why I had bought her champagne and I replied so I could invite you for lunch. Dominique laughed and we spent the next two weeks together until she had to leave. She had a very unusual way of saying yes. I would ask her, "Dominque would you like a glass of wine," and she would say in a very sexy French accent, "I don't see why not." "Dominque, should we have dinner at Mario's tonight?" and she would say, "I don't see why not." It got to the stage where everyone on La Baraka was saying when asked a question as Dominique would say, "I don't see why not," even years later people who had never even met her would say as Dominique would say, 'I don't see why not,' and laugh. I went to Belgium many times and she also came to England as we dated for a few years. Obviously, when she was not in Majorca, as with all of them, it was business as usual for me and my gang.

Many years later, probably ten to twelve years, I went to see one of my pals who had just moved into a new penthouse overlooking Palma. His name was George Harrison (not the Beatle). When I arrived at his house, he said you will not believe who lives in the penthouse next door. I said who and he replied, "I don't see why not." He didn't even say Dominque. I said you are joking. He said no, she lives in Cape Town, South Africa, married with two children. I couldn't believe it. I had to see her—one of the loves of my life when she was eighteen to twenty years old. I said to George, you must tell her I want to speak with her and he said he would do what he could.

A few days later, George came to La Baraka with her telephone number and said to call her. I was shaking, nervous but happy. I had no idea what I was going to say. She came down to the beach for lunch and told me the whole story of her life since we had last seen each other. She spends eight months a year in South Africa and travelling and four months in Majorca. I was embarrassed as my life was exactly the same as when I last saw her. Going to La Baraka, eating, drinking, sex drugs and rock 'n' roll but not too much rock 'n' roll. She looked sensational, and, if that was possible, even better than before. We had a four-hour lunch and arranged to have dinner the next night. Her husband was in South Africa, and she was selling the penthouse.

I went to collect her under the pretense of being a potential buyer. She showed me around the magnificent property, introducing me to her children and housekeeper as Mr. Rostron. Then we left and had dinner in one of the finest and most romantic restaurants in Palma that I had never been to that Dominique selected. From there, we drove to Puerto Portals where I had arranged to meet one of my pals and his wife, Steve and Ann Hayhurst, for drinks who were my neighbors in Rochdale but who also had a condo in Majorca. I must say, these are two of the sweetest people I know, and we have been close friends since we were teenagers. Ann tells the story that she was one of the girls who after school in Bury used to come outside Bensons of Bury, looking for little Frankie, the mod who parked his scooter outside the shop where he worked.

Dominique looked sensational in a full length, Versace, patterned dress. I can't imagine what it cost but it was worth every penny; she looked like a film star. As we walked down the narrow road in the port, with the boutiques and restaurants on our left and the yachts on our right, I could see Steve and Ann sitting at a front table at Cappuccino about fifty yards away. We waved but as we got about twenty-five yards closer to Cappuccino, someone calls out 'Dolly.' I look to my right and on the corner is a friend of mine, 'Cockney' Bernie, who lived in Monaco and Majorca, with a group of people. We walked over to him, and he introduced me to his friends, Rod Stewart and his wife, Penny. I introduced them to Dominique and even though Bernie had seen me with many stunning females even he was impressed with Dominique and, of course, Rod was. Then Bernie said to Rod, "Who have we been talking about all night?" and Rod says, Frank "the Shirt," to which Bernie replies, "Who do you think this is?" Rod looks at the wild-patterned shirt I was wearing and says, Frank "the Shirt." They invited us on their boat for drinks, but I politely declined as I was meeting Steve and Ann and didn't want a late one anyway, as I was thinking of bringing back memories with "I don't see why not" at my house later.

As we got to the table, Steve said, "Well, I've seen it all now. Rod Stewart calling Frank Rostron over to say hello." They had been watching Rod and his party for the last ten minutes. I didn't want to say that it wasn't Rod Stewart that called me over but my pal, Bernie, so I didn't. To this day, Steve still thinks it was Rod Stewart who called me over. But I will always be curious to know why Bernie and Rod Stewart were talking about Frank "the Shirt" all night over dinner. Unfortunately, I will never know as that was the last time I saw Bernie. He passed away shortly afterwards—a young man that was fun and very generous.

At the same time, Dominique and I arranged to meet in London the following month. She had a sister-in-law there and could use that as an excuse to be in London anytime that she wanted. She stayed at The Metropolitan hotel on Park Lane on my recommendation as it had a hot bar called The Met Bar. Unless you were a member, knew someone, or stayed at the hotel you couldn't get in. I thought that would be better than calling my pals in London to get us in as then they would want to be with us. I drove down to London and parked my car in the hotel's underground car park and went to her room. We had a bottle of champagne, showered, got dressed and went out for dinner. Afterwards, we spent the rest of the evening in the trendy Met Bar where Dominique signed the check to her room.

The next morning, we had breakfast in our room, and I went to see some clients and she went to see her sister-in-law. About an hour or so later, she called me in a panic and said her husband was in Brussels and she knows that he will come to London so for me not to come to the hotel. She said that she would call me later and before I could say anything, she cut me off. I wanted to say in case he does come, pay the hotel bill. But he did come and she hadn't paid it. Only then, he went and paid the bill and said to the receptionist that this couldn't possibly be his wife's bill as she doesn't have a car and breakfast is for two and she's alone. The receptionist explained to him that his wife's friend had a car and had eaten breakfast. She was busted. Dominique called me the next day telling me all this and that they had obviously had a massive row and he had flown back to South Africa, saying she could do whatever she wants. She was upset and not in the mood to talk and we never saw each other ever again.

The club, Babbles, in Palma, was a series of caves with small dance floors in the middle so four, six or eight people could each have a cave with a low table for drinks, large cushions, or chairs in the cave. It was a very cool looking place. One night, I am in with my crowd of mixed males and females. I went to the toilet and I'm at the stones having a pee and a guy comes next to me. He's wearing a one-piece cat suit with a zip up the front. So, to pee, he had to take it off his shoulders and roll it down to his waist which was strange as I have never seen this before. As he was getting dressed, he asked me if I would dance with his wife as she had been watching me dance and would like to dance with me. I said of course and he took me back to their cave which was two caves from ours; he had a crowd of people in his cave, and he introduced me to everyone.

He was Benny Anderson and she was Anni-Frid Lyngstad from Abba and this was at the peak of their world success. I got on the dance floor with Anni-Frid; my gang recognized her immediately and they couldn't believe that 'The Rock,' 'Dolly' or Frank "the Shirt" was dancing the night away with the dancing queen herself. We danced for three or four songs then I took her back to her cave. She said thank you to me and I said 'tack' to her which is Swedish for thank you. I picked up quite a bit of Swedish spending my summers in Majorca. She laughed and I went back to my cave to join my friends. That was another unbelievable experience in my life and another thing I didn't know was that she was Norwegian not Swedish. I always thought they were all Swedish. There are hundreds of stories that I can tell you about what happened in Majorca as these things happened nearly every day, but I am cherry picking just a few for the book, plus some really are unprintable.

A Spanish friend of mine called Tony is married to Angela McGrath from Manchester, the daughter of Paddy McGrath who owned the famous Mr. Smith's club in Catford, London. It's where the Richardsons and the Krays had the famous shoot out—one person was killed, and many others injured. Frankie Frazer was involved; the next day ending with Ronnie Kray shooting and killing George Cornell in The Blind Beggar on the Stratford Road.

Paddy was Hugh Hefner's partner in The Playboy Club in Manchester because in those days you couldn't get a gambling license, so for Hefner to open a Playboy club in Manchester, he had to have a partner with a license. Paddy had a license so that was the deal. Also, knowing Paddy and his family was another exclusive venue for me to go to and get VIP treatment. I didn't gamble but they had an incredible restaurant and, of course, very attractive bunny girls.

I have drifted there, so let me get back to Tony who owned a great club called La Serena in Cala Mayor where Paddy McGrath had a home along with Brian Clough and many others which was just outside Palma. I would often pop in to see Tony and have a drink on my way home. One night, I went in and when Tony saw me coming down the stairs sent one of his waiters to tell a girl to come over to him. This beautiful, blonde Swedish girl arrived and Tony said to her this is my friend, Frank, who plays football for Manchester United. The girl shakes my hand, Tony orders me a bottle of champagne, shows me and the girl to a sofa around the dance floor, and leaves. We drank and danced for an hour or so, getting on well with kissing and petting, so I asked her if she wanted to come back to my hotel. At this time, I had sold my apartment above La Baraka and for a year or so, while my house in Torre Nova was being built, we stayed in hotels. Except on one occasion when I stayed in a customer's house in Andratx which is another wild story that I will tell you about later.

At this time, I was staying at a beautiful Spanish hotel that a friend of mine, Martin, owned called The Bon Sol in Illetes, just ten minutes from La Serena. We went back to the hotel, and she was unbelievable in bed, with the greatest slim, tanned body, white-blonde hair, was very experienced and nearly killed me—she absolutely wiped me out. About 5:00 a.m., she said, "Frankie, I must leave now and go home before my mother wakes up." I asked why as Swedish girls and parents are usually very liberal and she said because I am only fourteen years old. I couldn't get my breath. She looked twenty-one and before you start, I was probably only twenty-three or twenty-four years old myself and the age of consent in Sweden was fifteen, so it wasn't that bad.

The next night, me and the boys go into Palma to have dinner then go to a few bars and clubs to look for girls. About 2:00 a.m., I thought, *what am doing with this lot looking for girls when I have the most beautiful Swedish girl waiting for me in La Serena.* I left Plaza Gomila and jumped in a cab to Cala Mayor. As I walked in the club, she comes running over and jumps into my arms saying Frankie, Frankie where have you been, I've been waiting for you all night. I quickly said I had to take my boys out for dinner and then get them into a club and they wouldn't let me leave but I got away and I'm here for you now.

We go on the dance floor and dance for a while then I asked her what she wanted to drink but she said she wanted nothing. I want to go to your hotel now. So not being one to argue, we walk outside and flagged a cab for the ten-minute ride to The Bon Sol Hotel. We go to bed, and she was again sensational—better than the previous night, more promiscuous, adventurous, and again she wore me out. It was now nearly 5:00 a.m., and I needed some sleep so I said to her get dressed, it's 5:00 a.m., and I will walk you to the taxi rank. She replied that it was alright, she could stay all night. "I told my mother all about you today and that you play for Manchester United so she said I can stay." Can you believe how easy these soccer players must have it with girls, but it's the same for rock stars, film stars, and I presume sometimes shirtmakers.

Once, a client of mine from London, but I knew him originally from Manchester, was named Eugene Rigg (this is the wild story I said that I would tell you about), offered to let me stay at his house in Port Andratx while mine was being built. It was a long way from La Baraka and even longer to Palma. It was free—no hotel bill—so I thought, *let me try and see how it works out*. It was a lovely, Spanish stone house in the old part of Andratx, with stone floors, stairs, and farmhouse doors with latches—very quaint and rustic. This trip was with four pals from Manchester, including John Moroney from Birmingham, and they were all staying as my guests at Eugene Rigg's house. They complained about the distance to everywhere, but I reminded them it was free, so they stopped moaning.

On La Baraka, we met lots of different people from all over the world. One of the crowds that used to visit every time they were in Palma were the officers of the US Navy's sixth fleet. These massive aircraft carriers carried four thousand to six thousand men, patrolled the Mediterranean, and came into Palma for rest and relaxation. The crew used to hit the town drinking, chasing girls and partying for the entire time that they were in port. The officers used to come to La Baraka, have lunch, drink, stay for the day and leave for their ship early evening. We got friendly with them and many times they invited us aboard these colossal ships: The USS Independence, The USS John F. Kennedy, and more. They were like floating cities. They had restaurants, kitchens, food, drinks, laundries, doctors, hospitals and, of course, accommodation for these thousands of men. One particular officer, called Steve, said to me one day after watching the fun, games, and partying that went on at La Baraka that his fiancé from America was coming in a day or so and that she would really like me. He said she loves a laugh and having fun so he would bring her to the beach to meet me. I said great and left it at that.

The next night, me, John Moroney, and the boys were walking down the narrow streets of Plaza Gomila, going to Sgt. Peppers when this girl came running up behind me and jumped on my back. I didn't know who she was, but she was hugging and kissing me, and the boys couldn't believe it. She was beautiful and her name was Cheyanne Pleasantfield. Walking a minute behind her, laughing, was Steve and another three officers from the ship. It was Steve's fiancé; she had arrived, and she certainly did like me.

We all went into the club, Cheyanne linked into my arm all the way and Steve saying didn't I say that she would love you, Frankie. We went to the bar, ordered drinks, and Cheyanne pulled me onto the dance floor where we danced as she hugged and kissed me all this time, with the boys looking on in disbelief. I had to stop and go to the bar and even though I had been drinking all night and was drunk, I needed another drink. We were at the bar about fifteen minutes when Cheyanne said she wanted to dance some more, took my hand and dragged me back on the floor.

After a couple of dances where she is kissing my face and neck and with her hands all over me, my pal, John Moroney, came over and said what the fuck are you doing; her boyfriend is there. I replied something like so what, there are four of them and five of us—no problem—to which Moroney replied, yes, but one phone call and there will be 4000 of them and still five of us. John walked back to the bar and I carried on dancing. Then suddenly, Cheyanne says to me, "You know, Steve really likes you. He told me all about you on the phone before I arrived, how handsome you are and all the fun you have on the beach and he is so right, Frankie. Do you know how much he likes you?" I said, "No, not really," and she said, "He likes you so much he would rather watch you make love to me than make love to me himself."

Immediately, I start to sober up as no one has ever said that to me before even though I know this sort of thing happens. Then she said, "What do you think, Frankie, would you mind Steve watching if we made love." I said, "Of course not, I'm game." Then, all of a sudden, it went like a business meeting; she walked off the dance floor, took Steve to one side, and talked to him. Moroney and the boys asked what had just happened and I told them the story and Moroney said, "Hey, pal, if it goes off, I can't help you out of this one.

I thought that the guys would be with me so I would be ok, plus she was beautiful, with that long dark hair and unbelievable body. The three of us left and got into their little rental car. Cheyanne got into the back with me, Steve driving, and she continued kissing and mauling me. Then she said that we would stay at their hotel which was only a few minutes away. I said no chance; we will go to my house in Andratx or there is no deal. I said you go to your hotel and get your clothes for the beach tomorrow and let's go to Andratx. Steve pulled up outside this small hotel in Palma with Cheyanne telling him what she needed him to pack for her; he went inside. By then, I'm sobering up more and more and thinking of all the things that could happen to me. They could kill me, throw me over a cliff into the sea—anything. I've read about these things; plus, I don't have my gang with me.

So, I said to her that since I have never done anything like this before, when we get to the house, tell Steve to go into another room for fifteen minutes whilst we kiss and have foreplay, otherwise I won't be able to perform. So, it's that or nothing. I thought if he does that, I will have done her and it will all be over when he comes in, plus the boys will be home by then. I am sure they would have left the club right after us. When we arrived at the house, it was completely dark and silent and she tells Steve the plan to which he agrees. We go upstairs, he goes into another bedroom, and Cheyanne comes into mine. We undress, get on the bed kissing, and I'm on top of her. It had only been a couple of minutes and we have just started when the door opens and Steve walks in stark naked. He walks past the bed and sits back on his haunches in the corner of the bedroom, and I thought to myself, *what happened to my fifteen minutes*. I carried on with one eye on him with her screaming fuck me, fuck me and him saying go on, Frankie, fuck my girl, she loves you. Well, it might be laughable now but at the time it was pretty scary.

After about ten minutes of this pantomime of him shouting orders, telling me what to do to her, and Cheyanne telling me how much she loves me, a car screeches up outside—the troops had arrived. They were all drunk and trying to be quiet saying *shush*, can you hear anything, as they come up the stone steps with one kicking the step and breaking his toe. Screaming out loud as he kicked the concrete step, the others were saying *shush* but making more noise than a herd of elephants as they get to my bedroom door. I can hear them saying can you hear anything, what's happening. Then the door opens with four heads sitting on top of the other like a cartoon movie looking into my room.

They cannot believe what they see. Me on the bed banging Cheyanne with her legs wrapped around my waist and an officer from the USS John F. Kennedy, her naked fiancé, sitting in the corner watching. They pile in and Moroney rips his clothes off, pulls me off her, and dives in himself with the US officer getting more and more excited, shouting and screaming more instructions. He is now telling Moroney what to do as Moroney and I are having a threesome with her. The other guys start undressing now; they know it's all ok. One friend, who I love dearly and is a perfect gentleman, said to me Frankie, this is not right and left and went to his own room. The rest of us took turns with her and had an orgy with this Native American Indian called Cheyanne Pleasantfield, whilst her fiancé got off just watching the circus.

The next day, we all went to the beach with her still hanging around me and within minutes, Claude and everyone knew what had happened. Claude taking me to one side saying is it true, are you fucking crazy. We could have four thousand guys down here wanting to kill you and this time I can't help you. I assured him there was no problem plus it was Moroney as well. I threw him right under the bus. They stayed all day on the beach having lunch and drinking and left for their hotel late that afternoon. That night we went into town, saw them in El

Rodeo and had a drink. I asked her to come to the bathroom with me, but she wouldn't unless Steve came with us. The only thing that turned her on was Steve watching and no way was I going into a small cubicle with the two of them. Other guys who knew the story were hitting on her all night, but I don't think any of them got a result. We didn't see them much after that but the next year, would you believe, I got an invitation to their wedding which would have been fun, but I declined. Eugene Rigg, my rich customer that owned the house, I saw again in New York years later, in unusual circumstances that you will find interesting later in the book.

Frank Rostron Shirtmakers Limited

I was eighteen years old and still living in our council house with my mum, Lena. My dad had passed away a year earlier, aged fifty-two. One night, she brought home from work some shirt fabric. It was plain blue end on end to make aprons for herself on her small, Singer sewing machine that she used to own. She made these aprons so she wouldn't wear her dresses out on the machinery she worked on every day. The fabric was slightly faulty, so they let the workers buy it cheap for a shilling a yard. Lena bought twelve yards. Working in Manchester, I knew a shirtmaker called Holroyd and Cooper on Spring Gardens who produced 'made-to-measure' shirts, so I asked Lena for three yards, took it to them and had my first shirt made.

At this time, the shop where I worked, John Michael, had a range of fashionable shirts from USA called Gant so I copied one of those. It had a soft button-down collar, half sleeves with a cuff and two pockets on the front, with a flap and box-pleat.

At the last minute after I had been measured, I asked the guy if I could have a smaller version of the pockets one on my left sleeve. He said of course. I don't know why I decided on that, but it must have been the designer in me coming out. I paid a pound to have this shirt made with my own material and six weeks later it was ready. I was excited as I went to pick it up not knowing or even dreaming that this would be the beginning of the rest of my life.

That Friday night, I went out with my pals from our council estate and wore it. Straight away, they all loved it, asking if it was from John Michael as no one had ever seen a shirt like that in those days. I said no, as I had ordered made-to-measure which freaked them out even more as no one had ever heard of someone having a shirt made. How much was it they had asked and again I don't know why I said this figure, but it was the first number that came into my head. I said three pounds, one pal saying get me one. He tried mine on and said make it a little bigger in the waist, a touch bigger on the neck, and that was it. I went to Lena asking for some more fabric which she gave me. I took it to Holroyd and Cooper and had another shirt made and six weeks later delivered it to my pal and he gave me three pounds.

I was on eight pounds a week basic wage at John Michael at that time so that week I earned 25% more. I didn't pay Lena for the cloth, so I thought *not bad*. Then a couple of the other lads said make us one, so I did the same and six weeks later delivered them. I got paid 6 pounds with 4 pounds profit that week—a 50% increase in my earnings at John Michael. The only problem was that when we went out that weekend, my pals and I were all wearing the same blue shirts as if it was a uniform. Lena had run out of the fabric and still had not made an apron for herself. She went back to work and bought some more, saying to me that it was the last piece. It had all gone, so I had to think of a plan B. Besides, we couldn't all be wearing the same blue shirt forever.

In those days, what is now a thriving Chinatown today was a square with nothing but textile merchants in every building. Upstairs and in the basements, hundreds of them selling every kind of fabric. Some were selling shirt fabrics; others were selling toweling and others suit lengths. They were mostly seconds with faults but cheap and sold in weight by the pound, bails tied up with string sold at fifty pence per pound. They would put the bail on the scales and if it weighed five-pounds then it cost me two-pounds fifty-pence to buy. That was ok but I couldn't afford to buy these bails without selling some shirts first. So, in my lunch time, I would take a pair of small scissors with me in my pocket and look around. Then if I saw a bail that looked promising, I would take small cuttings from the corners of each fabric without the owner knowing then hide the bail. I usually put it underneath a pile of others so it wouldn't be seen or sold. Then that night, I would show my customer half a dozen pathetic, little cuttings of fabric for them to choose from, saying these are my latest.

They would choose a couple then I would go back the

next day to dig out my bail hoping that it had not been sold. I would have it weighed, pay for it, take the ones that I had taken orders for to Holroyd and Cooper to have them made, the others going home for stock. By this time, all my mates plus their mates had bought shirts, so I needed new customers, and I would never sell them to customers of mine in John Michael. I put a small advert in *The Manchester Evening News* and started getting calls, so I was going out every night in my white Austin 1100 car seeing customers. I bought this when I sold my scooter. The registration was EVR 130D so I could go and see these new customers all over north and south Manchester. I had some cards printed with my home number and the words FRANK ROSTRON SHIRTMAKER to give out to people plus my new customers.

There was a time when my manager, Mr. Alan Gallagher, was sick off work for quite a while and our window dresser who didn't like me anyway was managing the shop in Mr. Gallagher's absence. He had heard on the grapevine about my shirts and got hold of one of my cards, telling the head office in London about me. The following week, the area manager from London came up, fired me on the spot, and gave me two weeks wages.

I was nineteen years old, unemployed but earning money, so I wasn't that concerned. I went to the dole office social security, and they paid me five pounds a week plus, by this time, I was earning twenty to twenty-five pounds a week selling shirts; I was rich. I was only getting about twelve pounds a week with commission at John Michael. Now, I was earning double that without going to work. Now, I could really tell people about my shirt business, in the streets, in clubs, bars anywhere and all this time, Lena kept telling me every day to get a proper job. I bought a sports car—a white MGC GT registration OOE 422G—the MGB had a 1800cc engine, but a MGC had a three-liter engine, so it was a flying machine. I didn't have a nine to five job so I would go into town about noon and walk around hoping that I bumped into someone to tell them about my shirts. I would then do the same every night in the bars and clubs. I had it made. I was earning good money and now dating a different class of girl but still living in my council house with my mum.

Most nights after the clubs closed, I still didn't go home but went to a coffee bar and restaurant called the Empire Grill in Albert Square. I was so cool, pulling up in my white MGC GT and parking immediately outside the window and the front door while most of the other patrons either walked there or got a lift. One morning about 3:00 a.m., we were all sitting at a prime table in the window having eggs and bacon or an omelette and looking across Albert Square when a Jaguar E-Type came speeding up John Dalton St. and crashed straight into the back of my car. It reversed then drove off at speed down Princess St. I sat there in shock and couldn't believe what had just happened. We all ran outside but the driver had turned his lights off so we couldn't see his registration and was well down the road. The manager had called the police who arrived minutes later and radioed ahead to other police about the incident. I was left standing there looking at my new MGC GT with the back all smashed in. About half an hour later, the police came back informing me that they had apprehended the driver of the E-Type who was drunk and was now in police custody.

The following week, I had to go to court as a witness about the crash because it was my car. I was sitting in the small waiting room at Minshull St. magistrates court, waiting for my name to be called, and a good friend and customer from my days at John Michael came in and sat next to me. His name was Geoffrey Uddin. He was a very wealthy Indian guy that owned a large and very busy Indian restaurant just outside town that everyone used to go to. I said to him Hi, Geoff, what are you doing in court? He said that last week he had been into Blinkers night club, was blind drunk, drove into the back of a car in Albert Square and drove off. What are you doing in here? he asked and I said that I had been in the Empire Grill in Albert Square last week and a car smashed into the back of my car and drove off.

We looked at each other for a couple of seconds and burst out laughing with Geoff immediately saying, I am so sorry, Frank, I had no idea it was you. He then said don't you worry about the cost and don't claim off your insurance but go to the best place to have your car repaired and give me the bill plus any other expenses that you might occur. I did exactly as he asked, and he paid like the gentleman he is, and we laughed about that for many years afterwards when he came into my shop or in a restaurant or night club.

On one of the days that I would walk around town, I was in Kendal Milne—Manchester's most exclusive department store owned by The House of Frazer which also owned Harrods before Mohamed Al-Fayed bought it. It was there that I bumped into Mike Summerbee's wife, Tina, who said that Mike went into John Michael looking for you and they said that you had left. I couldn't say I got fired so I said yes, I had to. I was so busy with my shirt business that I didn't have time for a day job as well. The natural spiel of a salesman just came out again. She said that Mike didn't know you made shirts; he would have some so call him and go down to the house.

One afternoon after training, I called him and arranged to go to his house in Timperley. The next day, I drove up in my white MGC GT and parked it in his drive. Mike like most people was impressed with things that made you look successful even though they could be financed like mine was or even borrowed. As a very successful Manchester businessman and a great friend of mine, David Johnston, once said to me, "Frank, 'you got to put a show on the road'" and even though I didn't realize I was doing that at the time, it was exactly what I was doing. I have probably done that most of my life ever since. Also remembering another saying that I learnt from one of my mentors, 'all that glitters is not gold.'

Mike chose half a dozen shirts and asked about my business, where I was having them made, and other questions.

I couldn't tell him I was taking faulty fabric that I bought at textile merchants to Holroyd and Cooper in Manchester and having them made, so I said I have a couple of ladies working from home making them for me. I told him that now I was looking for a location for my sewing machines. I didn't have any ladies or sewing machines to put anywhere. It was just the salesman again flowing out of me. He said how much will this cost you and again, like when I told my pals that the shirts were three pounds, I had no idea where that figure came from. I said 600 pounds. Again, having no idea where this number came from, he said if you let me be your partner, I will put up the 600 pounds. I stayed cool even though I was beside myself with excitement as one of the most famous soccer stars in England who also happens to be the star of my beloved team, Manchester City, had just asked to be my business partner.

He had just said that he would put up the money for my business. I couldn't believe it. I told him to let me think about it as I didn't really want a partner and I would get back to him in a couple of days. He then went on his own sales pitch to me saying how he could bring in lots of business from all the soccer teams including Manchester City and Manchester United and all his celebrity friends. I again said let me think about it. I left his house and had to park around the corner. I couldn't drive; I was so nervous but excited about this proposition and, of course, I was going to accept it. I knew I had to be careful and plan because for a start, I had no sewing machines, no machinists and he didn't even ask who cut them. I would need a cutter, as well, but what I really needed was a magician.

By now, I had left Holroyd and Cooper and was having my shirts made at a place called Arco Shirtmakers in Stevenson Square in Manchester because they could make the shirts in two weeks not six. They would also rush a special order through in a few days, if I needed it. Going into Arco most days taking in shirt orders or picking up shirts, I got friendly with the ladies and one had said to me a few times, if you ever start your own business, son, I will come and work for you. So, the next time I went in, I whispered to her can I have your address as I have something to tell you and she wrote it down and off I went.

That night, I went to her house in Cheetham Hill to see her. Millie Rhodes was about to become my first machinist and my savior in this deal with Mike Summerbee. I told her all about my new business and asked did she know a cutter to which she replied she did. The one whom she worked with for years at London Shirt Company in Cheetham Hill that had recently closed. His name was Fred Jones and he lived about ten miles on the other side of town. We arranged to go and visit him the next night. I went to Millie's and after dinner, we drove to Fred's house. We knocked on his door to be greeted by his wife, Joan, who said that Fred was now working at a petrol station just down the road. We drove to this petrol station in my MGC GT for this man to come and ask what grade petrol I wanted. When seeing Millie, he was shocked and asked her what she was doing over on this side of town. Millie then said that we need to talk with you. She told him all about me and my plans and asked if he would like to be back in the shirt business and of course, he would.

I said to both of them that I first have to get a room and a couple of sewing machines and get back to you. Millie told me that London shirts in Cheetham Hill still have some old machines that I could buy cheaply. I was off and running and my mum worked with a lady at the mill who also had a sewing machine to sell for twenty-five pounds, so I bought that and bought two from London shirts. I called Summerbee the next day and went to see him to tell him that I agreed to go into business with him. We arranged that he would give the money to his solicitor, Michael Horwich, who would then give it to me as I needed it to pay for things to set up this new business.

I had never met or been in a solicitor's office before, so it was all new but very exciting to me. Michael Horwich formed a company with 100 shares called FRANK ROSTRON SHIRTMAKERS LIMITED. I couldn't believe that all this was happening to me. Then he explained what we would have to do. He said with Mike being an equal partner with me, we should have forty-nine shares each and he would hold two shares in case in the future we had a decision that we both didn't agree on. Then, he would decide on my side or Mike's—whatever he thought was in the best interest for the company. I didn't care; I was so excited, Horwich could have had all the shares. I had a company in my name, business cards and shirt labels with my name. I still couldn't believe it and I was still living with my mum in our council house.

I found premises at Trevelyan Buildings, 52 Corporation St., Manchester—a 600 square foot room at the back of the building on the ground floor at ten pounds a week rent with a back door at the side entrance. My next-door neighbor, Winnie Kerr (who took me to my first football match at eight years old), had her husband, Terry, divide the room—one half for the showroom and the other for the workroom—and built a cutting table for Fred Jones. He built shelves for the fabrics; he also did the electric points for the sewing machines. I was going to Michael Horwich when I needed to pay a bill as Mike Summerbee had gone on tour to Australia with Manchester City. When he came back a month later, he said I can't believe it. We have a business with a brass plate at the building entrance saying FRANK ROSTRON SHIRTMAKERS LTD and a painted sign on the showroom door saying the same. I thought to myself, *he couldn't believe it. I couldn't believe it either, because when he left on tour, I had nothing but a dream.*

I also had no orders, so Fred and Millie agreed to stay working at their jobs until I was ready, but they would work in the evenings for me. I used to work in the office all day nine till five and take orders. Then at 5 p.m., I'd go to Stevenson Square and pick Millie up from work and take her home for her dinner. Then I would drive across town to collect Fred who had already had his dinner and drive him into Manchester, and he would start cutting the day's orders. I would then go to pick up Millie as she would have finished her dinner and take her to the office to start sewing the shirts that Fred was cutting.

When Fred had finished cutting the shirts, I would then drive him home then come back and start to button and buttonhole the shirts that Millie had made. When she was finished usually about 10 or 11 p.m., I would drive her home and then go back into Manchester to one of the clubs to relax and have a drink. When you are nineteen years old, it didn't matter that you worked fourteen-fifteen hours a day. I just loved it, plus it was my own business. This only went on for a couple of months before I could start Millie and Fred full-time. We had by then lots of orders and soon after that I started a second and then third full-time machinist.

People were walking in off the street to order shirts, plus my original customers, and Mike was also bringing in customers as he had promised. Celebrities and lots of soccer players when they played in Manchester came in to buy shirts because Mike Summerbee was a partner. We had only been in business a few months, doing well, and Mike wanted a new Jaguar saloon. With him being married and about to start a family, his Jaguar E-Type was great for a single guy but not a married man. So, he suggested that I take his E-Type and put up my MGC GT in part exchange for his saloon. I jumped at the opportunity; not only was I driving an E-Type Jaguar, the hottest car on the road, but Mike Summerbee's E-Type Jaguar. What more could a young kid want: I owned my own business, drove an E-Type, went to the top clubs around, dated models and beauty queens, yet still lived in my council house with Lena. I needed my own home.

About this time, Lena was off work sick and had to go into the hospital. This was the first time that my superhero had ever been ill or off work in her life and certainly in my life. I was worried stiff thinking that she must be dying because only death would make my mum not go to work. I didn't know this until years later because as a boy and our family not talking about these things, no one told me about her hysterectomy. I really thought that she was dying, plus I wouldn't have known what that was anyway.

I had never met him, but I knew I had an uncle in Guernsey who was one of my dad's ten brothers; he was called Harry. I found his telephone number in my mum's book and called him saying hello, Uncle Harry, this is your nephew, Frankie, from Manchester. I am Fred's son. With him asking what's wrong, Frankie, is your mum alright, I replied, no, Uncle Harry, she's in hospital and I think she's dying. But she's coming out this week and I wonder, if I bought her a plane ticket, could she come and stay with you for a week or two. "Of course, she can," he replied. "We would love to see her." When Lena came home, I told her she was going to Guernsey to see Uncle Harry. Little did I know but he had called the hospital and knew she wasn't dying. Now, I was the only one that thought that she was dying. I am twenty years old, and no one told me. She stayed with them for six weeks and I was so happy as this was the only holiday she had ever taken in her life. All that she had ever done was work in the mill and take care of me and my dad.

Before Lena went into the hospital, I had started looking to buy my first house for us to live in. I had the money and was ready to buy. I was going to make it a surprise for her and at first, I wanted to buy Summerbee's house in Timperley Cheshire as he was ready to move, and I loved it. Tina had furnished it so well and I could have moved in straight away. It was perfect but she wouldn't sell it to me. Tina had said that if there was ever a problem with the house, she would feel bad with me buying it so she would rather sell it to a stranger. I didn't agree with her, but I understood.

A new development was being built in Bamford near Rochdale, North Manchester, and about six miles from where we lived. I went to look at them and fell in love with the houses and the estate. They were mock Georgian, detached houses and I bought one—77 Oulder Hill Drive, Bamford, Rochdale. I got my friends like Terry Kerr to build the interior like I wanted with wine cabinets and bookshelves and to furnish it. I had it all ready when I went to collect Lena from her holiday in Guernsey. As I was driving her home from the airport, she noticed I was going a different way and asked why with me saying I wanted to show her something. We drove to Bamford to the house and into the driveway at 77 Oulder Hill Drive with Lena asking who lives here and as we walked into the hallway, I said we do.

She said that I couldn't afford this; take me home, my feet are killing me. But I insisted she look around because it was beautiful, and I was so proud. It was the first house that I owned. I had lived in Byron Road for nearly twenty-one years and Lena, since she was married, thirty-five years earlier. The hall was bigger than our front room in Middleton and the lounge and dining room were bigger than the whole house. It had four bedrooms and three bathrooms, with two *en suite*. Lena had never seen a house like this before and couldn't believe I owned it. But she still said that she would never live there and now take me home.

Every weekend, I would take her to the house and show her what was new since the week before. She still insisted that she wouldn't move in because if I ever couldn't afford the mortgage and lost the house, she would have nowhere to live and used to say she would end up in the poorhouse.

I was still living with Lena in our council house and used to date girls but at the weekends, after taking them for dinner and then to clubs, we would go back to my house in Bamford. I used to leave and take them home very early the next morning, feeling embarrassed about the neighbors seeing me. Years later, after becoming friends, they used to joke and talk about the guy who owned this beautiful house. They never saw him but that he would come home late and leave very early in the morning and only at the weekends.

After taking Lena every Sunday for six months, I finally talked her into leaving the only house that she had lived in since she married and move with me to the house in Bamford. But even then, she wouldn't move in until the Monday because she said it was bad luck saying, 'weekend flitting early sitting.'

So, I moved in full-time on the Friday and Lena followed me on the Monday. I must say living alone all weekend felt great with the girls staying and not being driven home at 7:00 a.m. but having a cup of tea in bed, walking around the gardens and going out for Saturday or Sunday lunch then home. It really did feel good, and I was so proud.

Everything was great and life couldn't be better. Then one day, about ten months after we opened the office in Manchester, I got a letter saying they were going to pull our building down to build The Arndale Center. This is now Manchester's largest shopping mall. I was devastated. I thought this new life of mine was too good to be true. That day, a customer came in and saw I was upset and asked me what was wrong. I told him and he asked if I had a lease and I said yes—for three years. He said good. Take it to your solicitor and the developers will have to pay you to leave, otherwise you could stay for the whole three years, and they don't want that. I took the letter to Michael Horwich who started negotiations for a compulsory purchase contract immediately.

They paid me 5000 pounds for my lease and to leave 52 Corporation St. which was a vast amount of money, seeing it cost less than 600 pounds to start the company less than a year earlier. I started looking around town this time for a retail shop. I had always imagined a shop with an old, curiosity shop, bowed window, a few bullseye glass panes, a brass rail, and velvet curtain inside like a Christmas card. I found a great location on Chapel Walks—a perfect location in the center of town. It was next door to a law firm called Copeland and Glickman and I knew a young trainee lawyer there called Ian Burton. I went to see Ian, telling him that I fancied the shop next door asking did he know who owned it. We do, he replied. I asked how much they wanted for rent, and he came back with a figure of forty-two pounds a week.

A vast amount of money. I nearly fainted but it was perfect. A retail store in a great location, with offices, toilets, a cutting room for Fred and a workroom for many girls. I had to have it. As I still do today, I had to get a better deal and cried poverty and asked could they do a better price. Ian came back with thirty-eight pounds a week. I said I would take it. I got Winnie's husband, Terry, to do my shopfitting again but with this newfound wealth from the developers, it was plusher, with my dream shop window looking like a hundred-year-old sweet shop in London. It was perfect. We moved in and had a sensational opening party. I had my model girlfriend at the time, Francesca Assumah, walking around with one of my shirts on that looked like a very short minidress, serving drinks that all the guys loved. Every player from Manchester City and Manchester United was there, plus stars from Granada Television and their top TV show, *Coronation St*. All the press from local and national newspapers were there taking photos of Francesca drinking champagne with the celebrities for their next edition, all courtesy of my famous partner. The first week, we took in 900 pounds and I was worried about paying the thirty-eight pounds rent. From then on, it was all up and up.

Besides all my old John Michael customers, plus businessmen I didn't even know, now every celebrity that came to Manchester would come into the shop—Jimmy Tarbuck, Michael Parkinson, Michael Crawford, Les Dawson, Freddie Starr, Jim Davidson, Dave Allen and many more. All the soccer players bought shirts from me—not only Manchester players but teams from all over the country. At John Michael, we used to have a visitor's book on the counter and every celebrity and star that came in used to sign their autograph. I did the same at my new shop and before long it was full of autographs from the people I mentioned, . . . plus Bobby Moore, Frank Worthington, Peter Osgood, Alan Hudson, Gareth Edwards, Bobby Charlton, Paddy Crerand, Denis Law, Brian London, Johnny Prescot and again many more. When I left the company, I gave the book to Fred Jones, my cutter. Today that book would be worth a fortune.

The Break-Up

Everything was great but I was ambitious and wanted Frank Rostron shirt shops all over England—Birmingham, Leeds, Newcastle, London, Glasgow and other major cities. I appreciated what Summerbee had done for me but, looking back, not as much as I should have. I had a couple of very successful Manchester businessmen that wanted to be my partner at the time and for many years I wondered where I would be now, if I had gone with them instead of Summerbee, especially after we split up. But now, older and wiser, I wouldn't have swapped it for anything. He had no business experience so he couldn't teach me anything. Everything I know, I had to learn through trial and error or by listening to my friends and mentors like Selwyn Demmy, David Johnson, Cliff Brierley, Martin Reynolds and more.

So now, I wanted to open my second shop in Birmingham and this time I didn't need Summerbee's money or a loan from a bank. I had some money of my own plus Terry Kerr said he would do my shopfitting and I could pay him a little up front and the rest as I had it. The cotton mill I was dealing with loved this young kid from a council estate who was going to be big in the business also said the same—that I could pay them when I had it, so I was ready to go.

I had to tell Mike about this new shop that I wanted to open but without him being my partner. He didn't do anything in the store; he came in most days after training, stayed half an hour, had a coffee and left. I thought that if he was my partner in my new shop, I would be doing twice as much work, running both shops travelling from Manchester to Birmingham, getting home at all hours and getting only half the money. Although I appreciated him setting me up in business in the first place, I didn't need him for my new shop. He would be getting paid for investing and doing nothing.

I told him and a couple of days later, he said that there was a meeting in St. Johns Street with Maurice Rubin, a lawyer in Manchester, and would I be there. I knew of Maurice Rubin but didn't know him personally. I turned up at 3:00 p.m. and an assistant led me to this conference room and sitting there was Maurice Rubin, Summerbee and two more people. Maurice Rubin very politely introduced himself and told me the reason for the meeting was because I was opening this shop in Birmingham and Mike wanted to be my partner. He said that Mike would put the same amount of money as me into it and I told Rubin the reasons why I didn't want Mike involved. He said in that case you are fired from Frank Rostron Shirtmakers Limited as from now, so leave your shop keys and your company car here as you leave my office. I said you can't do that. It's my company and I run it. But Rubin then said Mike owns 51% of the shares so he can do what he wants.

From the very first day of starting Frank Rostron Shirtmakers, Summerbee's wife, Tina, and I had become great friends, going out for dinner together and going to shows like Tony Bennett when he was in Manchester. We visited my mum when she was in hospital and even stayed home watching TV together. Mike was away so much playing or touring and she was only twenty-two or twenty-three years old, so we had a lot in common.

During this time one night when we were together, she suddenly said out of the blue, "I don't like the idea of Michael Horwich having these two shares in the company, I think I should have them." So, what did I care. I still didn't understand business even though I was a great salesman; it was my company, and I ran it. Tina was my very close friend and if a decision came up, I was certain being as close as we were that she would side with me anyway. So, before I knew anything, she had the two shares from Michael Horwich and that's how Summerbee had 51% of the company.

So, there I was, walking down St. Johns Street—no job, no business, no car, and had only recently bought my first house. This large, mock Georgian detached house in Bamford in an exclusive upmarket suburb of Rochdale, just down the road from recording stars, Lisa Stansfield and Graham Gouldman, from the band, 10cc, and beauty queen and model, Kathy Anders, who married the Liverpool chairman, David Moores.

So again, until this day, life couldn't get any better and now my world had come tumbling down. Knowing nothing about business, I didn't have a plan B or a move on the board like I have always had since.

About six months earlier, a customer and friend, Henry Weinstein, asked me to start a business with him, selling ready-made, Frank Rostron shirts. It would have no effect on my made-to-measure business, and we would have the shirts made in Ireland in a large factory he knew. I declined as I was focused on building my made-to-measure shirt business. So, there I was, walking down St. Johns Street unemployed, my mind working overtime and I remembered this opportunity. I called Mr. Weinstein and he suggested that I come to see him. I went straight away to his office; he asked me why I had changed my mind. I told him the crazy story of my day with Maurice Rubin and Summerbee. He assured me that this couldn't be done, especially with Michael Horwich not advising me the seriousness of giving up control of my company. Being as young and naïve as I was, I had no idea that was what I was doing.

He made a phone call to another lawyer, a friend of his called Nathan Marks—a partner in the Manchester law firm of Kuit, Steinhart. He briefly told Mr. Marks the story and sent me immediately to his office to see him. I had never met Mr. Marks but he had heard of me and my shop, and I told him my story in detail. He said that he couldn't believe that Michael Horwich had not sent me to another lawyer to advise me on what I was doing by giving the two shares away to Tina Summerbee. Nathan Marks and Michael Horwich knew each other well from the circles they mixed in and living in the same area of South Manchester.

Mr. Marks called Michael Horwich with me in a chair three feet away and Nathan started the conversation. Hello, Michael, how is the wife and family and everything else; Michael Horwich replying good, how is yours. Then, Nathan saying to Michael that I've just had a young man in my office who left in tears, so I thought I would call you immediately and hopefully nick this problem in the bud. Rostron said this and then Nathan went into the whole story about what had happened. He finished with . . . please, Michael, tell me this isn't true and that you did recommend he go to another lawyer for advice. He said because Rostron is now talking about professional negligence, having you struck off and suing everyone involved. Michael saying no, I didn't, with it being Summerbee, his wife, and Frank Rostron. I thought it would be alright. Michael Horwich crapping himself, saying what can we do, Nathan, to make this go away. Me sitting there all the time with no idea what was going on or even understanding what was going on.

Nathan started by saying, I think Rostron will listen to me so we will have our mutual friend and accountant, Cyril Hamburger, audit and come up with a valuation for the company. In the meantime, I suggest that Rostron keeps his company car and on full salary until Cyril comes up with the valuation then Summerbee will pay Rostron for his half of the company. What do you think, Michael, with Michael Horwich saying yes. Yes, that would be perfect. Thank you, Nathan, then Mr. Marks put the phone down. He looked at me and said now go and get your car. You are on full wages without going back to work. Open your Birmingham shop without having to draw a salary or buy a car which is a big saving with a new business. I will get back to you the day Mr. Hamburger has a valuation on the company and give you a check.

Wow, only four hours ago, I was broke, unemployed with no car, and walking the streets. It goes to show how a great lawyer is worth every penny. I opened my Birmingham shop in Edmund St. in the city center, getting paid from my old company and driving a beautiful car. I couldn't fail. It took fifteen months for Cyril Hamburger to come up with the figure for my shop in Manchester. I think he was told to take his time.

My Birmingham shop had been open a year and was doing very well. All this time, I was being paid by Summerbee and driving my company car. One day, I got the call from Nathan Marks saying to come and see him. He sat me down and passed pleasantries, asking how my mum was and how my shop was doing then told me that Hamburger had valued the company at 10,000 pounds. My share was 5000 pounds, and I was very happy with that but thought about the many times over the years that Summerbee and I went to London or Birmingham and got paid in cash and split the money. If we had banked it all, our company would have been worth a lot more than ten grand, and I would have gotten a lot more, but you can't have it twice. That was another lesson I learned. Again, at the end of my business career when I sold my company to retire, the same scenario happened again.

Nathan passed me a check for 4000 pounds. I asked where's the other 1000 pounds and he said that is my fee but today, young man, you have had a great experience that you will remember forever and experience is the best education in the world. But, unfortunately, it always costs money. But now you can go out and build your business with another 4000 pounds in your pocket. Nathan was completely right, and it was a great education and experience. One of many I had to come over the following years. To this day, I don't understand why all of a sudden Tina wanted those two shares. Did Summerbee organize it as a backup, knowing I was opening a shop in Birmingham and wanted to be a partner or was it that he just wanted me out of the way because of the close relationship between me and his wife. I presume I will never know.

Birmingham

Birmingham was a major city—the second biggest to London. I had a busy shop there and met many new friends, including the ones I already had such as John Moroney, Johnny Hart, Lenny Smith and Johnny Prestcott. When I told John Moroney that I was opening a shop, he insisted that I live at his house and not pay for a hotel or apartment. This is typical of John and to this day he is still as generous with everyone as he always was. Living with John was a roller coaster ride but fun at the same time. John and his wife, Mary, were constantly having fights but all loved up and happy five minutes later.

We went out most nights for dinner and then to clubs and John always paid as he knew I had little or no money because of the new shop opening. Every Friday night, it was a boy's night out, usually all car dealers. Then, I paid my way as most of them ordered shirts from me. Dinner was always at the motor auctions in West Bromwich that had a fine dining restaurant for all these wealthy car dealers with lots of cash. Then later, we would go into town to meet one of John's girlfriends; he used to chase a million girls then he would use me as the excuse for being home late. Mary would then be chasing me around the house with a knife for keeping him out when I had been asleep in John's car outside some bird's house while he'd been banging away. But he made up for it many times over, helping me out in fights or even having the fights for me and, of course, letting me live at his house in the first place.

At my shop, it was pretty much the same type of clientele as in Manchester with club owners, businessmen, lawyers, Barristers, and soccer players but from Birmingham City, Aston Villa, and West Bromwich Albion coming in daily. A few mentions of certain ones that I became friendly with: a young Trevor Francis, a sixteen-year-old star of Birmingham City that used to come in after training for a cup of tea along with the Birmingham captain and a real gentleman, Stan Harland. Tony Want and Mike Kelly from Birmingham City and Tony Morley and Gary Shaw from Aston Villa were also regular visitors to the shop. Once, Tony Want invited me to the PFA dinner in London at The Grosvenor House Hotel as a guest of Birmingham City Football Club and we stayed at Tony Want's mum's little council flat to save a hotel bill. Those were good times, but I was itching to get back to Manchester to see my mum and my beautiful house that I only saw at the weekends.

One day, a customer who came in all the time and that I became good pals with, called Micky Lewis, said he would love a shop like this, so I said buy this one. He asked how much and again without thinking or knowing where it came from, I named a price. He said that I think my mum and dad would give me that, so after a couple of months he owned it. Whilst this was going on, I was looking around Manchester for a location to open and to rival my old business and I found a great shop at 64 Bridge St, Manchester. Terry Kerr again did the shopfitting better and classier than ever but still with my signature bow windows with the bullseye glass panes, brass rail and velvet curtain—the works. I opened without any advertising or a party but from day one everyone was coming in to see me and buying shirts and ties and within a year my old business had closed down leaving me to run Manchester again.

Mike Summerbee in his early days used to spend time in Torquay and introduced me to a few people there, so I used to drive down most weekends, staying with a local soccer star who played for Torquay and Birmingham City. His name was Robin Stubbs. Robin was the George Best of the south. He drove a red convertible MGB and had a different blonde every week. At night, we went to all the clubs again being VIPs everywhere and played football on Abbey lawns during the day. This was another great time in my life and one I will never forget.

One of Robins many girlfriends was a model and beauty queen, Anthea Redfern. We used to hang out and I became good friends with Anthea, her sister, and of course all her pretty friends. Robin married her later on as he was the biggest star around which she loved but not big enough for Anthea. She was an ambitious girl. After she divorced Robin, she went on to marry Bruce Forsyth and starred in his hit TV show *The Generation Game,* but they also divorced after six years. We kept in touch and stayed friends and later she dated Louie Brown, the owner of the sensational London club, *La Valbonne*, in Kingsly St. just off Carnaby St. Louie Brown then changed its name to Anthea's *La Valbonne* so that was my club to go to for a long time.

One of my good friends from La Baraka was Wim Suurbier, a famous Dutch footballer who played for Ajax of Amsterdam and Holland, winning three European cups with Ajax and playing in three World cup finals with Holland, so you can imagine what a star and how famous he was in Holland and in the world football community. He called me one day as Holland was playing England at Wembley and asked if I wanted to go as his guest. Well, of course, I did. To see Johan Cruyff and this Dutch team playing total football, I would have walked to London. He also asked if I knew anywhere that the Holland team could go after the match to drink and party, so I said I do—Anthea's La Valbonne. I called Anthea and arranged this party for The Dutch FA; they paid the bill and what a night it was. The best champagne flowed, girls flocked around, Anthea was pleased I had called her and held the party at her club but I was not happy as Cruyff was the only player not to come and I had wanted to meet him.

Another very impressive guy that I became friends with was Bobby Moore, the West Ham and England's World Cup winning captain, who, with his beautiful wife, Tina, also used to come to Majorca and La Baraka for their holidays even though they had a place in Marbella. Bobby was one of

London's best dressed men and I was proud to make his shirts because all the players used to order and copy what he used to wear. Bobby once came to me with a design for a shirt and tie that he had seen in the movie, *A Girl in My Soup,* staring Peter Sellers and Goldie Hawn. This was a solid, pale blue shirt with a quarter inch piping around the collar and the breast strap in a darker blue and a plain tie to match in the color of the piping. This shirt was sensational, and you couldn't buy it anywhere. So, Bobby asked me to make him some in different colors. This shirt was so difficult to make and took twice as long as a regular shirt but I couldn't say no to Bobby Moore. But when all the players saw Bobby wearing this shirt and tie, they all called me wanting the same again in different colors, so I lost money on those Peter Sellers shirts that I made for Bobby.

I remember going to London staying at The Palace Hotel and Bobby and Tina picking me up in his Jaguar to take me to the business he used to own, making suede and leather coats called Harrison and Moore in the East End. He was like a Hollywood star standing there in the hotel reception. Everyone pointing and looking and getting autographs; he was so smart and handsome. Bobby and Tina were definitely the original Posh and Becks. Later, Bobby opened his own shirt shop in Upper Montague St. in London called Bobby Moore Shirts and Ties. I went to London for a week, staying at The White House Hotel on Marylebone Rd. He asked me to open it for him and to show the staff how to measure and run the shop. Another good time with great memories.

Whenever these London teams came to Manchester and stayed overnight, I had the pleasure of taking them out on the town. There was no such thing in those days of staying in before a match. I remember with Bobby and the rest of the team helping to carry Jimmy Greaves out of Blinkers blind drunk at 2:00 a.m., the night before they played Manchester City. I think Greaves still scored a hat-trick on his debut the next day and W. Ham won 5.1. The following week, they lost at Blackpool in the FA Cup and because they were out the night before as usual, the crap hit the fan. They all got in trouble with the club, and it was in all the national newspapers—Bobby Moore and all the West Ham players with Brian London in his 007 club, drinking until the early hours before the match.

It was brilliant for a kid from a council estate to move in these circles in London with the stars from West Ham, Chelsea, Tottenham Hotspur and Arsenal; sitting on the Manchester City bench at Stamford Bridge, Chelsea; walking down the marble corridors at Arsenals Highbury Stadium and standing in the center circle twenty minutes before kickoff with 60,000 fans in the ground; being in the Tottenham dressing room, measuring Martin Chivers, Joe Kinnear, Pat Jennings and other Spurs legends and going to The Boleyn Tavern near West Hams Upton Park after training for a drink with Bobby Moore, Harry Redknapp, Frank Lampard senior, Billy Bonds and other West Ham stars.

These are some of the reasons now that I am older and look back on my life that I would never have known, if I would have been a greater success or earned more money by going into business with the other people who wanted to be my partner. I might have made a lot more money, who knows, but the few years I spent with Mike Summerbee, even though he couldn't teach me anything about business, I learned so much about life and met so many wonderful people. I had so many great experiences, I wouldn't change it for anything now that I am here retired, living in paradise and many of these people are still my good friends today so, why should I.

Birmingham, as I said, was great, especially living with John Moroney who was a successful car dealer, always happy and always had a fat roll of readies in his pocket like all the car dealers in those days. His wife, Mary, used to nick (steal) a tenner, a twenty or even a fifty pound note out of his wad every night when John was asleep and John never missed it. He had no idea how much he had in his pocket. She used to say that was her pension or that she was fining him for coming home late. Obviously, I could never tell John because what you don't know never hurts you.

I had all the soccer players coming in but some really interesting people as well who became friends.

One of them was a judge from the law courts in Steelhouse Lane near my shop in Edmund Street. His name was John Field-Evans QC and we became good friends. He bought a lot of shirts for personal use and to wear in court. We went out for dinner and a few glasses of wine on a regular basis. I enjoyed his company very much usually ending up at his house in Edgbaston drinking port, with him telling me stories of cases he had presided over. One such case was the famous trial of the IRA Birmingham bombers who murdered dozens of innocent people. He represented them and he told me about the case. When he was finished, though they got life in prison, even I believed they were innocent.

I just loved to meet people with different lifestyles and backgrounds and hear their interesting stories. So that is why my life has been so colorful, exciting and sometimes dangerous but also blessed and so educational. One day, going for lunch to the House of Lords in London with Lord Joel Barnet or Lord Lester of Hearne Hill and that same night having dinner with the President of a Wall Street bank. The next night, drinking until the early hours in a club with some of London's most notorious gangsters or drug barons and the day after, delivering shirts to Lord Montagu of Beaulieu, the Queens cousin or going to Woburn Abbey to take shirt orders from Lord Tavistock. I enjoyed it all and made lots of shirts and money from every one of them.

Another customer that I became friends with was a very smartly dressed guy from London called Paul. He was away from home and alone in Birmingham as was I, so we went out drinking and for dinner sometimes. He was working in Birmingham and owned or was really fronting a wholesale warehouse doing a long firm. A long firm is when someone sets up an apparent legitimate business, buying goods, and paying promptly to eventually get credit. Then they would order lots of stock from many suppliers which usually went to the financier of the operation, a Mr. Big, then the warehouse would go bankrupt and close. If anyone got caught, it would be the front man, this one being Paul. He was well paid for his involvement and sometimes the front goes to jail but this one didn't go that far.

A very good friend from La Baraka was called Billy Bush. They even made a TV show about his life called *Market in Honey Lane* and the actor was called Billy Bush in the series. The show was based on Billy's colorful life on the market. Billy was a very successful businessman but a typical Cockney. A jovial character who had properties in Majorca worth a lot of money. But still he lived in his little council flat on the Old Kent Road in London where he had always lived. One day, we were talking about Birmingham and my shop and to cut a long story short it came out that Paul worked for him. Paul was fronting the warehouse and Billy was the 'Mr. Big'—what a small world again. I asked Billy how it went and he said that there was a fire and the place burned down by accident before the LF (long firm) could be completed. Billy saying yes and that wasn't on the menu meaning the fire wasn't meant to happen. Years later, I had a customer in London with a liquor and wine wholesale warehouse that I found out later was also a long firm, and he was fronting that for my pal, Billy, but they both made a ton of money from that one.

One of my customers in Birmingham who became a good friend and I went to his wedding was called Grahame Whateley.

He was a public schoolboy with a very posh accent who had offices in Edmund Street next to my shop, so he popped in all the time for shirts or just to chat. Before he got married, we had nights out going to one of the many great restaurants in Birmingham, his favorite being a sensational Italian place called Lorenzo's. This was also one of mine with Lorenzo Ferrari, the owner, becoming a friend and customer also. Grahame was a very successful property developer that I was fortunate to watch grow from reasonably small offices in Edmund St. to vast corporate offices in Halesowen on the outskirts of Birmingham. I also saw him go from a small but beautiful apartment in Edgbaston, five minutes from Birmingham city center which he built and lived in, to a stunning country estate in Bellbroughton, Worcestershire. Grahame today is the chairman of this vast property empire and is now named annually in The Sunday Times Rich List.

When I bought my building in Princess Street, Manchester, another typical Frank Rostron deal, I said to the trust fund that owned it that I would rent it for one year and then buy it, the reason being that as usual I had no money. But knowing, as always, that I would find it from somewhere in the next twelve months. My bank manager always said if you bought a building then they would finance it for me, so I wasn't worried. Well, business was great; I was going to America, taking lots of shirt orders and after about nine months, I thought I had better start organizing the finance with the end of the year coming up.

I went to the bank, but they had changed managers. The

new manager said that I would need a 30,000 pounds deposit and they would loan me the balance. I presumed a year earlier that they would loan me the full amount and now I have a few weeks to find thirty grand. Again, a lot of money in those days. Even though I had a house, car and boat in Majorca and a couple of cars, a house and an apartment in Manchester, I didn't have thirty grand in cash. I was in Birmingham seeing Grahame and whilst he was ordering shirts, I told him about my dilemma and about my building. He offered to loan me the deposit money and he had it all done very professionally with a contract for me to sign, witnesses, and the full interest shown. Plus, a typical trick of Grahame, he wanted a dozen shirts and ties thrown in as well that he didn't put in the contract. Even though he had tens of millions of pounds, Grahame was not like the Arabs in Manchester or the gangsters in London or even like me and my pals who didn't have money (even though people thought we did); he was very careful with his. He was never at the front of the line in a bar getting drinks. Even after I had repaid him the money, when we went for a drink, he would say go get the drinks. I loaned you that money remember which he did and I appreciated it.

Birmingham was great, especially living with John Moroney and going to all the clubs every night like the Elbow Room owned by our pal, Albert. The Rum Runner on Broad Street where our other pal, Norman, was the doorman and where the boys from the successful band, Duran Duran, all worked. They were barman, coatroom attendants and had other jobs in the club until they started their group with the brothers, Paul and Michael Berrow who owned the club financing them. Paul and Michael became their managers, with all of them making fortunes. Years later, when I started going to London every week seeing clients, I met and started making shirts for Simon Le Bon, the lead singer of Duran Duran. We kept in touch and since I retired to Florida, I have been to a couple of their concerts in Boston and Tampa when they were touring America. I took friends and had VIP passes and seats as guests of Simons. In Boston, we stayed up all night back at their hotel, drinking champagne and eating chip butties, courtesy of my wealthy pal, Bobby Stevenish, who I had invited to the show. Birmingham was great, but after selling the business to Micky Lewis, I couldn't wait to get back to Manchester and my friends.

Friends Helping Friends

I was so pleased to be back, and it was business as usual going out every night to clubs and restaurants with all my old pals like Cliff Brierley, Peter Smith, Robert McKirdy, Nigel Craig and more. I was drinking too much and getting into fights and other trouble. However, I think it was more because of the insecurity coming from my council estate, going to high-end places, and mixing with people who thought they were something that they were not that caused things inevitably to end up in conflict.

My close friends would do anything for me as I would do for them. One of the many funny stories: one night I was in a club and met this girl who wanted to play but I had nowhere to take her. A great friend of mine, Basil Burton, had a flat in Seymour Grove just a few miles from town. He said use it and I will come home in an hour or so. I thought, *cheers pal,* see you later and off we went. It was one of the worst Manchester nights ever—freezing cold and heavy snow. But when we got back to Basil's flat, he had left the gas fire on for himself and the bedroom was boiling. He had a big, white duvet on the bed.

We got in and it was so warm and cozy after the freezing cold of outside. We had sex and fell fast asleep. I remember waking up, looking at my watch, and it was 6:30 a.m. I couldn't believe it. I had to scrape the ice off the windows to look outside—it was that cold and Basil's car was parked there in the street. I got the girl up, dressed and ran to Basil's car which was a Ford Consul convertible to make things worse. Scraping the ice off to see inside, my pal was there, coat around his head, freezing. He had been there all night while me and this lucky girl had slept in his big, beautiful, warm bed. That is what I mean about what good friends do for each other.

One of the incidents that happened during this period of my life that I am not proud of but grateful that I have friends in high places or this one could have ended in a very bad way for me. I was seriously dating a beautiful girl, a model from Manchester, Karelyn Johnson, and had been seeing her for a long time. With me being an idiot and having no respect for anyone, I went off to Majorca whenever I wanted to get away or to see other girls. On one of these trips away, I heard she had been seeing someone else. I couldn't believe It. I was so arrogant and vain but looking back what did I expect. It wasn't only me that thought she was beautiful—all guys did. I came home from Majorca a few weeks later and she was dating this guy. I was shellshocked and angry but as I said before many times, it's more your ego and your reputation. I let it be known around town that if I saw him in any of my hangouts, bars, clubs, and restaurants, he would be in big trouble and I would hurt him badly.

The guy called me and said that you can't tell me where I can or cannot go to which I replied, of course I can. There are many places for you to go without coming into my places, so stay out otherwise you will be carried out. A few months passed and I had not seen or heard anything about them, and I was feeling better and getting over it. Plus, I was seeing another model from the same agency, Julia Mahon, from Sunderland. One night after dinner with Julia and friends from Blackpool, Mark and Debbie Darwin, we went to Bramble's nightclub which was definitely one of my places. We ordered drinks and within minutes people were coming up to me saying that Karelyn and her new guy were in the club. I said as long as they don't come to this end or anywhere near me that they will be alright.

About an hour later, Karelyn came over to us, had obviously been drinking, and shouted abuse at me and Julia who she knew from the agency. She was looking for trouble and to wind us up but then going back to her guy saying something like don't you be scared of him. Go down there and show him that you are not. In hindsight, she was sending the poor boy into the lion's den. He walked down towards me, and I just gave it to him, beat him badly and didn't stop until a couple of local gangsters pulled me off him. They could see how bad he was and said go out of the back door quickly before the police arrive. So, leaving him on the floor covered in blood, I went out of the fire escape at the back. When we got to our car, my pal Mark suggested that we drive the fifty miles to his house in Blackpool and lay low for a while.

We stayed there for about three days and were getting reports all the time about the incident from pals, saying the police were looking for me. I even had reports that he was on a life support machine and another one saying that he had died. It was a very worrying time. Then, I had a phone call from my friend and mentor, Selwyn Demmy, whose mother Millie told the world that she discovered Frank Rostron. Well, I don't think she would have been proud of her find on this occasion.

Selwyn knew the guy well and had spoken to him. He said this must stop now and told him if this goes any further then it would end in more trouble for him. He told him Frank's friends would take retaliation whether Frank wanted it or not so Selwyn arranged a meeting at his house in Wilmslow, just the two of us.

When I arrived at Selwyn's house, he was already there. I was so embarrassed and ashamed of the mess I had made of him. He looked terrible with his face badly bruised and scarred. Selwyn left us alone and I apologized, saying how sorry I was, and I really was. I couldn't believe what I had done to him, and he accepted my apology and said that was the end of it. I thanked him and we parted ways. He changed his story with the police, saying he didn't know what had happened to him. The police came to my house, and I said I didn't see the incident, that I couldn't help them with their enquiries and that was the end of it, luckily for me. But this was another instance of friends helping you out and my friend, Selwyn, certainly did that day.

One night, I was having dinner with another pal, Steve Albinson, and his wife. It was just before Christmas, and he was saying they had been Christmas shopping all day for their two teenage daughters and he was shattered. I asked what do you buy for teenage daughters these days? He said Take That albums, Take That calendars, Take That diaries, Take That posters, in fact anything that says Take That on it. At the time, Take That was the biggest boy band in Europe, a very talented band who had sold out concerts every night all over the world. They were working every day and making a fortune. I said that I know some of the band, particularly Jason Orange. He's the best friend of a good pal of mine, Neil McCartney. Neil and Jason used to dance together on the TV show *Hitman and Her* and both come from Wythenshawe, a suburb outside Manchester. Jason had been to Majorca with us and to the Hacienda and other places. He also once invited me as his guest in his box at Manchester City. We have been to their concerts, so I know him quite well. I said to Steve, "Would you like me to get him to your house one day to meet the girls?"

Steve went ballistic; he couldn't believe it and said that you are not joking are you and I said no not at all. Steve is a very successful guy with a great business, and he would have paid me ten grand to have a Take That member in his house for his daughters but I said leave it with me. To put it in perspective, it's like getting John Lennon or Paul McCartney to your house in the Beatles heyday. Steve called me the next day saying Frank, I've not told the girls but please don't say you can if you can't. I told him I had made a couple of calls so let's wait and see.

The band had not had a day off for six months and they had three days off for Christmas to go home and see their parents and take a rest. Jason said he would do it for me on Boxing Day, the day after Christmas Day. I called Steve and told him the news. He couldn't believe that I had done it. I said that's what friends are for, and Steve said but having a friend like Frank Rostron is an extra bonus. He told his daughters who told all their girlfriends at school who also didn't believe them—that Take That was coming to their house on Boxing Day.

Steve sent his driver and Bentley to Jason's mum's house in Wythenshawe to collect him and bring him to his house. Jason was brilliant. He walked up to the front door and rang the bell. The girls ran upstairs nervous and scared to death because this superstar was at their house. I think they didn't believe it either. Steve shouted at them to come down and answer the door and Stephanie opened the door and Jason said are Nichola and Stephanie in please; she said I'm Stephanie and he said Hi, my name's Jason, can I come in. She was petrified. Her idol was in front of her wanting to come into her house. He came in and stayed most of the day with the girls, signing the ton of Take That stuff that they brought down from their bedrooms and taking photos with them. As I said, he was brilliant and had far better things to do with his day off. But again, that's what pals do for each other. Jason did that for me, and I did that for Steve.

One day, I called one of my best pals who is my daughter's Godfather, Cliff Brierley, and said that I needed to see him tonight. I told him after work at six o'clock. He said I cannot, I have a meeting but I said that it was very important; you must come. At six o'clock he pulled up outside my shop in his new, gold Mercedes S Class AMG. I got in and he asked me where we were going. I said just drive and we went to a place on the other side of town. In Oldham Street, we stopped, and he asked what are we doing here? I told him we are going to an AA meeting; I think I am an alcoholic. He laughed and said I know you are but what are we doing here. I said be serious; let's go in.

We went inside and sat at the back. There were all these people, really sad down and outs, me, and Cliff, driving a gold car that cost 100 thousand pounds parked at the door. We are dressed in tailored suits, shirts and ties with them saying my name is George and I am an alcoholic, my name is David and I am an alcoholic—then telling their stories. I must say, I was an angel compared to these people but we stayed the full hour or so until it ended. When we were leaving everyone was leaving donations with the guy at the door, 10 pence, 50 pence and some a pound coin. Cliff put a fifty-pound note in the box; I thought the guy was going to faint. He said, "You will come again, won't you?" We got into the car and Cliff said I need a drink after that, and we drove to one of his steak restaurants in town called The Barnaby Rudge. We got a table; he ordered a bottle of Canadian Club for me and a bottle of vodka for himself, saying now let's start drinking. After going there, I can tell you, pal, you are not an alcoholic. We had dinner, a couple of bottles of wine, and I never went again, Cliff assuring me once more that I was not an alcoholic.

Two more stories about friends helping each other out when Manchester was going through a real bad period. Gangs roaming the streets just walking into smart clubs, ordering drinks, and not paying for them. Because there were ten or twelve of them, the doorman couldn't do a lot about it. It was also a waste of time for the owners to call the police as it only meant the gang would come back later and cause more trouble. These guys were usually wannabee gangsters that were really just bullies. On their own would have been helpless but with a dozen pals, they thought they were tough.

One day, a pal who owned a club called me and said some guys had been in and wanted to tax him. They wanted money or his club would have some real trouble. I said why are you calling me, and he said that he told them that Frank Rostron owned the club, and that he was just the manager and a front man so he couldn't do anything about it. I asked why on earth did you say that, and he said because they know who you are and with your connections, he thought that would be enough to scare them off. He thought it would all blow over, but it didn't. They came back so I said make a meeting and I will talk to them and front them up.

He made a meeting a couple of days later in a bar on Oldham St. in the city center. I know that these kinds of people are really nobodies and bullies who are intimidated just as much as they intimidate others. This is what I did this day on purpose to impress and intimidate them at the same time. I got my driver, who I never use during the day, put on a chalked striped suit, a great shirt with white collar and cuffs, cuff links and tie and turned up in my black, Daimler Sovereign. I was sitting in the back seat with Dale, my driver, pulling up on double yellow lines in the city center outside this bar. He got out, walked around to my side of the car and opened the door for me, in full view of my pal and the two guys who wanted to tax the club.

I walked in and introduced myself to them, shook their hands, sat down and started to talk before they had time to say anything. I started by saying my manager has told me what you want and there is no chance in the world of it happening. I admire your initiative though and have an idea where you can earn some money. Sunday, Monday or Tuesday, you choose, you can have the club one of those nights and all the money you take at the door is yours. You supply the doorman and reception to collect your dough and we will supply the barman, but we will have to have the bar money, otherwise we can't take stock and our accountants and bank would know about it. I said that, in other words, you would be club owners for one night a week and, as you probably know, the real money is what you take on the door. It's all cash and profit for you guys. But I know that the people they know have no money and certainly wouldn't pay to go into a club.

They looked at each other and had not spoken a word up to this point saying that it sounds great, we will get back to you, with me saying that I will be busy but make all the arrangements with my manager. I got up, walked out to the car, with Dale standing by. He opened my door and we drove off. Now, if they had wanted to do this deal then it would have been ok because Sunday we were closed, and Monday and Tuesday were dead nights anyway, so at least we would earn on the bar. But my pal never heard from them again. So, it never happened. But what I did to them was intimidation at its finest but warning my pal to never do that to me again and that he owes me one.

Another night, during these bad times in Manchester, I walked into my regular club, Bavadage. The girl who worked on the reception didn't like me but I didn't like her either, so all was good. She shouted at me, "Hey, you haven't signed the book." Everyone had to sign because it was a member's only club, but I never did. She knew that because the owner was one of my best pals and besides that, I was one of his best customers. As she said this, I looked up and walking up the stairs and coming in just before me were three black guys—real thugs and wannabee gangsters. I said I bet that fucking lot didn't sign the fucking book and just walked in thinking nothing more about. It didn't matter that they were black; they could have been white or Chinese, I would still have said it. A lot of my friends in town were black or Chinese anyway, it just happened that they had walked in at that time.

Two nights later, as I was about to walk into Bavadage, four black guys grabbed me by my arms, two at each side, lifted me up and started carrying me towards a waiting car about fifty yards away with another guy standing at the back of it with the boot open ready to throw me in. My pal, Robert McKirdy, who I was with, quickly ran inside and got another pal of mine, Thomas "Giro" Campbell, who is also black, and he ran out and before I was thrown into the boot, shouted out to them and came over. Now Giro, who is well-connected himself, knew them; they also knew who he was as he told them to let me go, it's not going to happen, otherwise there would be big trouble. Trouble that you guys wouldn't be able to handle so just go home and forget about it. They released me and drove off. We went into the club—but that was another instance of friends helping friends out and with my pal, Giro, helping me out big style that night. I still wonder to this day and I cannot imagine where I would have ended up that night without the help of my friend, Giro.

My pal, Colin Burne, had opened a club outside town called The Sandpiper. He had bought a plane for décor, so the inside of the club was like being in an airplane. It was really cool and original and typical of Colin. One night, I'm in there drinking with Colin and another friend called 'London' Neil Sollinger. We had a table and were talking and having a drink when Colin said follow Neil. I asked why and he said to just go and I followed Neil to the club kitchen. By now, the kitchen was closed. I remember it was all stainless steel, clean and shiny and Colin followed a minute behind us. Neil got out of his pocket this plastic bag, opened it and it was full of white powder and with a credit card, he put some on the stainless-steel countertop. He made half a dozen lines about three inches long with his credit card. He then took out a fifty-pound note, rolled it up, and snorted two of these white lines. Colin saying to me you next and that was it—the very first time in my life I had taken cocaine. Colin went next and the three of us went back to our table laughing and giggling like school kids.

At the time, after taking this white powder, this was the best night of my life. I couldn't fathom the experience, it was unbelievable. I can see how weak, vulnerable people could easily get addicted; this was now my weekend party piece—not every night like a lot of the guys in Manchester—but Friday and Saturday only. A date with a girlfriend, a great restaurant, a club, a bottle of champagne and a couple of lines of coke. Perfect and this was my new life thanks to "London Neil."

I didn't realize until I got into this scene that absolutely everyone was taking it. One night, I was in Bavadage in Manchester, a really high-end restaurant and bar, with a friend of mine from London who was the chairman of a public company. He was with his financial director in Manchester on business. The three of us had been out for dinner then ended up in Bavadage. After a while, I went to the toilet and my friend was coming out of the cubicle. Obviously, he had been having a line or two and said to come in. He locked the door and got his packet open. He gave me two lines of the finest Columbian marching powder. One of the many names people used to call it but saying, whatever you do, don't tell my financial director about this. I assured him that I wouldn't. Later that evening, I went to the toilet again and it was the same scenario but with his financial director coming out of the cubicle, obviously taking coke. He knew I knew and took me back into the cubicle with him, giving me a couple of lines and asking please don't tell the chairman about this, I will get fired.

I thought, *everybody really is doing this shit*. The chairman of a publicly traded company and the company's financial director both taking cocaine unbenownst to one another. After a while, one night after doing this every weekend and in Majorca, of course, someone gave me a pill to try and saying take a half and see what you think. Well, after twenty minutes, I had to take the other half. The experience was so unbelievable that after that the Charley (another name for coke) was history. My new party drug was ecstasy. The thing is that it was so good all you wanted to do was dance but the clubs like Bavadage and Brambles that I went to didn't play the type of music for this wild drug. You needed house or dance music. The only club for that was the world-famous Hacienda club in Manchester that I had never been to.

The Hacienda

It was the exact opposite of the places where we were going. No one drank champagne, no posing or fancy clothes, they just wanted to dance and be happy. They didn't care who you were, what kind of car you drove or what watch you wore, they just wanted to dance to this brilliant music after taking this unbelievable drug. By now, I had moved from Bamford, bought my mum an apartment in Middleton where I was born, and where she was much happier near her grandchildren who she saw every day. I bought myself an apartment on two floors in St. Johns Gardens right in the center of Manchester. Funnily enough, it was only fifty yards from St. Johns Street and Maurice Rubin's office where I was fired from my company.

I had met and knew the manager of the Hacienda as he also lived in St. Johns Gardens. He was a friend of a friend. A good guy, his name was Paul Mason. I called him and said Paul, I want to come to your club this Saturday with a girlfriend. He was speechless as he knew the sort of clubs I went to, the girls that I dated, clothes that I wore and was sure the Hacienda wasn't for me. But I insisted that I wanted to come and would he put me on the guest list.

I arrived in my jeans and a patterned shirt, trying to look like a raver instead of a big shot but let myself down by pulling up in my Daimler Sovereign, with my driver Dale. My date and I sat in the back as he pulled up right at the entrance with everyone looking and thinking who the fuck is this. Not one of them would know Frank Rostron because they wouldn't be made-to-measure shirt customers. My driver, Dale, got out, opened our doors for us, and we walked to the main door to be greeted by a giant of a doorman. To the left was a line three or four people deep going as far as you could see—hundreds of yards—and a line to the right probably fifty-yards long. I said to the giant my name is Frank Rostron and I am on the guest list to which he said that's the line to the right; get in it. Well, it was a shock and even though I was on the guest list, I have never been used to lining up but better a fifty-yard line than a two-hundred-yard line three-four deep, I suppose. Just as I was going to join the sheep, my friend, manager Paul Mason, appeared as if by magic at the door calling my name and introducing me to the giant whose name was Damien Noonan. Paul said to him whenever I come to the club to let me straight in. No guest list line for Frank Rostron.

Later on, Damien and I became very close friends and with him being one of the brothers of a major Manchester crime family, my reputation didn't suffer any harm either. My date and I went in and it was nothing like the plush clubs we usually go to. It had brick walls, scaffolding, and bare concrete floors—the walls wet through with the sweat of the hundreds of dancers. The music was sensational, and the walls were bouncing to the base of the music. We had taken our pills half an hour earlier, so they had kicked in and we were buzzing. We had started to dance, and it was the best night of my life again. After about an hour, Paul Mason, the manager, came to check on me making sure I was alright and as he got close to me, I hugged and kissed him. He ran away; that's how great ecstasy makes you feel. It was the happiest I have ever felt and, as I said, the best night of my life once again. But the next Saturday and the one after that were also the best nights of my life. That's how good the drug was. So instead of spending money on dinner, champagne and clubs, I was spending nothing only buying water which we drank by the gallon whilst we were dancing so we wouldn't dehydrate.

I never bought coke or ecstasy ever. When I went to London, delivering shirts to my clients who were in that business, they always gave me a big chunk or bag as a gift like a waiter would get a tip. When I was in clubs, there was always some guy who wanted to befriend me, offering to take me for a walk to the bathroom, give me a couple of lines and then tell his friends that he knew me. Things didn't change in the ecstasy world and before long, I became a friend of Damien, the giant. He would send one of his security staff to me a few times during the night with the pills that they had confiscated from the customers entering the club. They searched everyone coming in. They even had a metal detector you would walk through when you entered the club, making sure you don't have a gun or a knife on you. The doormen wore bullet proof vests under their jackets—a far cry from my previous clubs where the doormen wore tuxedos and black bow ties. On the other hand, this scene was so much better.

Before long, a few of my pals like Neil McCartney, Simon Haynes, Lee Tyson, Danny Nelson, Nick Jackson, Robert McKirdy and more, along with their girlfriends, started to come with me and it wasn't unusual for me to take a dozen or more people in as my guests on any given night. When my pals from London were in town like Ray Sullivan, Tony Tucker, Gary Norman (from Sky Television) and boxing champions like Nigel Benn, Billy Schwer, Glenn McCrory and Gary Mason, they all came raving and partying with me all night in the Hacienda. Tony Tucker, Nigel's close friend, was murdered in a drug deal a couple of years later. This was widely publicized because three of them were killed in a Range Rover in a farmer's field. Books were written about the murders calling it the *Essex Boys*. A movie was even made about it, but Tony was a good lad. Whatever he did for a living, he didn't deserve to die like that.

I even had my own area where we danced against a wall at the stairs going up to the DJ's box. When we walked in, one of the security staff would walk with us and if anyone was standing, dancing at, or near my wall, they just used to literally throw them to one side. I had my own table and chairs in the best restaurant in Manchester and now I had my own wall and dance area in the best club in the world.

One night, I was dancing with my gang, probably about ten of us and I notice a famous celebrity dancer and actor, Wayne Sleep, walking towards us. He recently had danced with Princess Diana on TV and it had been in the newspapers all over the world. As he got closer, I grabbed him and started dancing. I said, "Hi, Wayne, how are you doing, buddy, long time no see." Wayne was brilliant and danced with me like we were old pals and one of my gang, Neil McCartney, who danced on the TV show, *Hitman and Her,* along with Jason Orange from the boyband, Take That, couldn't believe that one of his idols was even in The Hacienda, never mind a pal of mine. That he was dancing with us was just another one of the many great nights in the Hacienda.

Once, and this is the only time I ever did this in all the years I went to the Hacienda, I went outside for some air. I didn't feel good. I must have had a reaction to a pill or did not drink enough water. Every night, there would be hundreds of people standing in line outside, knowing they wouldn't get in because it was full. But they were just happy that they could say I was there just like I did at The Twisted Wheel and The King Mojo in Sheffield, all those years earlier.

Well, on this night, at the front of the line, was the unmistakable face of Fergal Sharkey, a pop star from Ireland. Fergal had a number of hits all over the world, firstly, with his punk band, The Undertones, and then going solo. I said who are you with Fergal as if I knew him or that I owned the club. He replied just me and my pal, so I said come on, follow me in. Damien asked what are you doing? I said that this is Fergal Sharkey, Damien replying, who the fuck is Fergal Sharkey, I replied, a pal of mine. I will tell you later. When we got in, Fergal thanked me, and I said I will be over in the corner dancing if you want to join us. About ten minutes later, Fergal comes over to my wall where me and my gang were dancing our heads off, sweating like pigs after taking numerous tablets. My pal, Neil, and all the girls recognized him immediately. Fergal hugged me and started dancing again as if we were old pals. They all knew that I know lots of celebrities, so they thought that Fergal was one of them, just like Steve and Ann Hayhurst thought Rod Stewart was my pal when Cockney Bernie called my name in Majorca.

The follow up to this story was a few years later after the Hacienda had closed and that life was well behind me. One night after work, I went for a drink in the Midland Hotel that had a new restaurant with a trendy bar. As I was getting to the front to order my drinks, who was next to me with that unmistakable face but Fergal Sharkey. He looked at me and me at him; he's wearing a suit and shirt and me a suit, shirt and tie and he said that I know you from somewhere. I said I know you as well, reminding him where he knew me from and that I got him in the Hacienda one night as he was standing outside. He laughed and said you didn't look like that, me laughing with him saying and you didn't look like that either. He was now working as an executive for a recording company in London and was staying at The Midland Hotel on business. We chatted for a while and parted ways.

The Quality Street Gang

Before all this, having just returned to Manchester one night, I went on my own into a club owned by a friend of mine, Stuart Codling, called The Connection. Just like every club around at that time, I walked in cocky as hell and was standing at the bar near a gang of guys that I didn't recognize when one came over to me. He asked what's your name? I replied Frank Rostron and he said have you got any money? To which I replied, yeh why, flash and cocky again. He said you owe me five grand. What, I said, I don't even know you, but he said, yes, but Mike Summerbee gave you five grand and that was my money so I want it back.

This happens a lot in Manchester. Gangsters taxing people or collecting debts for people and taking a commission. Well, this was neither, so I started shouting at him that Summerbee got the best deal and he owed me—shouting because the music was so loud. I told the guy to come to the toilets; now, if you take someone to the toilets, its either for drugs or a fight. Again, this was neither but he nor his gang didn't know this. When we got inside the toilet, I gave him the full verbal saying Summerbee should have paid me a lot more; he got off light; we took loads of readies out and if we had left it in the company, he would have had to pay me a lot more. I wish I could have given him five grand for his half bla, bla, bla and I'm still shouting and pointing, angry with no fear, because I had no idea who he was.

When we left the toilet, he went back to his gang at the bar laughing and he said to his pals some spieler this kid is. I went to the toilet with him, and he owed me five grand. I've come out and now I owe him ten grand—unbelievable. They all started laughing and just at that minute Stuart the owner walks past. I grab him and asked Stuart to have a word with this lot. Stuart, shaking his head, said leave me out of this one and carried on walking. That night was the first time I ever met the famous Jimmy Swords, leader of Manchester's Quality Street Gang—street fighter, professional boxer, and the toughest guy around and I'm taking him to the toilet and having a row with him. With Jimmy Swords that night was his brother Joe Swords, brothers Vinny and Louie Schiavo, Joe Leach, Jimmy Riley, Ricky Gore, Mike "the Golly" Friend and Jimmy "the Weed" Donnelly—his full gang. No wonder they all laughed when Jimmy Swords told them what had happened, and Stuart said leave me out of this. Even with him being their good friend, he knew better than to get involved.

These guys were the inspiration behind the hit song, "The Boys Are Back in Town," by the band, Thin Lizzie, whose lead singer, Phil Lynott, and his mother were close friends of the gang. Phil's mother, Phyliss, said to him one day when he was visiting her in Manchester, ". . . the boys are back in town. Give them a call they would love to see you." Phil lived in Ireland and most of the QSG had villas in Marbella and Portugal and spent a lot of time there, so it wasn't that often that everyone was in Manchester at the same time. But this was one of those times.

Phil's mum had an upmarket but illegal drinking establishment on the top floor of a hotel in Whalley Range, just outside Manchester. You could only get in by going up the fire escape at the back, passing a security guard and then, only if you were known to him. No one went until after the clubs closed. So, at 1:00 a.m., it would be empty but at 3:00 a.m. until morning, it would be full and on any one night the QSG or Quality Street gang would be in there drinking with other celebrities both famous and infamous. George Best was a regular but I've been in when Tom Jones, Diana Ross and many more stars playing in Manchester have ended up in Phyliss's. Most of the guys from the QSG have gold discs of his hit records that Phil gave them hanging on their walls at home or in their offices. Every one of them went to his wedding and his funeral. Phil and his mother loved these guys.

Years later, I played Sunday football for a team called the Blackley Working Men's Club, a good team with all nice lads and we had a cup match against a team from another league, the Gorton premier league called New Cross Motors. They were a tough looking mob—scars, socks around their ankles, nothing matched. We were all smart and looking the part. It was a great match that they won 3-2. I scored our two goals and had a brilliant game taking the micky out of their players for the full ninety minutes. After the match, I was in the bar having a drink and one of their players, Steve Bowles, who is the brother of the England and QPR legend, Stan Bowles, who I knew slightly came over to talk to me and suggested that I should play for them. I told him that I liked playing for this team so, no thanks but after his teammates had joined us and a few drinks later, I was playing for The New Cross Motors in the Gorton Premier League. The team consisted of Vinny and Louie Schiavo, Ricky Gore, Norman Lowry and members of The Quality Street Gang that I had encountered in The Connection a few years earlier. Since that day forty years ago, all these guys have been my good friends that even now, living in Paradise, I still speak to them every week. I hang out with them every time I visit Manchester and Ricky Gore even came to visit me and Jane last year in Naples. We had a blast as Mancunians always do when they get together.

After that first match, when I played against them and they were in the bar asking me to join them, my Daimler Sovereign motor car was broken into and my England bag that Mike Summerbee gave me with the number 7 on the side with three pairs of expensive boots and all my cassettes was stolen. I found out months later that it was one of my new pals and teammates, Norman Lowry, who had done it but what could I do? Norman was now my buddy, the stuff was long gone, plus Norman was well over six feet tall, and a tough guy so I had to forget it. But the boys still made fun of it and still tell the story to wind me up today.

Also, that first Sunday when they broke into my car, they took me to a pub called The Kensington in the city center owned by a friend of theirs, Raymond Mancini. We drank for a couple of hours and when it was time to close, Raymond said we had to leave because he had to go home for his Sunday lunch with his family. They moaned as Raymond marched us out of the pub into the street and we watched him drive off and within a minute it was like circus acrobat act. One jumped onto another's shoulders then another one was pulled up onto his shoulders and he climbed into the upstairs window. He came downstairs and opened the front doors and within a minute we were all back in the bar. I had never seen anything like it before or since. Raymond had not been gone for two minutes and we were all back drinking in his pub. One of the guys went behind the bar and started taking orders making a note of what they drank and putting the money for each round of drinks by the side of the till. Three hours later, Raymond came back and walked into the bar, shocked at the sight of us, saying how did you lot get in here. Louie replying that it's a good job we are your pals, because as you left, you didn't lock the door properly and anyone could have walked in so we had to stay here until you got back. Every penny for every drink was at the side of the till. Unbelievable—as I said before, you could trust these guys with your life and your money if they were your friends and fortunately for Raymond, they were his very good friends.

These guys, my new teammates, were wild and another Sunday after a match and then drinking most of the day, we were driving in my car to another bar of theirs and Louie said to pull up, outside the Odeon cinema on Oxford Street. He called the girl over that was selling ice cream outside with her high heel shoes and short skirt with a tray full of ice cream and chocolate bars held around her neck by a leather strap. She approached my car asking what he wanted. He jumped out of the car, picked her up, and put her in the back, laughing along with the rest of the lads and telling me to drive off quickly. I didn't know what to do but did as I was told, worried that we would get arrested for kidnapping or something. We drove around Albert Square probably a quarter of a mile away then Louie said stop here. He then let the girl out to walk back to the Odeon in her high heels, carrying her ice cream tray. The boys burst out laughing, thinking this was so funny. They were fearless and me, the straight kid from Middleton, thinking we were going to get arrested. But this was a typical prank for them which I witnessed and was involved in many times over the next few years.

One time, I had a good friend, Paul Kelso, nicknamed Luigi, who used to have his own gang of armed robbers. One night, I went into a friend's club after hours and Luigi was in there with a few pals of his own. He introduced me and one of them was called Pete Heneghan. Heneghan was serving life for murder and had just escaped from prison that day with their help. His picture was in all the national papers and on the TV news that day. He used to work with Luigi before he got nicked. One night, a doorman at a club in Stretford near Heneghan's house wouldn't let him in so he went home, got his gun, went back and shot the doorman and the manager—the doorman died.

That day, they had just helped him escape from a prison van whilst he was visiting a hospital for a medical procedure and now, I am in his company, drinking in this club all night until the early hours. He was staying with Luigi until they could get him out of the country—which they did to Spain a few days later. Luigi himself got caught a couple of years later and I was spending more time at my house in Florida. I got a call from Ricky Gore of The Quality Street gang saying I believe on this certain day last year you came home from New York and Luigi picked you up from the airport and you went for lunch. I said yes, that's right, and Ricky said that they are looking after Luigi and would I come back to England as a witness at his trial. He said they would give me ten grand in cash and a first-class return ticket back to the States. I said, of course, I would but I wouldn't take the ten grand cash because Luigi is also my pal, but you can buy the plane ticket for me. I came home for the trial, and I was a great witness. The trial ended in a hung jury with a re-trial later. I flew back again for this trial to be a witness and they again paid for my first class return ticket home but unfortunately the new jury found him guilty and he got I think twenty-one years.

Lena Rostron
7 November 1916 – 26 November 2008

I mentioned earlier where my mum, Lena, was born, where she worked and how she had no life—just taking care of me and her invalid husband. She also spent a lot of time chasing around Manchester at nights and the weekends looking for her daughter, Maureen, who had given birth to her latest child. My sister, Maureen, had nine children in just over eleven years with four dying as babies and five today living great lives. They all took care of and loved my mum unreservedly whilst I was away and never a day went by that these five brothers and sisters, her grandchildren, one or more of them, didn't go to see my mum and take care of her until the day she passed away. For this, I will always be in their debt, and I am so thankful and proud of them. Two of the girls, Carol and Bernie, have opened a café on Boarshaw estate where I was born and where we all came from in my mum's honor and called it LENA'S KITCHEN.

I also said it would be impossible to make up to her for what she had done for me growing up and that I had no idea just how much. I just took her and everything for granted thinking this was normal. The older I got, the more I realized that what she did for me and my dad was far from normal. Afterwards, I did everything I could to give her a better life, a life that she never wanted or expected. Lena was such a simple and hardworking person; she would rather have sandwiches and a cup of tea with her grandchildren than come with me to the best restaurant in Manchester. She was the one that brought home that fabric from work that I never paid her for, that made my first dozen shirts; without that happening, I would never have even been in the shirt business. But then hopefully fulfilling my ambition of being the manager of John Michael Menswear.

I bought my first house in Bamford and talked her into living with me and I know now she hated every day of it, being so far away from her grandchildren. She also had an hour bus ride to Manchester to my factory to press shirts all day then an hour and two buses to get home at night. She didn't care about the size and how luxurious the house was. She would rather have stayed in her council house where she lived ever since she married.

After about ten years and many heated discussions, I bought her an apartment back in Middleton where she was born and had lived all her life and where all her grandchildren lived. From that day, I could see how much happier she was again. It was me being selfish and not seeing what she really wanted. When I had my factory in Turner Street, Manchester, upstairs there was a wholesale factory making fur coats—mink, fox, wolf and other exotic skins—and I wanted to buy Lena a mink coat for her Christmas present. I went to see the owner, chose the skins and had a beautiful mink coat made for her. I took it home in the box that they packed it in and hid it in my bedroom until the day I was going on my Christmas holidays which was three weeks in the Bahamas. I put the box on the stairs and said to her don't open it until Christmas Day so it will be a surprise.

I came home three weeks later, and the box was still in the exact place on the stairs. I said to her, "Lena, you didn't open your Christmas present that I bought you." She replied I didn't need a new vacuum cleaner. The one I have is still good. I looked at the box and the furrier had put the coat into a box that once held a vacuum cleaner. I didn't even notice. Obviously, they didn't have bags or boxes. Being a wholesale manufacturer, they had put it in the only box they had for me to take home. I opened the box, and she loved the herringbone patterned mink coat that was inside, and she wore it at every opportunity after that day.

I took her to all the restaurants, soccer matches, and even to the world title fight of my friend, Nigel Benn, against Chriss Eubank, along with over forty-two thousand people that night at Old Trafford. Everyone knew Lena and she loved it when she was out, and people came up to her in a restaurant or club, especially soccer stars and friends like Johnny Briggs, Geoffrey Hughes, and other TV stars from *Coronation Street*.

She made breakfast many times for them along with all my pals that stayed at our house, plus all the girls that stayed as well. She didn't even know most of them or what nationality they were or even how many there were. Once, coming into my bedroom one Sunday morning and saying to Bobby McAlinden who was in my bed that there are two girls in the next bedroom. Bobby said yes, so what and Lena said that there are two in the other bedroom as well; who are they? Bobby replied that the two in the next are mine and the two in the other room are Franks. Lena not bothering just asked how many for breakfast? Bobby replying, I don't know, you had better go and ask them. She got used to and enjoyed all this company and many times got up as we arrived home at 3:00 a.m. or later, asking if we or the girls wanted anything to eat before she went back to bed. A lot of the time she was just being nosey in case the girls were gone by morning or just to see who they were.

I took her to Majorca many times and we always stayed in hotels before I had my apartment above La Baraka and later at my house in Torre Nova. Sometimes, she would go when I wasn't there with her best friend, her niece Margaret. She felt so comfortable and relaxed there and everyone knew her like Claude and the crowd at La Baraka. Everyone else who went there on holiday, our neighbors, or that lived on the island all made a fuss of her and made her feel welcome. She also went to Miami and Freeport, Grand Bahamas, with me once. That was her first American holiday.

We went with three other couples because the girl I was taking and I had a fallout a couple of weeks earlier, so I changed the ticket into Lena's name and she came along with my six other friends. She enjoyed going to restaurants, clubs and bars like one of the boys, with no problem keeping up with us. I went to places over the years and always thought that I would love to bring Lena here one day so she could experience these wonderful things that I was so blessed to see. One of them was Disneyland in California but she never made it to LA. But Disney World in Orlando was just the same. It had the ride "It's a Small World" with all these dolls singing this catchy song going through different countries on a boat and the dolls dressed in their countries national costume. I knew she would love it. When we were in Miami, we chartered a small plane and flew to Orlando for the day and went to Disney World. We went on every ride, including "It's a Small World," and she did love it. I felt so good after taking her on that ride and another cross was ticked off my list of places that I wanted to take her. I took her to Mezzonotte where Madonna had danced on the table one night and even though there were no stars in the restaurant everyone was still getting on the tables at the end of the evening dancing. She loved it all.

Another night, we went to a club in Coconut Grove and we only got in by saying that we were from England, that it was recommended, and we only drink champagne, and other nonsense. We had a great night spending quite a bit of money and dancing past 3:00 a.m. We were going into the DJ's box, playing the music and making friends with everyone, including the manager who told us that we were welcome back anytime. The next night, we were having dinner in Coral Gables which was not far from Coconut Grove. One of the boys said let's go to that club again; we had a great time last night. So, off we went and when we got to the club there was a different doorman on, saying that we couldn't come in. We explained that we were in last night, spent lots of money, and that the manager had invited us back but the doorman was having none of it. I asked him would he please just go and ask the manager and tell him that the English guys from last night are here and he will tell you that it's alright to let us in but he still wouldn't let us in.

After a heated discussion took place and we walked away from the door, I had to have the last say. There was a great big pot, with a large plant inside. I got hold of the stem near the bottom as to walk away and pull the pot over along with the plant and soil spilling all over the entrance. Childish and typical of a Manchester yobo with aggression looking for trouble. But with the pot being heavy or even fixed to the floor, I ended up pulling all the leaves off instead, getting a handful of leaves and looking a right idiot. I turned around and threw the leaves at the doorman but they just went in the air and floated slowly to the ground like confetti; I now felt even a bigger idiot. With the doorman shouting and quite rightly attacking me, I was just going to throw my first punch when the giant doorman smothered me, pushed me onto the wall at the side, banging my head and half knocking me out, then falling on top of me. Lena jumped on his back and started to hit the doorman with her bag, trying to drag him off while shouting . . . "leave my son alone, you bully." Well, I wish I could have got this scene on tape; it would have been the funniest thing ever. Me starting trouble but coming second and an old lady smacking the doorman with her bag and whacking him as she tries to drag him away from me.

My pals picked me up and we ran off but going down the stairs, we heard police sirens circulating the mall near the club. The police ran past us towards the club as we were leaving, looking for the troublemakers. Not even thinking for one minute as they ran past us that three couples, smartly dressed, and an old lady could possibly be them. We jumped in two taxis outside and got over to our hotel in Miami Beach as fast as we could, joking later how funny it would have been with Lena in handcuffs, under arrest for assaulting the doorman and me for pulling leaves off a plant.

After a great time in Miami and Disney World, we went to Freeport, Grand Bahamas, and even though today it's a terrible place, in those days it was cool. Freeport had a large British pub, great hotels, restaurants, a casino, and the International Bazaar which was an area with shops, bars, and restaurants that featured different countries of the world like Epcot at Disney and, of course, beautiful, white, sandy beaches and sea.

We had another week there seeing all my old haunts that I used to go to with Erroll—Lesley had left long ago which was disappointing, but I met a couple of nice local girls to eat, drink, and spend time with. We went to different hotels for lunch and even had dinner in the casino one night. Although

I don't gamble, the others played for a while. We took a cab around the far side of the island to have local boys, six-seven years old, diving into the sea for conch for their mothers to wash, cut, and put lemon juice on, selling them to us raw just like I did with Erroll. Another thing to cross off my list of 'to do jobs' with Lena. As I keep saying, I couldn't possibly do enough to make up for what I owed my mum. In my letter I wrote when I was eight years old, I said that I was going to be a professional footballer and buy a big house for us to live in. Well, I had already done that even though I didn't become a footballer—all of these other things were me still trying.

For her 75th birthday, I wanted to do something really special. She had been on many holidays and to all the great restaurants in Manchester, Birmingham, and London plus all the ones in Majorca, so I had to really think. I saw an advert in *The Sunday Times,* saying Cunard that owned the QE2 had a deal: fly Concorde to New York with four nights at The Waldorf Astoria and QE2 back home. Perfect. I have always wanted to fly on the Concorde and sail on the QE2. I was really excited, so I booked it and told Lena. She was about as excited as taking her shoes off after walking for an hour. It was booked and paid for, so we were going and after a while, the idea grew on her. I told a friend of mine in London, Paul Berman, about the trip and he said that sounds great do you mind if my wife and I join you and, of course, I didn't. Paul was a great friend, and it would be more fun with a few of us.

We met Paul in the Concorde lounge at Heathrow airport,

and everything was just first class and perfect. We drank some Dom Perignon and had a smoked salmon breakfast before getting on the supersonic jet. I was like a big kid. I was so excited and impressed but Lena I know would rather have had a party with sandwiches in her small apartment with her grandchildren than flying on the Concorde to New York.

We arrived after about three hours at JFK, hearing the boom as we hit the supersonic speed of 768 miles per hour then reaching speeds of 1250 miles an hour, flying the rest of the way to New York. The plane was built for speed not luxury. Personally, I would rather be in a big comfy seat on a 747 in first class, with a flight attendant serving champagne and caviar as often as you would like. And then, have a bar to walk to and have a drink and talk to other first-class passengers rather than having a single, narrow isle, with one flight attendant pour you a drink and then having to wait until she reaches the front, turns around, and does the same thing coming back. In all, having to wait about thirty minutes for a second cocktail. Also, the seats were small although comfortable; they reminded me of Recaro seats in a sports car. As I said, built for speed not comfort.

When we arrived at JFK, we had a helicopter waiting to fly us into Manhattan and then a car to take us to The Waldorf Astoria. All first class and really impressive to everyone but Lena. In those days, what a distinguished, elegant hotel and building. It was in the middle of Park Ave. We checked in and were shown to our rooms and I was still as impressed as much as getting on the Concorde. Lena was still taking it all in stride, wishing she was home with her feet up on an ottoman, with a cup of tea in her hand. I had to keep reminding her this was all for her birthday.

We walked around Manhattan during the day, Lena not knowing that I had a few appointments for shirts and as we stopped outside a building that I had to go into, I would tell Lena to take a rest whilst I just pop in here to see a friend. I would then be back with her twenty minutes later to carry on walking the streets, then meeting Paul for lunch a little later. Nish Sawney, my pal who now lives in Monaco, also decided to join us in New York for Lena's birthday not to go on our deal but flying both ways commercially. He arrived and it was good to see my friend and now it made five of us for lunch, dinner and sightseeing every day.

Besides nipping into buildings and taking a few shirt orders, we did all the tourist stuff that I don't get time for when I go on business. We did the horse and carriage ride around Central Park, Trump Tower, John Lennon's Dakota building, The Empire State Building, Chinatown, little Italy and many more. Having dinner at The Tavern on the Green in Central Park, lunch at Bice with the Wall Street high rollers—we didn't stop with Lena still complaining about her sore feet and when can she go back to the hotel. After four wonderful days, we said farewell to Nish and went to the Brooklyn cruise terminal to board the QE2 home and another experience on this iconic British ship as well as another tick off my list of the things I have for Lena to do.

Talk about class distinction on the QE2. There were three classes and you could easily see the difference once you looked at the restaurants. It was like flying with Slim to the Gambia on British Caledonian—first class, club world and third world. The restaurant for the masses was called The Mauretania and held about 500 people and did two sittings. The second level that we were in was the Princess Grill and the top tier for the elite was the Queen's grill. Paul had so much front and style to go with it that he went to the purser to get us upgraded to the Queen's Grill even offering him a bung, I think, but with no luck. We had no complaints; the Princess Grill was sensational with excellent food and wine.

You were given a table that you could arrive at and have breakfast, lunch or dinner anytime during dining hours, but you always had the same table. At our table, three times a day, we became quite friendly with a man called Dallas Coors, later drinking in the bar until all hours. Dallas was a member of the Coors beer family, a tall, distinguished gentleman. I joked with Lena that she should marry him but she was disgusted that I even suggested it as she still loved my dad even though he died some twenty years earlier.

Dallas had a house in Belgrave Square, Knightsbridge, that he visited a few times a year, but he never flew. He always travelled both ways on the QE2 and although he could eat in The Queen's Grill, he preferred the people and the food in the Princess Grill. He was a charming man who liked Lena but although I was joking tongue-in-cheek that she should marry him and then we could retire, she wouldn't have it.

The seven days on board the QE2 were fantastic with shows every night, dancing in the night club, and, of course, first-class service and food. I even met a lady that I had fun and games with for a few nights whilst her elderly husband was either in their cabin asleep or at dinner when she would slip away for a while. What I didn't realize when I booked the trip, but it didn't matter anyway because it was Lena's birthday, 7th November, was that it was mid-winter and the Atlantic Ocean had its roughest seas during this time of year—not smooth sailing where you could sunbathe by the pool during the day and walk the decks during the evening. We had giant waves coming over the ship most of the time and the ship tossing up and down. Paul had a large, Sunseeker boat in Marbella so he was used to rough seas. He spent most of the trip home in his cabin or at the doctor with sea sickness along with a lot of the passengers but not tough, old Lena. She loved it.

When she did her interview for *The Middleton Guardian* newspaper about me being fifty years old at the Millennium and said, 'he's had me on Concorde twice,' there was another deal that I saw again in *The Sunday Times*. It was the Concorde Manchester to Paris with three nights in a four-star hotel and business class home on a charter by Air France—the Concorde flying over The Bay of Biscay to reach and experience supersonic speed then turning around and landing in Paris at Charles de Gaulle airport. The reason for this trip was that Fiona had told me she was pregnant with my daughter, Elle, and even though I was over forty, the thought of telling Lena was petrifying. I thought that the three of us would go to Paris and again Lena had not been so another tick off the list and one night over a few drinks I would casually slip it in that Fiona was having a baby. I thought that would be easy and the best way of breaking the good news. We did everything whilst in Paris: the Louvre museum, the Eiffel Tower, Montmartre, had an artist sketch us, and lunch at one of the brilliant restaurants even though touristy we loved it. In the evening, we had tickets for Le Moulin Rouge and another night, the Bateaux Mouches Seine River dinner cruise up and down the Seine as we are eating dinner.

From the first day at lunch when we got back to the hotel, Fiona would say, did you tell her, what was said, and me saying that it just wasn't right. I will tell her tonight. After that night, we returned and Fiona would ask again with me repeating myself that it didn't feel right. I will tell her tomorrow. This went on for the whole trip with me not having the nerve to tell my mum about me becoming a father and getting back to Manchester, with Lena being none the wiser. Two days later, I flew to Majorca and on the first night, I got home drunk from dinner and called Lena saying I forgot to tell in you in Paris but Fiona's pregnant. Lena replying that's great news, congratulations, and if you need a babysitter anytime call me. I couldn't believe it even though I should have known that she would have been pleased for us both.

After that, until the day she passed away, I still did as much as I could to make up for what I felt I owed her. Taking her to Majorca in the summer and every winter to Naples, she would come to Florida for two months or longer, going out most days and nights until she was too tired. One night before Christmas, she was staying home all evening whilst Rick Foreman put our Christmas tree up. She loved Rick and they got on famously. She would open wine for them both and later she would go on to her favorite tipple, Bacardi and coke, and Rick drinking anything he fancied. When we got home, they would both be tipsy, laughing their heads off, after having had a brilliant night together with Rick building a sensational Christmas tree. By this time, the tree had gone from 6' tall to 12' tall and was the centerpiece of the house, with every visitor having their photo taken by the tree.

Every day that she was in Florida, Lena complained that she missed her apartment and her grandchildren back home and wished she was there. The minute she got home, she was calling me to say she missed Naples, it was too cold in Manchester and she wished she was still here. You couldn't please her, but I didn't care. I know that she lived longer because of her two or three months in the Florida sunshine every year, rather than spending the same amount of time in the cold, wet, English winter.

The Millennium

Only twice in over twenty-five years, I did not go to Barbados at Christmas. One was when I spent six months in Naples and the other one was for my fiftieth birthday. Like Lena's seventy-fifth birthday, I wanted to do something different. It was The Millennium which happens only once in most people's lives and this one happened to be on my fiftieth birthday, so it was a very special occasion. I had fun as I still do today, looking at brochures for countries, hotels and flight prices with deals, and finally settled on a trip around the world, choosing places that I had never been to.

With Fiona and Elle, we flew business and first class everywhere. We stayed in first class hotels and ate in the finest restaurants for a month, and it still cost less than three weeks in Barbados. We started from Manchester, flying Singapore Airlines-Raffles Class to Singapore and what an experience it was, as good if not better than most other airlines' first class. The food, wine, but particularly the service was exceptional, and I was so happy I choose that airline arriving after a fifteen-hour flight feeling refreshed as if it was a five-hour flight. It truly was a pleasurable experience.

In Singapore, we stayed at the Shangri-La Hotel and like everywhere in Singapore the service was excellent but also humbling. The Singaporeans were born to serve and respect and how professional they were. Because of the price and the times that we travelled, we had midnight of the Millennium in Singapore. Originally, I wanted to be in Sydney, but it didn't work out. But what a night, the Singaporeans made it a truly world class event with a parade and fireworks display second to none that went on for most of the night. At 6:00 a.m. the next morning, the streets were swept and washed clean as if nothing had happened six hours earlier.

We loved Singapore, going to every tourist spot we could fit in, including lunch and cocktails in the world-famous Raffles Hotel and in their even more famous Long Bar and, of course, we had one of their iconic drinks, the Singapore Sling. Now, if you are not staying at the hotel, they don't allow tourists into the Long Bar, otherwise hundreds of people would be walking through taking photos and not buying a drink thus upsetting and disturbing residents that had spent a fortune to stay there. So, this was the first of many times during the trip that I pulled rank and flashed my American Express Black card, otherwise known as The Centurion card. Usually, I have to call my personal manager at Amex when I want something but Raffles reception just thanked us for coming to the hotel and led us into the Long Bar and gave us a table where we had a long, late, brilliant lunch and, of course, our Singapore Slings and wine.

Other days, we went shopping where everything was so inexpensive and most of the clothes custom made so I looked for a tailor that could copy my Versace trousers. I found one and took the plunge. I chose three fabrics that looked even better than my Versace fabric. The guy measured me; I left my trousers with him to copy the style and he had them ready the next day—unbelievable. I looked at the size of the stitching, the zip, the buttons and even the cotton thread he used and you couldn't tell the difference. Brilliant workmanship and he even put Versace labels in them. Talk about copyright—they have never heard of that in Singapore. The cost of my three custom pairs was less than half the price of one pair in Versace. What a deal. We bought lots of things for all of us and at great prices, walking into shopping malls, and down streets until our feet killed us. We stopped only for lunch and drinks then returned to the hotel for a rest then got ready for another night on the town.

Late one afternoon, when we got back to the hotel, I said to Fiona I think that I will have a massage in the health club. It looks great in the in-house magazine. I called the spa to see if they could fit me in and, of course, they could. I went upstairs to the health club thirty minutes later. I walked in and it was beautiful and very elegant as it should be in a five-star hotel. With a pretty receptionist taking my details, room number, name, soon an even prettier young lady walked in. She bowed and led me to a private room where she explained that she would be massaging me and if I would please get undressed and onto the table. She said to put the sheet over myself and press a bell when I was ready for her to come back into the room. All very professional and I was really looking forward to this massage after walking for six hours that day. She came back in and started to give me the greatest of massages. Nothing like the ones I used to have in Thailand that Mickey Gooch and Howard Marks used to organize for me, with sometimes three girls massaging and bathing me at the same time. This one was proper and very professional in one of Singapore's finest hotels.

After about half an hour, I was nearly asleep having this sensational body massage when she asked, "Are you enjoying the massage, Mr. Frank?" to which I replied its very good, thank you. "Is there anything else that I could do to make it even more pleasurable, Mr. Frank?" I couldn't believe it. I've heard those words many times in places in England, Hong Kong and Thailand but please not in the five-star Shangri-La Hotel in Singapore. I swear it had not even crossed my mind. I had my daughter and girlfriend a few floors below and here I have this beautiful young girl putting it on me. I told her that I had no money with me; she said that I could charge it to my room. She said those magic words "it can be charged." She was still massaging me but far more sensually and intimately by this time of the conversation, so it was difficult to refuse her.

I explained that she could only use her hands to massage me and not for sex. So, it was up to her and within five minutes she was kissing and licking my body from my chest to my feet and back for about fifteen minutes before she finished me off which didn't take that long. She was sensational and I was still in shock that it had happened in the first place. She left the room whilst I took a shower and returned when I pressed the bell with a spa receipt for me to sign to my room, for a massage along with space for her tip. Needless to say, she got a lot more than the twenty per cent that I usually give. I went back to my room wearing my white hotel robe and slippers, feeling very embarrassed about explaining to Fiona that my red face was from my extremely hot shower. I think I even said that I had a quick sauna as well.

After five great days in Singapore, we flew to Sydney, Australia, a place I have dreamed about going to for many years, seeing and hearing stories about Bondi Beach, Manly Beach, the Sydney Harbor Bridge, the Opera house, Darling Harbor and many more. We stayed at the Park Hyatt Hotel in the city's historic district called 'The Rocks' where you could see and walk everywhere. From our hotel room balcony, we had brilliant views of the Opera House and The Sydney Harbor Bridge which was breathtaking day or night. I had already chosen and booked the better known and trendy restaurants for the evenings but winged it for lunch during the day. No matter where we had been sightseeing, the one day going to the stunning Blue Mountains showed us scenery and views that we had never before seen or could imagine—absolutely beautiful and spectacular. We walked and got taxis, but most days went by boat to our destination from Darling Harbor which was a short walk from our hotel down the cobbled streets and hills.

Twice every day going out and coming home, we walked past this cool-looking restaurant, bar, night club that, early in the morning, people were seated inside and outside having coffee and breakfast whilst men in suits were rushing to work in banks or at the Stock Exchange. At noon, people were drinking wine and having lunch; late afternoon and early evening, the place was again busy with these people in suits, having a drink after work and at nighttime, it was a restaurant and night club. I wanted to go but having an eight-year-old girl with you limited the places you felt that you could go. Not like in Manchester where Elle, my daughter, could go and has been everywhere because of who her daddy is but, unfortunately, not in Sydney, Australia, where no one knows her daddy.

One afternoon after a great day out, we were walking home from Darling Harbor and as we got to this cool place that was driving me mad to try, three seats were vacant outside on the terrace. It was perfect for people watching and relaxing with a drink on this hot afternoon. So, I said to Fiona, sit here quickly with Elle. I will go inside and get drinks, hoping they don't see or mind that we have an eight-year-old girl with us, as all week whatever time we passed, I've only seen adults frequent the place. I walked up to the bar, looking around at this really cool restaurant, when the barmaid said to me what do you want, Frank, the usual—a Rye and Dry tall glass, with lots of ice and a slice of orange. I looked and couldn't believe it. She was my barmaid from, at the time, the hottest bar and restaurant in

Manchester called Mash and Air, as I exclaimed fuck me, what are you doing here? With her saying, you haven't even missed me have you.

She continued: "I left Mash and Air eight months ago and I was in Thailand for six months and here in Australia for two months. You didn't even know I had left." I said but what a small world it is with us seeing each other at the other side of the world in a major city and with a thousand bars for me to walk into and then I walk into your bar—even more fate in my life. She came outside and brought the drinks, said hello to Fiona and Elle that she knew already from Manchester, with Fiona saying to me you are unbelievable. Even across the other side of the world, you see people that know you. I smiled modestly and said it's not easy being Frank Rostron and laughed.

When I had my shop in Birmingham, I had a customer and friend called John Chapman who was the branch manager for Abbey Life Insurance. John was very successful and bought a lot of shirts from me and I had a couple of life policies with him. John was single and a really good guy that I liked a lot; we went out for dinner, some nights with John Moroney or other pals. As we talked about girls, John didn't join in, me thinking that he was just a gentleman and a little shy or modest about those things. Years later, when he was about to retire, we went out for dinner and he told me his plans for the future and that he was emigrating to Australia with his friend, Kenneth, as it was easier for two guys to live together in Australia than in England. Then it all fell into place—John, my friend, was gay.

It didn't matter one iota to me. He was my pal and I liked him a lot. We had even been on holiday together once—a cruise around the Caribbean with two pals from Manchester, flying to Madrid then on to Puerto Rico to board the ship, having a great two-week holiday. As he left for Australia, he promised to keep in touch which he did, sending cards and Christmas cards about how fabulous life was there with me also doing the same, saying I hope one day to see him again, not thinking I would ever go to Australia but here I was.

We had spoken a few weeks before my trip with me telling him that we were coming to Australia. John saying that we must fly from Sydney and stay with him and Kenneth for a few days at their home (as he said that they live and he laughed as he said that it was appropriate for them that they lived in) QUEENSLAND, only a couple of hours away by plane and, of course, we wanted to go. I had not seen my friend for over twenty-five years and I had never met Kenneth as John had kept him a secret whilst he lived in Birmingham. We arrived in Brisbane and were looking around the airport for John when this short, very flamboyant man came running over shouting Frankie, Frankie, waving his arms around like rag doll, with John about twenty yards behind him. John looked just the same but tanned. It was great to see him and being so happy. He introduced us to Kenneth who had already done it himself, giving me, Fiona and Elle the biggest of hugs. He got our bags and drove us to his home pointing out places on the way that we would see over the weekend, including the first in the world

Palazzo Versace Hotel that only opened weeks earlier and where we were having dinner the following night. We went to another couple of great restaurants where I was introduced to BYO (bring your own wine). I had never seen this or certainly never done it but apparently it was quite normal in Australia and I didn't come across again it for another ten years and that was in Naples, with a crowd that invited me to dinner at Bleu Provence, bringing their own very expensive French wines. We left John, Kenneth and the Gold Coast after a special three days with them. We flew back to Sidney to finish our holiday in Australia then went on to New Zealand.

New Zealand was never on my to do list like Australia but we were on the other side of the world, so we had to go and I'm so happy we did. It was brilliant. It's a massive country like Australia that you would need a month in each country to see properly and do them justice and we only had a week in each, but we saw all the landmarks and places people say you must go to and see. New Zealand is made up of two large islands—the North Island and the South Island—with 700 small islands in between and around. We stayed in Auckland at The Park Hyatt, again a fine hotel with a good location in the center of this vibrant city. We did the usual stuff: sightseeing, restaurants, shopping but something was happening in Auckland whilst we were there that I didn't know about or realize just how big it was. The America's Cup engulfed the whole city and country—every bar, restaurant, hotel, shop, store and anywhere that there was a TV. It was on twenty-four hours a day. If not live, then replays of the day's races with teams and races like The Louis Vuitton Cup and The Prada Challenge. This sport is not for millionaires but only billionaires. These yachts were coming into their bays after the days racing with damage such as a broken mast, with engineers and crew working through the night to replace it for the next day's races, costing nearly a million pounds to replace. We found ourselves getting ready in the hotel to go out for dinner and watching it on TV. You couldn't get away from it and it was on every channel. It was so exciting, and it really sucked you into the sport as everybody was watching the replays and the updates. It was unbelievable. One day, we were walking through the port looking for a lunch place and at the same time watching these magnificent yachts coming and going. We saw the perfect spot upstairs—an open-air terrace with the best view in town. It was the American Express 'America's Cup' Club lounge.

 The three of us walked in and were immediately greeted by an official asking what could he do for us and me saying a table for three, upstairs for lunch, please at the front, so we could eat and watch the races. He replied I am very sorry, sir, but this club is for members only and with a reservation. I was gutted as we were walking out but remembered that my black, American Express card could do anything—as it has done many times before like at Raffles Hotel Singapore and like it did in St. Andrews, Scotland, with Cliff, my daughter's Godfather, when he took me on The Orient Express to watch the British Open. We could not get into the hotel for lunch because Tiger Woods and all the other star golfers were staying there for security reasons. So, I called my Amex black card manager and we were seated down having lunch thirty minutes later—to say Cliff was impressed is an understatement. I turned around to the official and flashed my black card, saying does this privilege American Express card get me a reservation. It was like magic, the guy saying it certainly does, sir. Please follow me. He led us up the stairs to easily the best table on the terrace. He brought the menus and wine list. I ordered a bottle of French rosé for myself and Fiona, a Shirley Temple for Elle and we sat back and enjoyed our four-hour lunch whilst watching the Louis Vuitton, Prada and team New Zealand yachts coming and going in and out of their docks all afternoon. It was better than being in an executive box on the halfway line at Wembley Stadium for a FA Cup final. It was that good and this was a sport that I didn't really know existed three days earlier.

We were told by friends that we must go to the South Island, but it was impossible as we just didn't have enough time. You would need at least three or four days just to see the basics, so I got a private charter plane with four other people, and we flew there for the day. It only took about thirty-five minutes, so we left early and spent the whole day looking around and at least I can say that I've been there. The pilot was pointing out and explaining different landmarks there and back and one very important and impressive thing to see was this world class golf course that was built in the middle of nowhere by an American billionaire—a Wall St. Investment banker—that no one ever played on. Only the banker and his friends used it. He has full-time staff and groundsmen, a clubhouse to change and shower, and nothing else. He flies in on his plane or helicopter, plays a round of golf and flies out. You cannot get in by any other way but by air. He didn't know the American billionaire's name, but I did. It was Julian Robertson, the President of Tiger Management, in New York that was a friend and a very good customer of mine for over twenty-five years.

Julian is a wonderful man and had told me and shown me photos of this golf course many times. He uses it for himself and friends only. Talk about wealth, even though he has his own jet, he lets his friends and staff go in the jet and he flies commercial first class. He says because he finds it more comfortable and relaxing and then meets them there. Once when GQ in America did an article about me, they wanted to interview me with a client. I asked Julian if he would be photographed by GQ with me, whilst being interviewed. Although being flattered, he said he would rather not. Julian is a very modest billionaire and thought it wouldn't look good for his business to be seen ordering custom shirts even though he donates twenty-five million dollars at a time to his old college. He is a very generous man. When his sons found out that he had declined to appear in GQ with me, they were angry with him. Saying Dad, you are in *The Wall Street Journal* and other financial magazines and newspapers every day and this is much cooler. You should have done it. Every time I saw him after that, he says how he regrets not doing it and how much stick his sons gave him for ages.

We went back to Auckland for a couple of days and had a great time but then it was time to go to the next destination on our World tour. This was Rarotonga in the Cook Islands. I had never heard of it before but when talking to my travel agent, he suggested that since we were in New Zealand, we must see it, if only for four days—so we did it. It was a beautiful island with white beaches, lagoons and reefs. We stayed at a Polynesian beach hotel and just relaxed on the beach and had dinner in the hotel. After a hectic three weeks of non-stop travelling, this was the perfect place to do just that. The only night we went out for dinner was to the Te Vara Nui village, which was a Maori cultural site, with evening shows. They had Maori dancers performing on floating stages whilst you are having a dinner of their local cuisine and it really was worth the night out. The dancers as young as six and eight years old in their full Maori dress, giving a wonderful show along with male and female adults dancing between fire and waterfalls. It was really spectacular.

After Rarotonga, the next stop was Tahiti which I was really looking forward to. I had always wanted to go there after seeing movies like *Mutiny on the Bounty* that featured beautiful girls with long dark hair. These days, the hotels are mostly with bungalows on stilts going out to sea, with white sandy beaches and coral-fringed lagoons just like you see in magazines. We were booked to stay for two nights in the capital Pape'ete and when we arrived even before we got to the hotel, I couldn't believe what a dump it was. After we checked in, we walked around town and I was right. It was an absolute shithole and there was no way we were staying two nights there. I even went to see if we could leave immediately to our hotel on the island of Moorea but we had missed the last launch. We had to stay that night but left on the first boat early the next morning. I cannot believe with such beautiful places like Bora Bora and Moorea that you would have to land and even stay in a place like Papeete. It really was disgusting and dangerous. On the island of Moorea, we again had a bungalow on stilts, stretching out above a turquoise blue sea. We had a glass floor in the lounge that lit up at night so you could see all the colored fish swimming below. We had a golf buggy to drive us to and from the main hotel. It really was brilliant. The French food was excellent and the only night that we went out was again to a spectacular, Polynesian dinner show—very touristy but well worth going to. During the day, we spent swimming and lying on the beach getting a tan and still relaxing after all the travelling.

After a week, it was time to leave and the launch picked us up but this time, we didn't have to stay in Pape'ete and got a car straight to the airport for our flight to Los Angeles. I had been to LA lots of times but Fiona and Elle hadn't so we would have had to stop there to get the flight to London anyway. I thought why not show them LA and stay a few days as opposed to just changing planes and flying straight home.

We stayed at my regular hotel, The Beverly Hilton, and went to my favorite restaurants: Spago, No Bu and Mr Chow.

Elle loved them all. During the day, we did no more sunbathing even though the Hilton has a sensational pool. We went to Malibu, Santa Monica, and walked up and down Rodeo Drive, Beverly Drive and Cannon shopping but didn't do any serious damage, just a couple of things for Elle. We flew home with Air New Zealand, an excellent airline from LAX to London, on the last leg of our holiday. We had first-class seats and beds on this flight, but it was the only time during the whole months holiday I was sick. I don't know if I ate something the night before or that morning, but I was sick and ill all the way home. It was a twelve-hour flight and I didn't get to enjoy the experience of the full flat beds, the bar, wine or the excellent food. Fiona and Elle had a ball, but I don't remember the flight home at all and spent most of it in the bathroom.

Leeds

After a couple of years in Bridge Street and after my old shop that I had with Summerbee had closed down, we were busier than ever, so I opened a second shop in Leeds. I already had a few customers there: Martin Reynolds, John Luper, and the Burton family but then met friends like Robert Lemoine who I took to LA on holiday and he still lives there today. Also with Howard Symonds, John Hubbard, Phil Butterworth and Lenny Cohen along with their friends, I thought I could do well in Leeds. I was going over and staying two or three nights a week even though it was only an hour drive home so I could circulate in town, going to clubs, bars and restaurants, meeting people, and telling them about my Frank Rostron shirt shop.

One night, I went out in Leeds with Martin Reynolds and a few friends to a new club that had opened recently called Cinderella Rockerfella's. It was a very elegant and exclusive place that cost a fortune to open, and they suggested we go there for dinner. They had a fine dining restaurant with very pretty waitresses and hostesses, so it was just up my street. We had a great booth overlooking the dance floor and ordered drinks when one of the guys said he's here—the owner was walking down towards us wearing a white tuxedo jacket and an open neck shirt, with his long blonde hair looking like a rock star. These guys had been in several times trying to meet him so that they could become his pal just like the guys who used to give me coke in clubs. As he got to our booth, he looked and smiled at our table then did a double take, looked at me and said, "Little Frankie!" I said to him, yes. Then he said to me I'm Peter from The King Mojo club. I then said, fuck me, Peter, what are you doing in here. He replied that he owned it. The last time I saw him he was in jeans and T-shirt and me fifteen years old sitting on scooters outside his club. He was brilliant at remembering people. That's why he became a multi-millionaire and the world's biggest night club owner, with clubs in Manchester, London, New York, Los Angeles, Miami, Paris and Ireland. He ordered me a bottle of champagne. I introduced him to my friends and preceded to tell him what I had been doing since I was fifteen years old. I told him that I had a shirt shop in Manchester and now I had just opened a shop in Leeds. After he left to circulate the club, my friends, all successful Leeds businessmen, said that we can't believe it; we've been coming in here, spending bundles trying to meet him and you come in for the first time and he comes to you and buys you champagne. I don't know why but my life has always been that way since I lived in my council house. Getting these privileges, I felt blessed and I still do to this day while living in paradise. Later, Peter opened another sensational club in Manchester called The Millionaire Club and everyone from Manchester wanted to get in on the opening night. The club was full, but the restaurant was closed to the public and only Peter's personally invited guests had dinner with wine and champagne that night. Myself and my girlfriend, Stephanie Serene, were the only people from Manchester in the restaurant VIP section on the opening night. The others were his friends from Leeds and Sheffield. I also went to the opening of his other clubs in London and in America.

There are many stories of nights out in Leeds, with Rob LeMoine, John Hubbard, Martin Reynolds and Phil Butterworth. In Lens Bar, Madison and Cinderella's and restaurants like The Terrazza, The Flying Pizza, and Bibbi's and the stories in Majorca, England, Barbados, and America—the stories are too numerous to tell—otherwise this book would be thicker than the Bible.

One fun story that nearly ended badly was a night out in Leeds, with my shop manager Peter Rushby. We were in Madison's night club having dinner when two girls came over to talk to us. I bought them drinks and they sat at our table for the rest of the night. At two o'clock when the club was closing, they asked us if we wanted to go back for a drink to their house in Armley, just outside Leeds. They had already told us that they were married but that their husbands were working in Wales and were not at home. We drove them to this little, two-bedroom, terraced house in a cobbled street in Armley, in the shadows of the Victorian Armley Prison. We parked the car a couple of hundred yards up the road so that the neighbors wouldn't know that they had company. During the evening, their husbands had been calling them regularly and were not impressed that their wives were in Leeds city center at nightclubs drinking and partying.

After pouring the drinks, I went upstairs with my girl and Peter did the same with his. About two hours later, we were in bed asleep and all of a sudden there was banging on the front and back doors, with guys shouting and screaming. I thought it was a dream, but the girls jumped up saying that it was their husbands outside trying to get in. Peter and I were trying to get dressed but panicking as the banging and shouting got louder and louder with the doors nearly crashing down. I said to Peter that there are two guys: one at the front and one at the back. The one at the back had already smashed the window. So, we will open the front door quickly and rush out. You turn left, I will turn right and hope for the best. We did that, knocking the guy over as we brushed past him and running for our lives, going our separate ways through the cobbled streets of Armley—Peter having no shoes on and me having no shirt on at 4:00 a.m., with two guys chasing us. Then, all of a sudden, a police car sees me and flashes his blue lights, wondering what I was doing in the middle of the night half-dressed. I ran over to them telling them what had happened and that two guys were trying to kill us. They said get in and we drove around looking for Peter for about fifteen minutes before we found him hiding behind a wall.

The police took us back to the house with Peter and me in the back of their car. One of them went inside to get our clothes that we had left behind in the rush. The police warned the guys who were builders and big guys at that to stay to one side whilst the police officer rescued our belongings and told them in future to manage their wives better. They dropped us off at my car and we drove back to Manchester, laughing and joking about the experience but also about how close we were to getting a battering from two bricklayers. Peter also saying that working for Frank Rostron wasn't like any other job. It was a lot more fun and exciting but also very dangerous.

Barbados

Back in Manchester, things were going along smoothly, and I had a great team run by my friend and manager, Richard Shaughnessy. Business was good and I was spending the Summers in Majorca and Christmas in Barbados, with whoever was my current girlfriend at the time. But with a boy's trip to Barbados at least one time a year as well. These two trips were like chalk and cheese—at Christmas, a proper family holiday, staying at Glitter Bay, being on the beach all day, having lunch, dressing up for dinner and going out with my rich friends and clients from London and Manchester. Then home to bed after dinner, sometimes a night cap at the hotel bar before retiring.

The boys' trips were completely different; somedays not even making the beach, going out at night with my Bajan gang to take care of us, with names like Artifus Flavios, Ralph, Satan, David, Andy White and Wayne Alleyne. They would take me and my boys to clubs that white guys or tourists didn't know about like The Warehouse, with the legendary Splash Band playing. I loved this music. We would send drinks to local girls in there with the Bajan boys saying our rich friends from England want to buy you all a drink. I could buy everyone in the club a drink and it still cost peanuts compared to the places we would go at Christmas that cost a fortune. Then, the boys would go and get coke (the drug). It was easy to get and cheap on the island since it was near South America, and we would give it to everyone in our company. Then, about four in the morning, we would go to a very rough and dangerous area in a street called Baxter Road but we were safe because I had my Bajan boys with me. We would take the girls with us and whichever bar we chose to go in, the owner would lock the doors so no one could come in the place. It was just for us, and he knew we would spend more than he had taken all day and night. He didn't want us disturbed or having trouble with the local Bajan thugs looking around for a move.

We would take the girls back to the hotel after Baxter Road not even making the beach. Just partying in the suite for a day or two then starting again with new girls that were always Bajan. These girls wouldn't be allowed on the beach anyway with the chic clientele. I could have pulled rank and insisted being a great customer, but I wouldn't have done that, plus it would have been embarrassing considering the state that we were in. Another bar we used to go to which was nearer to our hotel and a lot safer was Crocodile. This place was a local Bajan chattel house converted into a bar that all the celebrities on holiday used to visit. The toilets were disgusting and smelled but I have been in Crocs when Joan Collins has been behind the bar serving drinks along with John Cleese, Julian Lennon, Cliff

Richards and many more. I knew Julian and his mum, Cynthia, from Majorca where they spent a lot of time and when Julian used to date a girl whose British parents owned a local shop, selling belts and gifts in Magaluf. I even hung out with him many years before that in London with Mark Macauley going to The Embassy club and Toyko Joes. Thus, I had known him a long time before Majorca and Barbados. One New Year's Eve, I was walking into a club in Holetown where I had a table for my birthday and who was in the long line waiting to get in but Julian and his mum, Cynthia. I couldn't believe that Julian and Cynthia Lennon were lining up to get into a club, so I said to the manager that they were with me and took them in.

One day after two days of partying, sex, drugs and not rock 'n' roll but reggae, I made the beach and I looked terrible. I was unshaven, pale and drawn but needed some food. I used to have a girlfriend in Manchester back in the day called Moya, a model who moved to London that I never saw again. But I read in the newspaper that she had married a very famous, successful actor and writer called George Layton. Whilst I am getting my orange juice, I noticed George on the beach. I looked but couldn't see Moya. Anyway, I might not even recognize her after all these years, or they could have divorced by now who knows.

After a few minutes, a young man who I saw on the beach with George stood next to me getting breakfast. I was curious; so I asked him is your mother called Moya to which he replied, no, my mother isn't but my dad's wife is called Moya. Just at that moment, George walks up to his son who said, "Dad, this guy knows Moya." I thought to myself *what have I got myself into here.* He asked, how do you know her to which I replied, she used to be in our crowd when she lived in Manchester. George then says what is your name and told him Frank Rostron to which he replied Frank, Moya talks about you all the time. He tells his son to go and get Moya quickly. I want the ground to open and to bury myself. I looked like shit and this beautiful woman walks over to us, looking like a million dollars. She is wearing a straw hat, sunglasses, and a sarong and looked sensational. She gives me a peck on both cheeks and said come and join us. I made up an excuse saying I have been in bed sick for two days and I don't feel good but perhaps later. I couldn't say I have been drinking and taking drugs in a shebeen with local girls and having an orgy for two days. As she was walking back to the beach, she turned and asked are you going to the Pavarotti concert? I told her no; she said that she would see me later.

On this trip, I was with two pals, and I always stayed at Glitter Bay. But a girl, working in the office whom I once dated and came to Manchester to see me named Shernell, called me in England. The general manager knowing that if he needed a favor from Frank Rostron then Shernell was the one to ask me. She had already called me weeks earlier to see if I wanted tickets to a very prestigious event that they were having in Barbados. Luciano Pavarotti was performing at the very first Barbados opera and it was by invitation only. Today, I would cut someone's hand off for such an invite but in those days the stupid, ignorant Frank Rostron would rather be on the beach drinking and surrounded by girls than watching a fat Italian sing in a language I didn't understand in 90 degrees of sunshine.

The favor she wanted was that Glitter Bay was overbooked and the manager wanted to know if I would swap my two-bedroom suite for two one-bedroom suites at their hotel next door, The Royal Pavilion. It is beautiful hotel, a little more expensive than Glitter Bay but more formal and not as much fun. I politely said, no. She said that it's important. What would I want to stay next door? I thought for a minute and said the two one bedroom suites are fine but they must be adjoining as three pals at the end of the day want to sit and have a drink on the terrace. We want to be looking down onto the beach and out to sea so they must be next door to each other. Anything else, she said sarcastically and I said, yes. I want the hotel Mercedes to pick us up from the airport and take us back. Anything else? she asked, I said, yes, a bottle of champagne in my suite every night and breakfast for the three of us. I thought I would go in strong as I don't want to stay there anyhow. She replied, he will never do all that with me saying good because I want to stay at Glitter Bay anyway. Thirty minutes later she called me back saying, ok, you got it and that was that. We were staying at The Royal Pavilion with all the Royal privileges.

The first morning I got up and walked onto my terrace and looked down on the beach and who was there in the tiniest pair of Speedos but my old pal from London via Leeds and

Manchester, Peter Stringfellow. I called down to him and he looked up saying what are you doing up there. I thought they were all suites on that floor; have you got a suite? I replied, no, I have TWO suites and laughed. I went down and we had a chat. Peter asking, are you going to the Pavarotti concert, me saying, no, are you? He said, of course. I told him I was invited but didn't fancy it and then a few days later, George and Moya Layton asked me the same question. I thought am I missing something here, only later realizing what I missed and how stupid I was.

The next month in the celebrity *"Hello"* magazine, there were a dozen pages in color photos of the invited VIP guests and celebrities with Pavarotti. Full page photos of Peter and his girlfriend, Frisbee Fox, and George and Moya with Pavarotti in the middle with the edit saying Millionaire club owner, Peter Stringfellow, and actor, George Layton, with his wife, Moya, with the star, Luciano Pavarotti. I was pissed that it could have been the same but with me in the picture with them saying millionaire shirtmaker to the stars, Frank Rostron. What a mug I was missing, not only the publicity and prestige but also the sensational Pavarotti concert.

It was always good to go back for our annual Christmas in Barbados. I love the island, the locals, and the restaurants. But now, it's just me and Jane; no more boys' trips. But saying that, I had five days last year with a pal from Naples. Not wild like the old days but still seeing a few old friends. We stayed at The Royal Pavilion and went to some of the excellent restaurants

My mum, dad and sister showing off the new baby, Francis Rostron.

Every year
Whit Sunday
in my new
clothes.

My soccer teams from eight years old and onward.

▲ Top photo, a young me wanting to be a goalkeeper in my cap.

Me, front row, number 6. ▼

Me, back ▲ row, far right.

▲
Boarshaw Hotel football team late '60s early 1970 (named "Harvest" after the band "Barclay James Harvest"). Three of the lads sadly have passed away—Alan Smith (Smeller), Mike Heed and Graham Soothill.
L to R—back row: Jimmy Halliewell, Neville Crook, Brendan Waterfield, Frankie Rostron, Alan Smith, Mike Heed.
L to R—front row: Not sure, Colin Ashton, Pete Trussell, Graham Soothill, Pete Roach.

Sunday morning, looking good.

The original Wheel, 1964, in Brazennose St., Manchester.
Spencer Davis spelled wrong along with Rod Stewart.

THE TWISTED WHEEL CLUB

6 WHITWORTH STREET, MANCHESTER 1

Tel. CENtral 1179   (Opposite Fire Station)

✷ GRAND OPENING ✷

of New Twisted Wheel Club Premises on

SATURDAY, 18th SEPTEMBER, 1965

THE SPENCER DAVIS GROUP

The Club in Brazennose Street will Close on
SATURDAY, 11th SEPTEMBER, 1965

with

JOHN MAYALL BLUES BREAKERS

PLUS

GUEST ARTISTS

ADVANCE TICKETS ARE NOW AVAILABLE FOR BOTH THESE DATES

The opening of the new Wheel in Whitworth St., 1965.

Opening Leeds Store

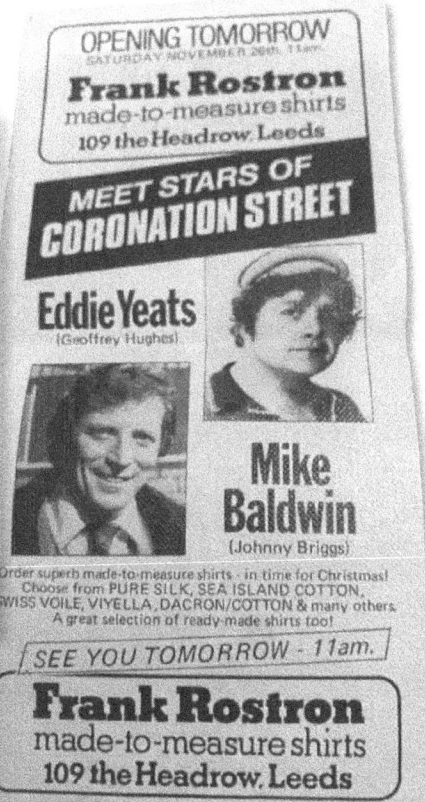

Famous actors Johnny Briggs and Geoffrey Hughes opening the shop and the poster advert that closed Leeds city center down for a day.

Brian Johnson's Leaving for California Party

L to R—Alex Grunfeld, Peter Smith, me, Brian Johnson, Martin Reynolds and my hero Don Wilson.

My first trip to California.

▲ With Brian Johnson at Disneyland in the film studio.

◄ Me and David Soul on the set of *Starsky and Hutch*.

Kentucky King

My trip to Owensboro, Kentucky. Kentucky welcomes the King of England—me in my crown.

Crazy Days in Majorca on La Baraka

Majorca

Wally Gordon with the champagne I gave him for not believing when he told me Billy Idol sang for him. ▶

◀ A cloudy day on La Baraka; me plotting with Barry Faulkner from Middlesbrough to have some fun.

▲ Lunch on La Baraka with Claude and some Swedish guests.

◀ A day on the beach with Tina and Roberta Moore, wife and daughter of the late great Bobby Moore, England's World Cup winning captain.

St. Tropez

Me outside Senequer in St. Tropez after coffee with George Michael.

Hi Dolly

▲ Me and two friends on my boat, *Hi Dolly*.

▲ Marley Marquis, from Sweden, getting some sun on my boat; it was Marley who dragged me out of BCM when I judged the Miss Wet T-shirt contest.

◄ After lunch on my boat, *Hi Dolly*, with friends from Sweden.

◄ The magic American Express "Black Card"—the Centurion card that opened so many doors and impressed girls from Manhattan and Beverly Hills.

Girls...

Julia Mahon in Ft. Lauderdale. ▶
Julia was with me in Brambles nightclub when I had the fight with my ex-girlfriend's new boyfriend.

◀ Fiona Blackshaw, my daughter's mother in Stringfellows in New York.

▲ The wonderful Caroline from Sweden in Majorca.

▲ Dinner with Marlen Gannem in Miami.

Girls...

▲ At Palma Nova Beach club with Caroline from England.

▲ On La Baraka with Marley Marquis from Sweden.

A day on the boat in Majorca with Anita ▶ from London, who I also took to Barbados.

◀ In Atlantic City with Marlen Gannem.

Girls . . .

▲ Dinner in Majorca with Claudene from France who had a shop in Magaluf, Majorca.

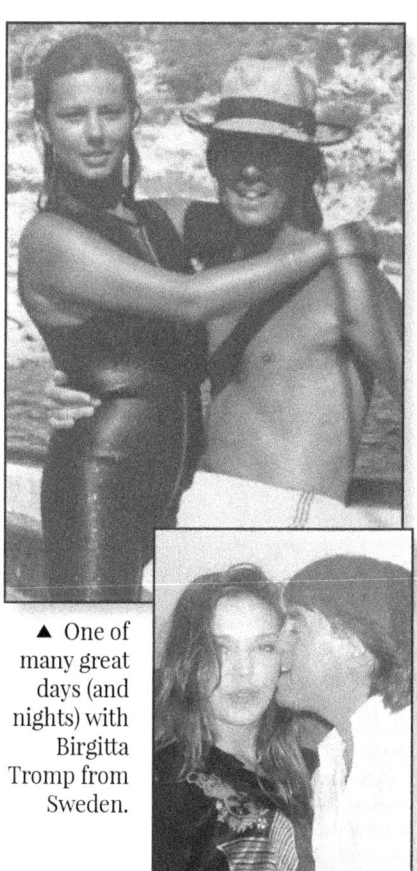

▲ One of many great days (and nights) with Birgitta Tromp from Sweden.

▲ More fun with this beauty in Manchester.

▲ On the beach with Gabriella from Sweden. She came to Manchester twice.

▲ Julia Mahon in Majorca.

Girls . . .

▲ Karelyn Johnson my ex whose boyfriend I had the fight with.

▲ The London beauty, Anita, in Barbados with me.

▲ With Gabriella from Sweden.

◀ On La Baraka beach with Jackie Hall from Manchester.

Girls

▲ On the boat with Maja from Sweden.

▲ In New York with Jean Clark from Kentucky.

Dinner at Mario's in Palma with two Swedish beauties. ▶

▲ Dinner at Mario's in Palma with Birgitta Tromp.

▲ In Barbados with Jackie from Leeds. In one month, I took this girl to Barbados and New York.

Celebrities

▲ Me with Harry Connick Jr. helping me sell shirts at his kid's school in Connecticut.

▲ Me with Governor George Pataki in his New York office.

◀ With Jason Orange from the band Take That who came to Steve Albinson's house at Christmas for his daughters.

▲ Me and the world's greatest jockey, Frankie Dettori, having fun in Barbados.

◀ Marvelous Marvin Hagler ordering shirts in my shop.

Me with undisputed heavyweight ▶ champion of the world Lennox Lewis in his home in London.

◀ My schoolteacher and hero, Don Wilson, at his son's wedding.

The giant who became my ▶ pal—Damien Noonan of The Hacienda.

◀ Some of the many letters from Ronnie and Reggie Kray ordering shirts from prison. The blue slip is from Broadmoor Hospital where Ronnie was serving his life sentence saying his letter has been opened and read.

▲ Some of The Quality St. Gang who Thin Lizzy named the hit song "The Boys are Back in Town" after.

Jimmy Swords, center, with me and ▶ Brian Kidd (the Man United European cup winner), the morning after City won the championship after beating QPR.

Jane

▲ Me and Jane at the Make-A-Wish Ball.

◀ A wild shirt night in Naples.

◄ Dinner in Naples.

Waiting on porter in Venice to put Jane's luggage on the boat.
▼

The Frank Rostron Golf Invitational

Dear Mr. Rostron,

Mr. Trump received your invitation to attend The Frank Rostron Golf Invitational on October 25-26th through Mr. Keith Schiller. While we truly appreciate you bringing this even to our attention. Mr. Trump usually does not attend events not hosted at one of his clubs and unfortunately has a prior commitment during that time. We thank you for reaching out and wish you the best of luck with this Invitational!

Best,
Chelsea Frommer

TRUMP
THE TRUMP ORGANIZATION

Chelsea Frommer
Executive Assistant

◀ The letter from Donald Trump saying thank you for the invite but couldn't make my tournament.

At the step and repeat wall ▶
at my golf tournament.

▲ With celebrity guests Super Bowl winners Ed Marinaro and Tom Matte.

Two Proud Days

Being made an honorary ▲
deputy sheriff.

◀ Becoming a US citizen.

Home & Cars

Friends for Life

▲ Robert LeMoine from Leeds, who I took to and now lives in LA, visiting me in Majorca.

▲ Giulio Nobilio the owner of La Terrazza my friend 50 years later.

▲ Paul Hanly Jr. who walked into my shop and changed my life, who brought me to New York and introduced me to his friends.

▲ Two of my greatest friends—my daughter's Godfather, Cliff Brierley, who took me to AA and my friend and mentor, the late Martin Reynolds.

▲ Black Lives Matter, especially for two of my oldest and loved pals, Basil Burton and Selwyn Stephenson.

▲ "London" Neil Sollinger who gave me first line of Charley.

like The Cliff, Tides, and Chin Chin that would hold their own against the finest restaurants in London or New York. We also went to Bombas, of course, a great Bajan restaurant owned by my pal of over thirty years, Wayne Alleyne, who was one of the original members of my Bajan gang when we used to go to The Warehouse and Baxter Road. Wayne has been out with me in Manchester many times when in England visiting his many girlfriends.

Another time, I arrived in Barbados and after checking in at my hotel, Glitter Bay, I went straight to see Michael Morris and friends at Sandy Lane. When I got there, Michael said you have just missed our old pal that we grew up with from London and went to school with. His name is Robert Earle; he would have loved you. We had a blast. He was so much fun, and he only left last night. You missed him by less than twenty-four hours. I knew the name. When they said who he was, it all came back to me. A billionaire who opened and owned The Hard Rock Café and later Planet Hollywood, with a mega range of superstar actors as his partners.

I love meeting characters like him, so I was sick that I had missed him. But one character I did meet many times at Sandy Lane (I met many going there to see my pals like Michael Morris, Wally Watson and Stuart Marks) was someone that Stuart introduced me to—Jack Walker. The Blackburn lad that made millions in Walker Steel, selling it, and amassing a personal fortune of over 800 million pounds. But even with all that money, Jack was still one of the boys who loved a drink.

I think that's why he liked me because I would drink with him whatever time he arrived on the beach. He bought his boyhood football club, Blackburn Rovers, and pumped enough money into it to win the English Premier league. His wife, Carol, who was a bit of a snob, said many times, I wish you would have bought Arsenal or Tottenham Hotspur instead of Blackburn Rovers so I could have been nearer to Harrods.

One year, Blackburn was playing Manchester United on Boxing day and Jack flew back to England on the Concorde in the middle of their Christmas holidays to watch the match and flew straight back. She went mad with him and the following season, Blackburn played United again but she wouldn't let him go. So, the day of the match, he sneaked off the beach, went to his hotel suite and phoned his housekeeper in Jersey. He told her to put the phone next to his TV and he listened to the match and came back to the beach two hours later. His wife didn't even miss him. That match we had a bet of a bottle of Dom Perignon, and I lost but to spend a couple of hours with Jack drinking it was well worth it, plus with Blackburn beating United.

Many years later, on a trip to New York and then Las Vegas for the Ricky Hatton world title fight, I was with my pal, Ray Ranson, the ex-Manchester City star, Ray's dad, Terry Byrne, and a pal of his from London. We were staying at The Hotel at Mandalay Bay but went for dinner to The Strip House, a steak restaurant at Planet Hollywood Las Vegas. I wanted to go there because they were opening a Strip House in Naples a few months later. I asked the lads if they objected and they said, of course not, so off we went. We had just started a cocktail and ordered dinner when Ray said, look who is walking over to our table, Robert Earle. Robert comes over and says, Hi, guys, is everything alright? I think he had heard our English accents and with everyone wearing loud, patterned shirts, gold and diamond watches and gold chains, he wanted to know who we were. He informed us that his name was Robert Earle and that he owned the hotel.

I said to him, Robert, you don't remember me do you. He looked at me, saying yes, I do, but can't remember where from. I told him that we met in Barbados years ago at Sandy Lane, with Michael Morris, Phillip Green and the rest of your old pals from London. My name is Frank Rostron and Robert replied, of course, I remember you, Frank, how are you? Do you still see the guys and I said, of course—every Christmas in Barbados. Robert then saying call me a flash bastard if you like but I don't go to Barbados anymore because I own my own island. Robert continued with Frank, you look great (even though he had never seen me before), I love your shirt and then he said I'm having a private party downstairs. You must come and bring your friends. He called his general manager over and said to him this is Frank Rostron, a good a friend of mine from England. When they finish dinner bring them to the party.

Well, now I am a good friend of Robert and he's never met me. But that's what we Manchester lads do. We are great salesman and con artists—especially with girls. As Robert was leaving the restaurant, he came over to my table and introduced us to his pals, Sylvester Stallone, Bruce Willis, Wesley Snipes, Charles Barkley and Stallone's brother, Frank. I nearly had an altercation with Frank Stallone years earlier in Stringfellow's in New York but that's another story and he didn't remember me as did Robert, so it didn't matter. Robert then saying see you downstairs and my GM will bring you when you have finished dinner. About an hour later, we finished and were led through corridor after corridor down then upstairs until we came to this massive room with a couple of hundred or so people drinking and dancing.

The room was divided into two by security ropes and we were led to the half where Robert and his merry men were sitting on throne-like chairs, watching the proceedings. The party was two-thirds women and one-third men—all partying and obviously snorting illegal substances by their facial expressions. Their half had an open bar and our half had only two drinks: Dom Perignon and Cristal Champagne. If you wanted anything else—vodka, whisky etc.—you went into the other half and to the bar. All the girls were young and attractive—all hookers—but everything was free, so after a couple of drinks, I started dancing with a very attractive Eastern European girl. Robert saying earlier that whenever we want to leave, the hotel limos are outside to take us home with as many of the girls as we wanted. After about an hour, Ray came over to say his dad was tired and they were going back to our hotel, obviously with no girls but they had loved the night. Ray's dad couldn't believe that he had met Stallone, Willis, Snipes and Sir Charles Barkley.

I stayed about another hour then went over to Robert to thank him for a great evening and for my Eastern European present. Robert saying only one, you are having only one? I said, yes, and it's enough. Robert saying don't go yet, I have another forty-eight girls coming shortly. I replied to him thanks, pal, but this one is good for me. I got into a limo and went back to The Hotel at Mandalay Bay.

Another character that I met in Barbados and who became a friend and customer was Michael Winner, the film director, writer, and TV personality who directed the *Death Wish* movies starring Charles Bronson. Michael was a very strange man; one minute the most charming person you could ever wish to meet and then an absolute piece of work the next minute. He lived in this sensational house in Holland Park, Kensington, which had the biggest bedroom I have ever seen. You could have played four-a-side soccer, it was so big. Adjoining this enormous room was another bedroom of a reasonably normal size and I once said to him what is this bedroom for Michael—to which he replied in his very posh English accent "that is where they wait until it's their turn"—meaning girls. I don't know if that was true or he was just showing off but he certainly had a thing for the ladies. One of these ladies was a model and former beauty queen from near Liverpool. I had seen her as a young man in Blinkers nightclub in Manchester and thought she was beautiful and she was, but it was before I had the confidence or money to date such a girl. When I first went to Michael's house, she answered the door and immediately I thought that I recognized her, but didn't know where from as it had been many years since I had seen her and that was only across a dance floor. She showed me to Michael's drawing room and that is where he introduced me to Dinah May. She was his personal assistant and still beautiful and lived at the house during the week going home to her husband and family at the weekend. I thought this was very strange, but it obviously worked for her and the pay must have been good. Michael would order shirts in fine cotton or silk and entertain me with great conversation and cocktails until I had to leave. Then he would ask me to stay for dinner, with a promise of a bigger shirt order which was not possible as I always had plans. A few weeks later, I would call him to say the shirts were ready and make an appointment to go to his house and deliver them. Again, he was the most charming and complimentary man as he tried his new shirts on saying how beautiful they were and what a great shirtmaker I was. Again, suggesting that I stay for dinner and drinks, again with me politely declining. The next morning my manager, Richard, would call me saying call Michael Winner quickly. He's called the shop saying the shirts were shit, that they didn't fit and using every swear word in the book at my staff, being rude and insulting. I would call him and he was perfectly alright talking to me, saying could you find five minutes to look at his shirts, please. I went to the house and Dinah May would open the door and take me to his enormous bedroom. Michael would greet me as if nothing had happened and again very charming, thanking me for coming back and asking if I had a good night the previous evening and where I had eaten dinner and how it was. He would say the shirts are fabulous, Frank, but what do you think of this button placing or this monogram to which I would say and mean it that I thought it was perfect and I loved the monograms. He then would say good; I just wanted your opinion then ordered more shirts. Michael was a complete lunatic, with no rhyme or reason about his behavior or his dual personality. It was a shame because he could be a real gentleman entertaining me and my friends in Barbados for hours at a time.

Freeport Grand Bahamas

Before Barbados, my first taste of the Caribbean was Freeport, Grand Bahamas.

One day, a customer and friend from Manchester, Raymond Abrahams, came into the shop and had been to Freeport on holiday. He went to see his friend from school whose name was Erroll Keel. I used to make Raymond fancy, flowered shirts, with big, rounded collars and wide, bishop sleeves. I know they sound terrible but, in the day, they were great, especially for holidays in Spain and the Caribbean. He was wearing his fancy shirts in Freeport and Erroll and his partner Mario Pasquini went crazy about them, just as my pals in Middleton did the first night, I wore my blue shirt with Lena's fabric. Raymond gave them a couple of his own and when he got back to Manchester, he came to see me and ordered a dozen for his friend, Erroll. This was a present for taking such good care of him in Freeport. Raymond chose the fabrics, paid me, and said post them to Erroll Keel in Freeport, Grand Bahama Island. Again, just like my first and second holiday in Majorca, I had no idea in the world where this place Freeport was.

When Michael Morris and I met Carla Argosy and Liz Ing, from Connecticut on our second holiday in Majorca, they invited us to visit them in America and the year after we went to see them. They picked us up at the airport and drove us into Manhattan to show us around. I don't think these schoolgirls knew New York too well as they were driving us up and down Second and Third Avenue not Madison and Fifth as I know today. We ended up having dinner of no note in a restaurant on Second Avenue. Then they drove us to where they lived in Newington, Connecticut. They both went to Southern Connecticut State College and Liz was that year's homecoming queen. They also shared a small apartment near the college, but their parents lived in Newhaven, CT. We were so excited just to be in America, we thought it was fantastic. We didn't care about this tiny apartment. They took us to their local bars, to their college and to Mystic Seaport and Newport which was brilliant. One day, they took us on a friend's boat whose family name was Fisher. He said they had just bought a toy company from England called Price and now their company is called Fisher-Price. What a world-famous company that was and it never crossed my mind to keep in touch with this young man. What a fool I was.

A few weeks before we were due to go to America to see the girls, I was in my office and my manager came in and said that there were two guys in the shop to see me. He said they looked strange, sun-tanned, with white linen shirts outside of their jeans, sandals and beads on their wrists—not what a

Mancunian would wear in town. I went out and the taller of the two said, "Frank, it's wonderful to meet you" and he put his arms around me gave me a hug and said, "I'm Erroll, Erroll Keel from the Bahamas." This man was so sweet and kind and softly spoken, he could have been Jesus Christ in the movie and his friend with him was Peter Bizzell who was Freeport's veterinarian. Erroll said that the shirts you sent me courtesy of Raymond Abrahams were beautiful. Everyone in Freeport loves them so I would like to order some more please.

We went for lunch and he explained he was in town visiting his mother. It turned out I knew his sister. She was beautiful. Her name was Helena Keel; we used to call her Lenny. I asked him where this place called Freeport was located and how do you get there or more like how did you get to Manchester from there. He said that we flew from Freeport to New York then New York to Manchester. I replied, my pal and I are going to New York in three weeks to see two girls that we met in Majorca last year. He insisted that we come for the weekend to visit him and perhaps bring his new shirts. What could I say—of course, we will. I called Michael and said that when we go to New York on the weekend, we are going to Freeport. He asked, where's that? I replied, I have no idea but its only two and a half hours flight from New York. When we arrived in New York, we told the girls that we had to go to Freeport for the weekend to deliver some shirts and see friends. It all sounded very flash and impressive. The following Friday, they drove us to JFK airport for our flight to Freeport still having no idea where it was.

We arrived and as we were landing, we could see all these beautiful, white, sandy beaches, with turquoise sea like I have never seen before not even on TV. As we got to immigration, the officer looked at our passports and said you cannot enter as you don't have a ticket to England. I replied, we are not going to England but back to New York for three more weeks and to England from there. The inspector said, you can't go back to America either because you only have a one visit visa for the USA in your passports and you have used it already. I was shocked, upset and had no idea what to do. We had been with immigration now for over an hour and suddenly, Erroll walks in and says what's the problem, George, to the Inspector. Everyone knows each other in Freeport and Erroll had no problem walking through security to see where we were. The Inspector told Erroll the problem. He left and came back five minutes later with two British Airways return tickets to England and showed them to his pal, George, who then stamped our passports and said have a nice time in Freeport. As we walked past the British Airways desk, Erroll gave the two tickets to the agent there who ripped them up and tossed them into the trash. Driving home, Erroll explained that his mate at BA wrote the tickets out just to get us in and we will sort everything out on Monday. He also said that he would have to drop us off at his apartment as it was Friday and a very busy day. He had to do the wages at work and that he would be home by six o'clock. He took us to his apartment at Alamanda Court, saying quickly, there's the pool, the beach is just through those bushes, I will see you later and rushed off.

We didn't even unpack—just put our shorts on and ran to the pool. We couldn't believe how beautiful it was not even thinking about Monday, the girls or Connecticut. Still naïve and lacking in adventure, after about thirty minutes, Michael said shall we see if we can find the sea. We walked thirty yards to the bushes and there it was—pure, white sand and turquoise blue sea like I've never seen before, with no one on it for as far as you could see. I ran and ran into the sea until the waves wouldn't let me run any further then dived under water and I swear I was brown when I came up—well, I thought I was. We walked up and down the beach diving into the sea every 100 yards and couldn't believe it. I looked at Michael and said to him that I'm not going back to Connecticut; I'm staying here, and he replied, me too. We stayed on the beach all day and about five went back to Alamanda Court. Erroll came home shortly after and asked if we had a good day. I said that you are joking aren't you—its paradise. That night he was having a dinner party to introduce us to a few of his friends. His partner, Mario Pasquini, Mario's wife, Barbara, and her beautiful, blonde friend, Lesley, who happened to be English and Peter Bizzell. We watched Erroll prepare the salad, the conch (which I had never seen or heard of), pineapple, peppers, strawberries and fillet the fish that he was going to grill later. It was a show I enjoyed, and I still love watching cookery shows today.

Erroll and Mario were croupiers at the Princess Hotel &

Casino but also had a business employing Bahamians cleaning the marble floors of fancy hotels at night whilst guests were sleeping. It was called M & J cleaning services. They used to have vans with the logo, "M&J we are on your way," plastered down the side. The next night, we were going to a restaurant called The Rusty Pelican and I asked Erroll would he invite Lesley for obvious reasons—she was blonde, tanned and beautiful. I think for the first time I was in love. She came and sat next to me, and we talked nonstop all night and after that we were together all the time. That evening after dinner, we met a friend of Erroll's who was a witch doctor from Exuma, a nearby island. He wrote 'Island folk songs,' they were brilliant, and he gave me one of his tapes. In those days, it was the big eight track cassettes and one of the tracks was called "Brown Girl in the Ring." It was a Bahamian folk song and I told everyone that if this was out in England, it would be a number one hit. I played it in my car all the time when I got home, and everyone loved it. A few years later, it was a number one hit sung by Boney M. It read "written by Frank Fariani," the German record producer and manager of Milli Vanilli who the world found out couldn't sing when on one US TV show, the tape stopped and they didn't know the words or couldn't sing either. But what I do know is that the witch doctor from Exuma wrote "Brown Girl in the Ring." We told the girls back in Connecticut about our visa problem and to send a box with our belongings and that we were sick. We couldn't come back to see them. They were sad but the truth was we had the choice between being in a small apartment in Newington,

CT, or being on the beach in Freeport. We were staying in a large apartment with a pool, two minutes from the beach and seeing Lesley every night. Well, it was a no-brainer—Freeport won. We stayed about six weeks and loved every minute. I went to Freeport regularly after that. The next time was with Micky Lewis who bought my Birmingham shop and another time with the British middleweight boxing champion, Gary Stretch. I even took my mum, Lena, once. I loved it so much. The local Bahamian girls plus Lesley made the holiday even better.

The time I went with Gary Stretch, we met some fun people from Owensboro, Kentucky. We drank Bloody Marys on the beach all day with them and one night arranged to go out with them thinking we were going for dinner and then somewhere drinking. They asked us to go to their hotel, The Bahama Princess, first for cocktails and then go out from there. When we got to the hotel, we went to their room and had a couple of drinks then about an hour later, we all left together. This is a story about the fate I believe so much in. We pressed the button for the elevator and there were four elevators. We got in the first one that came. The elevator had an absolute stunning blonde, wearing a black minidress, black, high heel shoes with no tights, and the most perfect teeth and body with a guy who I have no idea what he was wearing. When we all got in the lift, I couldn't take my eyes off her—she was that good. She smiled at everyone as if to say hello and when we got to the ground floor, they said bye and walked away. Me, Stretch and my friends from Kentucky stood for a while deciding where we were going. I asked which restaurant should we go to, they said, we are not eating; we are going to the casino to gamble. I said I thought that we were going out for dinner but no, they wanted to gamble so then I said that Gary and I would go and have dinner somewhere and see you all in the casino later.

We had no reservations and had no idea where to eat so we just walked through town seeing which place took our fancy. We passed a couple then decided on a French one that looked classy with a pretty hostess. We walked in and asked for a table for two. A guy in a tuxedo and bow tie came and said follow me and he walked us through this very large restaurant passing many tables and sat us down, gave us the menus and walked away. Who do you think was sitting on the next table but the blonde from the elevator with her lump of a boyfriend. I couldn't believe it and that must be fate. She could have been in any elevator—one five minutes before or five minutes later but no, she was in ours. She could have been in any restaurant in Freeport and on any table but no, our restaurant and on the next table. I tried to get her attention to smile or say hello, but she didn't even look our way talking and laughing with the lump all the time. Gary turned his chair around so it was facing away from our table and directly staring at them so she would notice us. I said to Gaz what are you doing, turn around and he said, why, what's he going to do about it. I will knock him out. With him being the British and European Super Middleweight boxing champion, he could have easily done that but it's not the way I wanted to get her. I could have done it that way myself.

They left the restaurant and didn't even notice or acknowledge us. We finished dinner about an hour later and went to the casino to look for our friends. When we got there, I couldn't believe how big the place was—just like Las Vegas, bigger than a soccer pitch. I thought that we would never find them. We walked for five minutes and bumped into two of them, asking where the others were. They said, over on the far side somewhere, playing blackjack. We walked in that direction and saw them at the far side of the casino which was packed with about a thousand or more people playing slot machines, roulette, craps and blackjack.

My friend, David, was standing behind his wife as she played and standing next to him, behind her boyfriend, was the blonde from the elevator and restaurant. I couldn't believe it. Of all the hundreds of tables in the casino and she is standing next to my pal. As we approached, David said to me, do you remember this girl; she was in our elevator. I nodded yes, as if I didn't remember her, with me saying to her, I saw you in the restaurant. She smiled and said, yes, I saw you as well. David said, can you believe it? Jean is from Louisville, Kentucky, like us. Her name was Jean Clarke. I said to David I need a word with you please; come to the toilet. He followed me and asked what's the problem? I told him he must get her telephone number. He said what for, she has a boyfriend, also, she lives in Kentucky, you live in England. I cannot believe how dumb some guys are, I said. Please, just get it for me, ok. He nodded and we walked back to the gaming table. I said goodnight to

Jean and David's wife and said I would see them tomorrow. Then Gary and I went to a club, but I couldn't get this Jean Clarke out of my mind.

The next day, I went to the hotel hoping she was there, but I didn't see her. David said that he didn't get her number because her boyfriend was with her all night, but he would get it later today. We left Freeport and didn't see them again but when I got home, I immediately called David in Owensboro, asking for her number. He said whose number. I said the girl, Jean Clarke's, from Louisville. He said, "Oh, that; I didn't get it, sorry. I didn't think it was that important to you." I couldn't believe it. He shouted upstairs to his wife saying that blonde from Freeport, didn't she have some kind of shop in Louisville. His wife shouting back, yes, a nail boutique. He said, yes, she owns a nail boutique in Louisville. I said thanks and put the phone down. Now this is what a lunatic I was in those days; I did this many times. It was all a game but a serious game that cost me lots of money over the years. I couldn't help it, but it was always a challenge that I loved.

I called International Directory Assistance and asked the lady on the phone could I please have the telephone number for the Nail Boutique in Louisville, Kentucky. She said just a minute then came back and asked me which one, I said how many are there, she replied twelve. I said give them all to me and I wrote them down. I called the first one nervous as hell and a voice said hello, the Nail Boutique, can I help you. I replied could I speak to Jean Clarke, please, the girl saying we don't have anyone called that here, sorry. I called the next one then the next—all giving me the same answer—no Jean Clarke here. I called all twelve Nail Boutiques but no Jean Clarke.

I called David back the next day and said that she doesn't work at any nail boutique in Louisville. He said who doesn't? I said, fucking Jean Clarke doesn't. He must have thought I was mad, and he would have been right. All over a girl as if there were not enough girls in England and Europe for me. I said to him think, where does she work? He asked his wife again and she said that it's not the Nail Boutique, it's the Nail Place in Louisville. I said, thanks. I called International Directory Assistance again and asked for the Nail Place in Louisville, Kentucky. She gave me five. I called them all, one by one, getting despondent and on the fifth call, a girl answered, "Hello, The Nail Place." I asked if Jean Clarke was there, and she said, who's speaking? I nearly dropped the phone. Frank Rostron from England, I said. A second later, Jean came to the phone saying Frank is that you, from Freeport? Yes, I said. She asked what do you want; are you in Louisville? I replied, no, in England. I just wanted to speak with you in case I am ever in Louisville, it would be good to see you. She said, oh, that's so sweet of you. I had her number that she gave me, the shop address, and I then said goodbye, and I hope to see you soon.

The next day, I sent her flowers so that she would know that I meant business. I put my name, address and phone number in the flowers. I got a call from her that afternoon, thanking me and saying no one could get into her shop for the flowers.

There were so many, it looked like an Interflora shop, with flowers everywhere. At least, I made my point and to let her know I was serious. She said that if you are ever in Louisville to call her. I was never going to be in Louisville but a few weeks later, I was going to New York on business, so I called her to see if she wanted to come for the weekend. She couldn't make it for some reason or another. A couple of months later, I was going to Miami and called her to see if she wanted a holiday in the sun, but she couldn't make that either. I called her every time I was going to the States but every time she had to work, or she was going on holiday or some other excuse.

A year had now gone by with me calling her every time I was to visit America. I again called her, saying that I was going to New York and would she like to come. It was probably the fifth or sixth time I had asked her. No one can ever say that I am not a tryer. She asked what dates and I told her, and she said, yes, I can come on those dates. I nearly dropped the phone again like the first time I got through to her.

This trip, I was going with my manager, Richard, and by this time, I always took one of my staff because we were so busy. Also, being on your own for weeks got lonely and a little depressing. It doesn't matter how much money you were taking; it was good to have company at the end of the day for dinner rather than always being alone. It was winter, very cold and we were staying at the Hotel St. Moritz, overlooking Central Park. It's now The Ritz-Carlton. I had an early dinner with Richard and then went to JFK to pick up Jean Clarke. I was nervous and excited at the same time because I had been chasing this girl for over a year to date, so I was hoping it was worth it. It never usually was worth it but as she walked down the ramp towards the baggage hall, she took my breath away. She was wearing jeans, knee-length boots, a white polo neck sweater and a full-length wolf coat. She looked a million dollars, with her long, blonde hair blowing behind her. She kissed me saying how happy she was to see me and to be in New York as she hadn't been here for ages. She said that she was really tired with the travelling and just couldn't wait to get to the hotel, drop off her case, and to take her boots off.

When we got to the hotel, I asked if she had enough energy to go for a drink and meet some friends at a club. I said that I had arranged to see them which I hadn't; I just wanted to go to Stringfellow's. I wanted to impress her with the VIP treatment I got in there from my pals, Julian Russell, the manager, and Jeremy Jarvis, the restaurant manager from England. I was also hoping that she would have a few drinks to loosen her up. She said it would be ok for a short time only. We jumped into a cab to East 21st off Park Avenue South and driving down there, she told me just what I had always thought. That she couldn't see me all the times that I had asked before because she had a boyfriend. They had now broken up and that she was hoping I would call her again with another invite. We arrived and as I expected and hoped for there was a line to get in, with a rope holding them back. I walked to the front of the line with the doorman opening the rope saying, welcome, Mr. Rostron, then have a good evening. As we walked in, Jeremy came over and shook my hand. I introduced him to Jean, and he took us to a great table overlooking the club and brought me a bottle of champagne. I know Miss Clarke was suitably impressed.

I had booked her a room of her own and I would have done that anyway even if I had been alone as not to take it for granted that she was sleeping with me. I had no choice anyway as I was sharing a room with Richard. So, after a couple of hours, and Jean loving Stringfellows, we went back to the hotel. I walked her to her room, stopped at the door, gave her a kiss on the cheek, and said goodnight and that I would see her in the morning. I went back to my room lying on my bed with my trousers, shirt and shoes still on with Richard waking up and saying why aren't you getting into bed and asking why do you still have all your clothes on. I replied that I am hoping to get a call to go somewhere. He shook his head, turned over and went back to sleep. I have done this many times, so I was hoping the Stringfellows experience, the VIP treatment, and the champagne, were enough to impress her and clinch the deal.

Five minutes later, the phone rang, and it was Jean, saying that she was cold and lonely and would I go to her room. I yawned and said let me get dressed and I will be there shortly. Bingo, it had worked again. I went to her room; she opened the door and looked sensational—just like a Victoria's Secret model in their latest white lingerie. I went in and stayed the night and what a night it was; Richard had his own room for the rest of the trip.

After New York, we saw each other long distance for a couple of years. She came every time I was in New York, but we also had a few fun holidays in Miami Beach as well. In those days, we stayed at the Fontainebleau where she always caused a sensation, walking around the pool and beach, with guys getting a dig from their girlfriends and wives for staring at her. She was that sensational and whatever time we got home from clubbing, she would be in the Fontainebleau gym at 7:00 a.m., working out to keep her Victoria's Secret model-like body. She never came to Manchester which is strange because she would be one that I would usually fly in to show her off to my pals and everyone else in town. I cannot remember why; the only thing must have been because at that time I had a regular girlfriend in Manchester.

Erroll was dating a beautiful, Bahamian girl, Gwen Saunders, who also worked at the casino. She was the prettiest and nicest girl; Erroll and Gwen made a lovely couple. One day, I got an invitation to their wedding and Erroll asked if I would design and make his wedding shirt. This was an honor and I made him a white, silk shirt like a pirate's shirt, with wide, bishop sleeves, along with an attached tie neck that was about two feet long that you wrapped around your neck, tying it into a loose bow. It was sensational looking and he loved it.

The invitation said attire: "dress cool and comfortable." Everyone was in white and mostly linen and what a great day it was. The only disappointment for Erroll was that he was Jewish, and his family disapproved of him marrying a non-

Jewish girl but, in addition, she was black. They didn't come to the wedding but his sister, Lenny, attended, so I am sure she went home telling her parents what a beautiful and wonderful girl Gwen was. He had a priest and a Rabbi conduct the service with a half-Jewish and a half-Catholic wedding, with Erroll standing on the glass and the full bag of tricks. It was a really special day.

I saw Erroll many times after that but on one trip he told me he was leaving Freeport to go and live in India. He was following an Indian guru he had met at a religious convention like the Beatles did. I asked what he would do there and he said that they would build a house in the Maharishi's compound, pray, go to school every day and grow vegetables and flowers. Erroll was very spiritual like that saying to me that there must be more to life than living in Freeport and eating, drinking and smoking marijuana. Well, I couldn't think of anything better even though I didn't smoke. We kept in touch, and he loved his life in India. A few years later, about the time I had Cliff take me to AA, I was going through a period of thinking that I was missing something in this life. Was there more to life than sleeping with different girls, partying, drinking, going to restaurants, Majorca, and by then Barbados. So, I asked Erroll to call me. I told him I would like to know more about his new life with the Maharishi. Erroll saying that, in a month, they are going to be in London, and he would call me and make a time to come down to see him.

Now this must be the funniest part of the book. He sent

me details of where to come in London and on what date. I turned up at this mansion worth probably twenty million pounds on Avenue Road in St. Johns Wood. I had many friends who lived nearby so I knew it well. I went to the door and asked for Erroll. These two giants that looked like Jesus but were obviously security asked me to come in and they had the softest of voices. They all did. Erroll did even before he joined this cult or whatever it was. I had to take my shoes off and leave them on the stairs with another hundred pairs and went to the second floor to meet Erroll.

It was great to see him even though we had spoken on the phone and written letters; it had been a few years. He looked happy though a little drawn, explaining that I wouldn't be seeing the Maharishi today but in France in the next week or so. I thought that this was a little strange, but Erroll said it was for security. That's the way it was done but someone would call me at work with the details. The following week, I had a call from a guy, again softly spoken, saying that I should fly to Paris on Wednesday, and someone would meet me at the airport. They would then take me to a hotel and leave me there and not to leave the hotel under any circumstance. The next morning someone would pick me up and take me to a safe house fifty miles outside Paris and there I would be joined by two other followers and stay two days. I would then rent a car and drive south to an address that they would give me later. After that, we would get a phone call telling us where the meeting was to be and to call and let them know the details of my flight to Paris.

I was scared to death after this phone call with the instructions. It was like an FBI, secret service or even a James Bond movie. There so was no way in the world I was going. I had to stay living this life of excess. I never found out if living in India, going to school every day, praying for hours upon hours and growing vegetables in my own garden was better than the life I was living. About ten years later, I got a message from Freeport that Erroll had passed away, still a young man, with Gwen staying in India living that life.

St. Tropez

After La Baraka closed, Majorca wasn't the same. During the day, everyone was walking around, looking for where to go and meet but nothing could replace it. I found a bar restaurant on Maguluf beach and hung out there for a summer. There were lots of girls but not in the class of La Baraka. By then, I had sold my house and paid Graham Whateley back the money he loaned me for my building in Manchester. I was invited to a wedding in Leeds and was seated next to one of the guys I knew from the old days in Lens Bar and other places when I had my shop. His name was David Walker, and he was now living in St. Tropez but still had investment property in Leeds that he came to see periodically. David invited me down to stay at his house with him and his wife—an offer I couldn't refuse. I had never been to St. Tropez and was going to a place with someone who lives there or knows it well like—myself and Majorca. It was always an advantage. Because then, you go to places and meet people that you wouldn't normally see by going on a two-week holiday. With Majorca and La Baraka finished, I thought that this would a great opportunity to check out the South of France and hopefully find somewhere new to spend my summers.

I stayed once or twice with David then started going to St. Tropez for a couple of years, staying in hotels around the port or in the area. I loved it and still do. The restaurant's bars and clubs in St. Tropez are fantastic and you talk about money, but this was a league above Majorca and La Baraka. The beach clubs like Club 55, Nikki Beach, Byblos Beach, Tahiti Beach Club and Moorea Beach Club were fantastic and on a daily basis, young people would be spraying magnums of Louis Roederer Cristal champagne over everyone, costing thousands of pounds. It was an unbelievable flaunting of this obscene wealth.

Once, Michael Inwards, my great friend, who I loved for over thirty-five years and who passed away this year, invited me on his boat for a holiday. I flew to Nice where his driver picked me up and took me to Monaco where his boat was moored, and we had two weeks cruising around the Cote d'Azur. We mainly stayed in the port of St. Tropez and moored opposite the famous coffee bar, Senequier, where one morning I had coffee and croissants with George Michael and his friend. Michael Inward had four crew on his boat and even though one was a fine chef, we still went out for dinner most nights to all the hotspots yet had breakfast on the deck every morning. The tourists would walk past taking photos, wondering who we were, drinking champagne on the deck at breakfast and before we went out for dinner. Whatever time we got home after a night out, which could be very late in St. Tropez, at least one of the crew was always waiting to greet us, asking if we wanted anything to eat or drink for a nightcap. Whatever time we woke up in the morning, it was the same—at least two crew members were there to say good morning and ask what we wanted to drink or have for breakfast. I miss that boat.

It didn't matter how much money you had or how big your boat, in St. Tropez, there is always someone with more money or a bigger boat. I thought that Michaels was one of the best with a prime mooring outside Senequier but one day a boat came in and moored next to us owned by the Chelsea Football club owner, Roman Abramovich. It made ours look like its tender. It was five times bigger than ours with twenty or thirty crew and on board was the Chelsea captain, John Terry, with all his London mates. Roman must have let him use it for winning the league and cup that season. The sickener was that Abramovich had four more boats, and this was the smallest of them all. Again, talk about real money. It's the same on the beach—if someone is squirting bottles of champagne, someone else will squirt magnums. There is no end to this flaunting of wealth.

I have been to St. Tropez a few times since but not on a regular basis like Majorca. After that, I started to have my holidays in America. About three years ago, Michael was a tax exile living in Monaco, so I flew down to see him. We spent a few days there at his new apartment and at the same time I arranged to see an old friend, Nish Sawney, who was also living in Monaco who I had not seen for over twenty years. It was Nish who came to New York for Lena's birthday. It was also Nish who bought my St. Johns Street apartment when I moved to Salford Quays and we became close friends. It was good to see him and catch up having some great dinners in Monaco's finest restaurants. Then, after a great time in Monaco, Michael and I went to St. Tropez for a few days to all our old haunts, reminiscing about the old days. It was as good as ever with new beach clubs and restaurants and I cannot wait to take Jane as it's one of the few places she's never been.

California

I have been to the States hundreds of times, since that first trip with Michael Morris to visit the girls from Connecticut. Shortly after that, I went to California for the first time with Brian Johnson, my pal from Manchester who used to be the manager of the first wine bar in town, the Cellar Vie in Lloyd St., Manchester. We went for three weeks, visiting San Francisco, Los Angeles, and Las Vegas. Places we had only seen on TV and in the movies but never dreamed that we would ever be going there. We were so excited.

Our travel agent had a deal from the Hilton Hotel chain with perks, if we only stayed at their hotels. The perks were transport to and from the airport, breakfast and I think an arrival drink. So, in each city, we stayed at the Hilton Hotels which was luxury and a big deal for us in those days. We arrived in San Francisco and got to the hotel about 7:00 p.m., unpacked our cases, and were out and about at 8:00 p.m. Now we have been travelling for about eighteen hours and it was 4:00 a.m. real time for us but we were rocking and ready to hit the town. We had reservations at The White House, one of the finest French restaurants in San Francisco, which was stupid and a waste of money, seeing it was now 4:30 a.m. in the middle of the night real time for us. We had been eating and drinking on the plane all day and were not even hungry but we didn't care.

After dinner, we got into a cab and we asked the driver for a good club to go to and he said, "Dance Your Arse Off." I asked what is it like and he said you will like it. He said that it's a kind of polysexual place, I had no idea what polysexual meant but we arrived, went in and it was fantastic, great music, some good-looking girls and even better-looking guys. They were all smiling at us. Now don't forget even though we and other people think we are big shots, we are still young, naive guys, with none or very few life experiences. We bought these two African American beauties a drink who happened to be sisters. We danced and drank for a couple of hours. Then suddenly, the music stopped, and the lights came on. I said, "what's happening," and they said, "it's over, the night is over." I couldn't believe it. I said that its only 2:00 a.m.; our clubs in Manchester are open until 2:00 a.m. For some reason, I thought a city like San Francisco would never close or at least stay open until 4 or 5.

I said to them there must be somewhere open that we can go to, and they said in Oakland where they live is a club that is open. Let's go, I said. We jumped into their car, over the Bay Bridge, and twenty minutes later arrived in Oakland. Now, I had never heard of Oakland but forty-five to fifty years ago, it was one of the most dangerous places in the USA where no white people ever went, especially at night. They took us to a building with no lights or signs but outside were parked Bentleys, a Rolls-Royce and even a Cadillac, with bull horns on the front grill. It was called The GQ or the Gentleman's Quarters. They knocked on the door and a square box peephole opened. A guy looked through asking who are these two, the girls saying friends of ours from England.

I heard about four bolt locks being pulled back and the door opened. He ushered us in and slammed the door behind us. The place was packed with everyone dancing and I didn't see one white face. Again, no fear. I didn't know any difference. We followed the girls across the ground floor up the stairs to the second floor which was a bit more relaxed—a few sofas and people still dancing, then up to the third floor like the VIP room. No one dancing, just drinking and sitting on large, leather Chesterfields. There were drinks on every table. They took us over and introduced us to a party that included their brother and the owner whose name was Alti. I asked everyone would they like a drink but only me, Brian and the girls wanted one. The others all had full ones. I went over to the bar and ordered the drinks. The barman told me how much and I gave him a crisp 100-dollar bill. "This money is not good," he said. "You need the REAL money," me saying this is real money but he kept saying, no, the REAL money. I went back to the table and told Alti about the money and he said, "Oh, I forgot, go down that corridor and you will see a serving hatch. My wife will change some money for you." I couldn't believe it. I gave her my 100-dollar bill and she gave me a mixed 100-dollars back. It was exactly the same but instead of having the president's picture in the middle of the notes, it had a picture of Alti wearing a fedora. I paid for the drinks and back at the table, Alti explained about the money situation and the reason for it and it was brilliant.

By law, selling drinks after 2:00 a.m. is illegal so no one is paying because it is not real money. It's like monopoly money; also, none of the staff can steal because it's no good to them, only his wife handles the money. He said the authorities had taken him to court in the past and he won the case so all was good. In the club, tonight and every night, are judges, lawyers, basketball players and baseball players—hence the cars outside. Everyone was African American and it's the place to go in Oakland, IF you can get in. We had a brilliant night leaving The GQ about 6:30 a.m.; the sun was up and we hadn't slept for over twenty-four hours and been up all night with the girls. They took us to a diner down the block for coffee and it was only then I felt intimidated with the dregs of the area all hanging around the diner looking menacing. After coffee, the girls dropped us at a taxi rank and we went back to San Fran.

We showered and got a couple of hours sleep as we had to meet a guy called David Thorla for lunch. He was someone I had never met but was a friend of Gary Thompson, an American friend from Majorca who said if you go to San Francisco you must see my pal, David. Everyone used to do that in those days, not so much anymore. We went to his office, a nice guy, and he greeted us, saying you must be tired after all that travelling? Did you crash out last night? I said, no, we went to The White House for dinner then to Dance Your Arse Off, then we went to Oakland to a club called the GQ, with two girls we met. He stood there with his mouth open and couldn't believe what we did on our first night in San Francisco, saying you are joking. He said that he had a friend driving through Oakland in the middle of the day and at the traffic lights was dragged out of his car, robbed and his car taken in broad daylight in a busy area.

We went for lunch and saw him a couple of times after that but the next day, it was pouring down and we had a late lunch at a place called Tuxedo Junction. David Thorla was with us, and we had been in the restaurant about four hours eating and drinking, hoping the rain would stop but it never did and now we were getting bored. Brian suggested a game where, at the bus stop across the road, we would have turns trying to pull a girl and get her in the restaurant for a drink. Thorla went first. It was pouring down and with an umbrella, he went to a girl in the line said whatever he said and came back alone. We waited for the next line for the next bus and Brian went with the umbrella, chatted to a girl and came back alone as well. Now it's my turn and it's still absolutely throwing it down. I take my jacket off and I am in a shirt only and with no umbrella. I run across the road, and I don't speak to the girl at the front of the line but pretend without success to get a newspaper out of the machine getting soaking wet. She asked if she could help and gets me a paper in two seconds. I say thank you, that's really kind of you. Will you please come have a drink for doing that for me over there with my friends. She agrees and I walk back into the restaurant soaking wet but with my trophy.

Her name was Donna Coccozello, and she spent the next five nights with us; she worked for Coldwell Banker during the day as a secretary. On this trip, there were many girls but three that were special, all with strange names. There was Donna Coccozello, Sharon Lazzoya and Dahlia LaCoco—names that you would never hear in England. I have great stories to tell you about both Donna and Dahlia. Brian and I had a routine in the hotels because we shared a room. If one of us pulled a girl, he would say goodnight, see you tomorrow, and the other would sit in the bar or foyer for about half an hour or so. Then later, banging on our door, saying can I stay with you as John arrived and took my room. I have nowhere to sleep. You can only get away with this for one night because after that the girl would know there was no John. So that night, Donna stayed with me and we did the routine but after that I stayed at her apartment. This was the first time I realized how promiscuous American girls were. I thought Swedish girls were easy, but the Americans leave them in the dust.

One day, we went for lunch to a restaurant called Macarthur Park which was in Macarthur Park. We went there because of the song by Richard Harris. It was a great place, and we had this hot barmaid named Sondra. I was looking at the drinks list and there was a drink called a Sondra special. So, I asked her what that was. She said and I quote for you, "Cutie, with that accent, it can be anything you want." With me flirting back, she asked where I was staying. I said around the corner at the Hilton. She took off her apron, threw it on the bar and said to her co-worker that she would be back soon and walked out, taking me with her. Leaving Brian at the bar, we walked to my hotel, up to my room, had sex, washed and walked back to the bar, all in forty-five minutes. I couldn't believe it and neither could Brian. I presume I had just had a Sondra special, so I had a glass of red wine next.

David Thorla had told us about a few great places to meet girls; one being called, Henry Africas. Another place he said we must go to before we leave is a bar called The Body Shop. I said in England that's where we take our cars to be repaired, he replied, here it's where you go for a body. We turned up at The Body Shop that night looking cool and confident, we or I should say I was on a roll. The place was really plush and upmarket. Brian got a table, and I went to the bar for our drinks and as I was waiting to be served, this good-looking girl—I must say all American girls were good-looking whether it was because it was our first time to California, or they really were I cannot remember, but in those days, they really were—asked where I was from and I told her England. That was such a great pull in those days, it was like having a black American Express card later in life. I asked if I could buy her a drink; she replied, asking where are you staying. I told her The Hilton and she said that you have a minibar in your room why don't we go there for a drink. I said should we have one here first. She said, no, let's go and she got her friend. I went to Brian and said come on these girls want a drink in our room and we left and walked to our hotel. We went to the room, put music on, poured drinks, lowered the lights and partied. I had sex with my girl and Brian with her mate—all in this small, hotel bedroom. Afterwards, they dressed and left. David Thorla was right; it was a place to go for a body. Still to this day, if anyone says a body shop meaning their car needs mending, a smile comes to my face.

From San Francisco we drove to Los Angeles down the coast road, stopping in Carmel to see where Clint Eastwood lived and to visit his bar and restaurant that I had heard so much about. It was called The Hogs Breath and it was as exciting going in there as seeing Clint himself which I did many years later in New York. There were photos on the wall of Clint in all his movies, particularly *Play Misty For Me,* the one he made in Carmel. All the drinks had names like The Dirty Harry and Magnum Force, named after all his films. I have been a few times to The Hogs Breath since even taking Jane a couple of years ago and it still impresses me every time.

We arrived at the Downtown Hilton, and it was terrible. The outside looked more dangerous than walking the streets of Oakland, but we didn't know when the travel agent said there are two Hiltons in LA. The Downtown Hilton and The Beverly Hilton. Well, big shots like us wanted to be downtown. It sounded better; so, I said downtown. In those days, it was a rough and dangerous place; not like today, hot and elegant with fine restaurants and shops. The next day, I asked if we could move to The Beverly Hilton and they transferred us, taking us on the hotel bus. But that morning, before we left for Beverly Hills, we spent the whole time with David Soul and Paul Michael Glaser on set filming *Starsky and Hutch* in a dirty car park behind the hotel which again was another great experience. We arrived and it was like chalk and cheese. I thought this is more like Frank Rostron. I didn't know one person in LA at that time, so it was all trial and error. But we did alright with the hotel concierge pointing us in the right direction for bars, clubs and restaurants. We went to Nick's Fishmarket on Sunset Boulevard that had a great restaurant and an adjoining night club. It also had a long line outside trying to get in but if you had dinner in the restaurant, they would walk you into the club through a private door—no lining up and a VIP table around the dance floor—more my scene. The waiters and managers were all handsome—six feet plus tall. They were all would-be actors and scriptwriters, waiting for their big break so they were working at Nick's until that day arrived which for most of them never did.

Another hot club in those days was Pips in Beverly Hills and very exclusive. We were friendly with the concierge at the hotel. I had bunged him a few times and he called Pips, saying he had two very important guests from England and could he send them down and to put them on the guest list. Pips was great, and on another level compared to Nick's Fishmarket.

I stood at the bar and next to me was Eric Estrada, a heart throb actor and a massive star in those days, appearing on the hit TV show *California Highway Patrol* (Chips) as Frank "Ponch" Poncherello. I was like a big kid while looking at him starstruck, but he was cool, saying hello to us. We got a drink and walked around checking the place out and came across this big room with giant backgammon tables and large pieces and drink holders on the side for your drinks. We played on the beach at La Baraka most days, so I said to Brian, fancy a game? Looser pays for the drinks. We sat down and started to play.

Can you believe that we are in the hottest club in Beverly Hills and these two jerks from England are playing backgammon. After about fifteen minutes, this absolutely sensational looking girl walks up to our table, or I should say glides. She leans on the table saying have you two got nothing better to do than play backgammon. Her name was Sharon Lazzoya; she also was an actress waiting for her big break. I looked at him and he looked at me like the two lumps we were and I said to her actually, no, we haven't. She replied looking at me saying I can think of something better for you to do than play backgammon. I got up and left the club with her, leaving Brian behind once again. I thought to myself, *I just love these American girls not even dreaming that one day I would marry one.*

We went to our hotel; Brian arrived two hours later, saying John had arrived, taken his room and could he stay in my room as he had nowhere to sleep. I asked Sharon if it was alright, but she said no—she had to go anyway. She got dressed, kissed me and left. I saw her the next night, took her to Nick's for dinner and dancing but never saw her again. I often look at names of actresses in movies and on TV, but I have never seen her name come up. I was told many of them change their name, hoping for more luck so I will never know. The next day, we were driving to Tijuana in Mexico. It's about a three-hour drive from LA and a hellhole of a place. The only reason I wanted to go was so I could have a Mexican stamp in my passport and I could say I had been to Mexico. In those days, I thought it was cool to have all these stamps from countries I had visited.

On the way down, we were thirsty and saw a sign that said San Diego, so Brian said, "let's pull off the freeway and have a drink." We did and within half a mile saw a bar that said "Girls, Girls, Girls." I said to Brian that place looks good, so we parked and went inside. We were greeted by this beautiful girl from the Philippines; her name was Dahlia LaCoco. She sat us down and took our order for two Rye and Drys, lots of ice and a slice of orange. We drank them and about twenty minutes later got up to leave when she asked in broken English, where you going, stay, have another drink with me. She was hustling but cute, so we thought why not. She sat with us saying where are you from? We then replied, Beverly Hills. Dahlia saying, ah, Beverly Hill that is where all the film stars live. Do you live near the film stars, do you know any film stars, I've always wanted to go to Beverly Hill. Dahlia saying Beverly Hill not Beverly Hills in her broken English. I asked where she was from and she said the Philippines to which I replied, I've always loved South

American girls (me not knowing my geography) and Dahlia saying Philippine not in South America. I said quickly, I know it's not in South America. I was just saying that I love South American girls, but I love girls from the Philippines as well. I got out of that by the skin of my teeth, once again. Dahlia was really beautiful—long, dark, silky hair, pearly white teeth and a great skin color, working in this sleazy bar and speaking poor English. If she only knew how beautiful she was and six inches taller, she really would be a top model or a film star.

I asked if she would she like to come to Beverly Hills and see some film stars. She was excited saying, yes, please, I would. I gave her our hotel and room number and she gave me her home number and we promised to call each other the next day. Dahlia called the next day and we arranged for her to come to LA that week. I bought her a ticket for the short flight from San Diego, and she was due to arrive at the hotel at 7:00 p.m. I got a call at 6:00 p.m. from her brother saying that she had missed the flight but was on the next one arriving now at the hotel at 8:00 p.m. We went to the bar to have a drink about 7:45 and a few minutes later there was a commotion in the foyer, with security running all over the place. A minute later, Dahlia was pulling on my shirt from the side of my stool and the hotel security immediately behind her trying to grab her, while I'm asking, what's happened?

Apparently, when she walked in the hotel, security asked to speak with her probably thinking she was a hooker. With her seeing these guys in uniform about to accost her, she ran and ran and ended up beside my bar stool. I assured the guys that she was with me. They apologized to her and that was that. I took her upstairs to my room, left her to shower, get ready and then come down to the bar. About thirty minutes later, she walked into the bar and looked like a supermodel. When we met in her bar, she had on these tacky shorts and T-shirt and now she's wearing a black minidress, black, high heel shoes, no tights with her tanned, shiny skin and a perfect body. Even though her outfit probably only cost a few dollars she looked a million dollars, and I was so proud of her.

We got a cab to Nick's Fishmarket where I had reservations. As we walked in were greeted by the future James Bond as if we were his best ever customers. He showed us to our table like we were celebrities. These guys had so much style and class and made you feel so important.

While standing by our table, a waiter arrives asking what we would like to drink. Rye and Dry for me and Brian and when I asked Dahlia, she said cup of tea, please. The waiter gasped and James Bond said to him, if madam wants a cup of tea, then bring it. A little later, a beautiful, silver teapot arrived on a silver tray with a silver sugar pot and milk jug—sheer class. He poured her a cup of tea then Dahlia put about six cubes of sugar into the cup, some milk and stirred it with her spoon, leaving the spoon in the cup. When she finished, we all looked at each other and after a few seconds, I took the spoon out of her cup and placed it by the side of her saucer. Dahlia having no idea what she did wrong. Obviously, Dahlia had never been into a hotel the standard of The Beverly Hilton or a restaurant like Nick's before, but she was great and didn't pretend to be anything else other than what she was and that was a very special girl.

During dinner, she told us that when she had enough money saved that she was going to take English lessons so she would speak better English. This was because it was her life dream and ambition to be a flight attendant and travel the world and she knew she would never get a job speaking poor English. After dinner, we went into the club, had a table by the dance floor, and ordered drinks. Dahlia said to come and dance. She kicked off her shoes and pulled me onto the dance floor. She was dancing in her bare feet. She looked spectacular and every guy in the place was looking at her. We had the best of nights, and I was looking forward to getting her back to the Hilton to make it an even better night. We got back to the hotel, Brian saying goodnight, see you both in the morning, Dahlia and I are going up to my room and Brian is going to the bar. She looked sensational with her long, dark, silky hair and tanned skin and was everything I had imagined. One hour later, the knock at the door came with Brian asking if he could he stay in my room as John had arrived and locked him out. I laughed and said, of course, come in. Unlike Sharon Lazzoya, Dahlia couldn't get dressed and go home.

The next morning, we were going to Disneyland and wanted to get an early start so we could have a full day as we had never been before. So, I left Dahlia in bed as her flight wasn't until later that morning. As we were driving down the freeway to Anaheim, Brian said that we don't really know Dahlia. What if she steals everything in our room? I replied, I know her, and she won't. We had a great day at Disney, going on nearly every ride. It was brilliant and we stopped for dinner on our way home, getting back to the hotel about 10:00 p.m. When I met Dahlia, I was wearing a T-shirt with Ted Nugent World tour on it. I bought it for the color having no idea who Ted Nugent was but Brian reminding me that she went mad for it, saying Ted Nugent was her favorite star.

Could you believe nothing was missing from our room? Only this T-shirt when she could have had much more valuable things. I believe she kept it as much as a memento of me as of being a big Ted Nugent fan. About ten years later, I was in LA when there was a plane crash. A commuter plane flying from San Francisco to San Diego with 135 passengers and eight crew aboard all died. The LA Times named the passengers and crew and one of the crew members was called Dahlia LaCoco. I am shaking writing this now and wondered if it was my Dahlia, hoping it wasn't. But a friend said to me and he's right that if it was Dahlia then she did something that most people in their life never achieve. She fulfilled her ambition and life-long dream to become a flight attendant.

After LA, we went to Las Vegas and again had a brilliant time. We had some great food and drinks, and in those days, everything was so inexpensive—not like today, with the finest and most expensive restaurants in America. It was my first time in Vegas, so everything was exciting and in our Hilton hotel there was a Japanese restaurant—Benihana. It was the first time I had ever been to one. The chefs were throwing the food into the air, catching it, setting the table on fire with five-foot flames and sitting at a table with twelve people you didn't know. It was all so new and exciting, and I loved it.

Las Vegas was all so different, from the slot machines as you got off the plane to Martha Reeves and the Vandellas playing in our hotel lounge in full costume. You could just walk in and out having a cocktail while this superstar was singing with no cover charge. There were a few girls, of course, but there always are in Vegas—things have not changed today. But the shows are one of the things we were told you must see but all the shows with the big Vegas artists around town were sold out and we couldn't get tickets. The only one we could get tickets for and that was because it was at our hotel was Liberace. To this day, after seeing all the biggest stars in the world in concert, this was the best show I have ever seen. On every set, he came on in a different mink outfit, with a different piano, being driven on stage in a different vintage Rolls-Royce—absolutely spectacular. He played the piano but more than that told stories about his flamboyant life. It was a real Las Vegas spectacular show and the best I have ever seen. We had four days in Vegas. We then flew home after a memorable first and certainly not the last holiday in California. We had lots of stories to tell our friends back home. Some had to be seen to be believed but I had Brian Johnson to confirm each one.

A good friend of mine, Alex Grunfeld, and his cousin, Norman, were going to San Francisco a few months later and asked did I know anyone who could show them around and of course I did—Donna Cocozello. Alex thought she was great and even invited Donna to Manchester to work for him in his company, Precious Metals Limited, an invite Donna jumped at so she could see or be with me. She obviously didn't realize that I am a confirmed bachelor in Manchester and a permanent girlfriend was not on the menu. It was great to see her and introduce her to my friends, take her out to dinner and show her around Manchester. She sometimes stayed at my house but that was it. So, we had lots of problems and arguments. She was thinking there was going to be a lot more between us once she landed in Manchester but unfortunately not. I think she stayed about a year before finally giving up and moved back to San Francisco. About ten years later, a friend in NY said he had just met a girl who knew me at a trade show at The Plaza Hotel. Her name was Donna Cocozello. I went to The Plaza, and it was good to see her. We talked about the old times. She asked about Alex and Norman and my friends in Manchester but that's as far as it went. I didn't want to lead her on again even though I didn't the last time.

When we got back from California, Brian called every day saying that he couldn't get over LA and couldn't stop thinking about it. I know, I said, I was the same, but we have jobs and can't live there so just get on with your life. About a couple of months later he said I'm going, I've put my house up for sale and as soon as it's sold, I'm going to live in LA. He sold his house and, as good as his word, he went. We had a going away dinner at Blinkers Bijou for him and waved him goodbye two days later. He bought a house in a new up and coming town in Southern California called Irvine and we kept in touch every week. It was probably about nine months before I could go on holiday and visit him and I was excited about going back to California and seeing my pal. I flew to LAX and got a helicopter from there to Orange County airport with Brian there waiting to greet me in his American car which he was proud of from the car dealership. He was now working at Bauer Motors in Costa Mesa. Brian's mum who had been a month earlier to see him had come to me before I left with things she wanted me to take for him. Also, to ask me to speak to him about his girlfriend that he was dating that she didn't approve of, knowing he would listen to me if not her. I arrived at about 7 p.m. and Brian wanted to go back home to show me the house and change to go out. I said no, I'm excited, let's go straight out—take me to a few bars then we will have dinner. We did this and I loved it. Some hot bars, great restaurants and we ended up in a club that was about to become my favorite club in Newport Beach called, Bobby McGee's. We arrived and there was a line of about twenty people waiting to go in. I walked to the front of the line and asked the doorman, "do you have a VIP lounge in this club?" in my finest English accent. He said yes, so I asked him to put two bottles of champagne on a table and show me the way. He called over the manager, and repeated my request, and he took us to a table by the dance floor, ordered my drinks, and gave me his personal card, and a VIP club card. The manager said that you are welcome anytime and don't join the line just walk in and show your card. Brian had forgotten how it was done, but that being said, Brian was never at the front of the line buying drinks and didn't like to spend money that easily. He always had to be shown or pressured. Within minutes of arriving at the table and a couple of bottles of champagne placed on it, it wasn't long before the California girls were hovering around. The local boys were drinking beer out of the bottle and here were these two good-looking English guys drinking champagne. Well, as you can imagine it was no contest. Before long two, pretty, sun-tanned CA girls were sitting at our table enjoying our accents and champagne. We danced, drank and when the night was over, they came home with us. Brian briefly showed me around the house then I went into my bedroom with my girl and Brian into his with her friend. Within thirty seconds, an almighty argument started in Brian's room—screaming, shouting and banging. I couldn't believe it because Brian wasn't like that with girls. I rushed in and like magic there were two girls there, one making all the noise, and the other standing back looking petrified. What had happened was that the previous weeks, Brian had been telling his girlfriend whose name was Elaine all about his pal, Frank Rostron, who dates lots of girls, spends money on dinners and champagne for them and is coming to stay for a few weeks. She had sneaked into his house and hid in the closet and when Brian walked into the bedroom with his girl, she jumped out and confronted him, scaring the new girl to death. I asked, "Who are you?" She replied that she was Brian's girlfriend, Elaine. I said to her, well, Elaine, you were on a three-month lease and that lease expired at 7:00 p.m. this evening. I am on a ninety-nine-year lease so it's time for you to leave. I got hold of her by her collar, and walked her to the door, and said goodbye. I then went into Brian's bedroom and said normal service resumed see you both in the morning and left with Brian saying: "I've been trying to get rid of her for three months and you did it in three minutes. You are unbelievable."

I loved Southern California; it was so different than Beverly Hills where the girls looked like models in their fancy, expensive clothes with beautiful make up. In Newport Beach, Corona Del Mar and Laguna Beach, the girls were younger with either none or hardly any make up on and most went to college with part time jobs behind bars or waitresses in restaurants. A completely different scene between the beach and Rodeo Drive girls. We went out every night and were always successful, Brian couldn't believe it, as well as how much it was costing him. As I said, he was very careful with his money. I understood that he had to go to work every day so it wasn't long before three or four nights a week, I was going out alone or with girlfriends that I had now met. One night in Bobby McGee's, I was dancing with a girl and this big lump of a guy was dancing, bumping into people, swinging his date around, taking up all or most of the dance floor. After bumping me twice, it was time to have a word. I said to him, "Hey, you are not the only one on the dance floor. Don't bump into me again." He said, "or what" and I replied or you will be in trouble. Now, usually the threat is enough but this guy said outside now. I looked at him, and he was twice my size but I couldn't back down now so I said, "follow me outside." One on one, I wouldn't have stood a chance, so as we were leaving the dance floor, I spun around and hit him right on his jaw and he fell like a ton of bricks on his back, spark out. The manager and doorman came rushing over to see if I was alright. I explained he was pushing everyone around on the dance floor and was about to whack me but I got him first. The manager was full of apologies saying things like this never happen in here, I am sorry, please let me get you a bottle of champagne, and walked me back to my table taking care of his best customer. The next day, I went to Brian's car dealership as I usually did before lunch to tell him what I did the night before. He asked did you go in Bobby McGee's last night because one of the guys from here was in and said there was a fight, did you see it, I said not only did I see it but was involved. He said Oh No, are we banned now? I said that no, the manager apologized, bought me a bottle and said the guy was a troublemaker and banned him from the club. At this time, I was going to southern California on a regular basis seeing Brian and enjoying my new playground and my new playmates of which there were plenty. One night about a year later, I'm in Bobby McGee's on my own and who comes over to me to say hello but Brian's old girlfriend, Elaine, and she looked fantastic. She asked how I was and how was Brian. I told her all was good. I asked her if she wanted a drink; she said why not so we got a table and spent the night drinking and dancing. To cut a long story short we ended up back at her apartment and I stayed the night. The next day before lunch as I usually did, I went to Bauer Motors to see Brian and report in. I said you will not believe who I pulled last night and stayed with—Elaine, your ex. He said I don't believe you; she hated you. When Elaine finished college, she and her girlfriend toured the USA visiting all fifty states taking a year to do it and had a great time. Her favorite state was Texas and the two girls had a very small tattoo done on their groin area of a Texas star to remind them of their time in Texas. Brian repeated that he didn't believe me. I said, really, then how would I know about her tattoo at the top of her leg in her groin. He was devastated even though they had finished a year ago when I first arrived but as I've said before, its only male ego especially when it's your pal. So, the few years I spent in southern California were great but it was time to move on and working in New York by now and going to different cities, I started spending more time in Miami with Nigel Benn and Ray Sullivan. I've been back a few times when in LA with Jane once for a wedding and other times, just for old times' sake and to see my old haunts.

London

In my La Baraka days, I had met a tailor from London called Barry Scott, yet another person who enriched my life and bank account in many ways. One day, I asked Claude about a Rolex watch. He said to ask Barry; he might have one. I said I thought he was a tailor. Claude replying, he is but he also sells more jewelry than anyone in London's Hatton Garden. I asked Barry about an intermediate size, yellow-gold Rolex watch, usually worn by Japanese men. He replied, I think I might have one in stock call me when you get home. I called Barry the following week and he said to come to London and that he would have me picked up at Euston station and brought to Neasden to his tailor's shop. He said bring your shirt patterns and you will sell some shirts.

I was about to embark on another period in my life that would bring me new experiences, friends, contacts, customers, and money. Barry had this shop on Dudden Hill Lane in Neasden in a row of about five shops, with large, wide pavement outside that was always filled with parked, luxury cars. The owners of these cars were inside talking or doing deals which Barry always took a cut on and buying suits or anything else that was on the shop floor. These ranged from diamonds, watches, any kind of jewelry, mink coats, crystal decanters, crystal cut glasses, leather coats, paintings or anything else that people brought in to sell or that Barry bought. I was picked up at Euston station by 'silk shirt' Ted, one of Barry's staff, the other being Rodney. 'Silk shirt' Ted was nicknamed that because he always wore a silk shirt not necessarily always pure silk, many times polyester, but shiny and it looked like silk. Rodney and Ted worked full time making coffee and tea for whoever was in the shop, going for toast or bacon sandwiches, in addition to delivering or picking up goods from all over London.

Barry was the greatest salesman I have ever known and earned a fortune every week all in cash. He would never allow anything illegal to happen in the shop but many of the guys went outside and did private illegal deals of their own. I arrived and Barry had the watch I wanted saying, take it and pay me next week. Everyone owed him money and he never wrote it down. It was all in his head; he was a one-off and I have never met anyone like him before or since. The people who went into this shop that had the windows blacked out so no one could see inside were the who's who of London's underworld: Hatton Garden jewelers, police detectives, millionaire travelers and beyond. Taking phone calls all day from as far as Scotland, people asking for watches and diamonds, even a Nigerian diplomat used to come from his London hotel when he was in town for suits, shirts or jewelry. Many times, the Hatton Garden jewelers came into the shop for stuff that they couldn't get.

I started making shirts for everyone who came into the shop, and also some that couldn't come in like the Kray twins, Ronnie and Reg, who were in prison for life. Later, I made shirts for their older brother, Charlie, Mad Frankie Frazer, his nephew, Jimmy Frazer, and many more that I cannot mention because they are still alive. I am talking about some of the most famous and biggest gangsters and crime families in the south of England. They all used to frequent Barry's shop. Barry said to get your shirt patterns out and spread them on that table and sit down. I met every single person who came in that day, and they bought shirts. Some six, others ten and twelve, it was unbelievable and everyone paid cash, no credit cards or checks. I think I took in six or eight grand that day which was a week's takings in my shop at that time. After that, I went every Wednesday for years and started staying in London two or three days a week at The Goring Hotel, Beeston Place. I would work one day at Barry's and two or more days seeing other people I had met in Majorca, Barbados or in Barry's that wanted to see me at their homes with their friends who wanted shirts.

I heard stories of people that used to come into the shop. One of them was called Rolex Ray Sullivan who was in prison in Belgium at the time. Now, Ray's a great friend of mine but everyone knew him, talked about him, and loved him long before I had even met him and now knowing him for over twenty-five years—I now know why. When Lloyd Honeyghan shocked the boxing world by beating the champion, Don Curry, he screamed down the microphone while still in the ring "that was for my friend, Ray Sullivan, who could not be with us tonight." That's when Ray was in prison in Belgium and that's how much he is respected. I remember clearly the day he walked into Barry's shop after he came home from Belgium and meeting him for the first time was like meeting a celebrity. I had heard so many stories about him.

We became friends and the first time I went to Miami with Ray; he was on the plane when I met Jane. That story will come later in the book, but I went to stay with him and his best friend at the time, Nigel Benn, the British and World super-middleweight boxing champion. We spent months every year there with Nigel watching him train and fight. We would go out for dinner then Nigel would go home to sleep. We would go and party until the early hours getting home with girls about 5:00 a.m. and Nigel is there getting ready to run ten miles on the beach and train all day.

Nights out with Mickey Rourke and other Miami Beach party goers was the norm in those days. That's when Miami was hot with Versace, the models, the gays, and, of course, drugs. We would go to Warsaw, a massive gay club on Collins Ave., because all the models went there with the male models that they worked with. They said it was because they felt safe with them and we would be the only straight guys in the place, dancing and drinking champagne. So, with luck and drugs, sometimes we went home with the girls.

We have been in restaurants when Madonna jumped on the table, dancing and singing. Another night, Ray and I are in a restaurant called, The Strand, on Washington Ave. with two girls. One says, look who just walked in—Mickey Rourke. There he is, looking around the place, seeing who is in and he notices us and walks over. I introduce the girls to him, and he says come and join us for dinner. I replied, that's ok, Mickey, we have ordered already. So, he says meet us upstairs in the VIP later. I said, ok, see you then. When he left, I came out with the old, classic, Frank Sinatra joke, saying to the girls he (Mickey Rourke) is always driving me mad and pestering me and won't leave me alone when I am trying to have my dinner. They believed me but life in Miami Beach wasn't real in those days. We were partying day and night but it's not like that anymore—it's tired and rundown. Miami now lives in the past and by reputation only.

One night, we were all in a club in South Beach called Club Nu that was owned by the husband of my ex-girlfriend from Manchester, Stephanie Serene. We had a table: myself, Nigel, Ray and a couple more guys and I went to the toilet for a line. This club didn't have regular toilets but a full-size bathroom as in a house. It had a bath, shower, toilet and sink but no one in Miami went to the toilet for a wee anyway so there was always a line to go in. After about ten minutes, a crowd came out and it was my turn to go in. As I started, a guy bumped into me also going in. I said, excuse me, it's my turn with him saying the same. I said, let's go together using yours. He smiled knowing exactly what I meant, and we went in together. He introduced himself as Rob and got out his coke and cut four lines; we had two each and then talked nonsense for half an hour, saying nice things about each other like you do when you have had Charley.

We leave the bathroom and go back downstairs to Ray, Nigel and the boys and Rob to his table. Nigel then asked how do you know him. I replied that I just met him in the toilet; he seems like a good lad. Nigel saying that was Rob Lowe. About an hour or so later, my new pal, Rob, comes over and said are you ready, Frank, it's your turn. We go back to the bathroom and repeat what happened earlier—four lines, talk nonsense and go back to our tables.

About a month later, I am in New York with a girlfriend called Marlen Gannam from Miami. It was quite serious; she had been to England to see me and now we are in New York going to Atlantic City to see Nigel Benn fight Doug DeWitt. A funny note about Marlen was when she was coming to Manchester, I said to her, if you fly American Airlines, I can get you upgraded to business class. Marlen replying, I only fly business class. I thought, *Wow, this girl's paying three grand or more to come and visit me for a few days. She's either madly in love with me or just has too much money.* I think it was both. One night in Manchester at dinner with my friends, she threw her Platinum Amex card down to pay the bill. We had never seen one before and we thought we were big shots with our gold ones at the time. Of course, I didn't let her pay but what a nice gesture it was of her.

Anyway, in New York, it was Saturday noon, and we went to a trendy bar/restaurant called Columbus on Columbus Ave. for lunch where all the TV and celebs go because it is near the studios. We are at the bar having a drink waiting for our table and Marlen says look whose over there—Rob Lowe. I said to her, I know him. She asked, where from, I replied, it's a long story, I will tell you later. He was with a guy, so I went over excused myself, reminding Rob who I was. He remembered and introduced me to his pal then I went back to the bar. A little while later as he was leaving, he came over to say goodbye. I introduced him to Marlen, but I never got around to telling her how I met Rob Lowe.

I was in New York that week with Ray in a club called Au Bar. We were going to Atlantic City a few days later to watch Nigel fight for the world title against Doug DeWitt. Nigel wasn't supposed to win but stopped DeWitt in round eight. In Au Bar, I was with a girl from Columbia, and she said look whose over there—Michael Douglas. Ray said, I know him. I asked Ray how and he said he walked into Tramp, in London one night, and he was with one of my exes. She called me over, we drank, did some coke and I took them to Café de Paris in Leicester Square. We stayed there until the early hours then went back to his hotel for a couple of days. I said to go and say hello. Ray being modest as he is said he probably wouldn't remember me, but I insisted and pushed him over. Within a minute, Michael Douglas hugged him then Ray called me and my date over and introduced us. We drank some champagne then the three of us spent the next half hour in a toilet cubicle. We left my Columbian girl at the bar in the company of Michael's 6'5" security guy who I found out later was an actor in his film *Wall Street*.

That week we stayed at The Plaza Hotel which was at the time owned by Donald Trump and in Atlantic City, we were staying at The Trump Taj Mahal. We charted his black, Trump helicopter to Atlantic City, not knowing that only six months earlier the Trump helicopter had crashed killing two pilots and three of Trump's executives. It was scary when we found out.

Back in England, when Nigel had a fight, I used to always organize his after-fight parties in a top club, whichever city the fight was in. Manchester, Glasgow or London—the tickets although free were more sought after than the fight tickets and every celebrity and underworld figure who was at the fight was at my party. We had DJs from The Ministry of Sound in London come to Manchester in Madonna's tour bus to DJ. The Manchester parties were at Idols Bar, and it was open season for drugs—you would think it was legal. Everyone was doing lines on the bar top not even bothering going to the bathroom with everyone dancing. The parties were the best ever, going on all night then carrying on back at our hotel. I cannot mention names but football stars from London, Manchester and Glasgow were coming back to our hotels, taking coke until the early hours in full view of everyone.

As I said, in Manchester, we had the party at Idols on

Oldham Street because my pal from Newcastle, Keith Gibbons, owned it. He would close early at 11:00 p.m., get everyone out, clean and re-stock the bars, with the security on the doors ready for my private party that started at midnight. The limos and lines to get in were outside much earlier, waiting for the doors to open or me to arrive—whichever was first. This night, 'Mad' Frankie Frazer, who I made shirts for plus knowing it was my party, came up to me and said that he didn't want to put his girlfriend Marilyn's mink coat in the coat room with everyone else's so for me to put it somewhere safe. I got the manager to take it away with the same instructions and we all went back to partying. I must just say that Marilyn was the daughter of Tommy Wisbey, one of the great train robbers, so this was a heavy team. Four hours later, after lots of alcohol and a ton of drugs, people came looking for me, saying 'Mad' Frankie can't find the mink coat and he wants to see you. I found him and he said, "Frank, where is Marilyn's coat—find it, sharpish."

Now, if you don't know the stories of 'Mad' Frankie Frazer, he was the enforcer for the London crime family, the Richardson Gang, and he used to pull gangster's teeth out with pliers to get what he wanted. So, I thought I had better find this coat quick. I found the manager and asked where the fuck did you put 'Mad' Frankie's mink? He said that it was in the safe in my office. I gave a sigh of relief and said that's good, go and get it. I gave it to Frankie. He said, great party, Marilyn gave me a kiss and they left in one of the many limos outside.

From Poverty to Paradise

64, Bridge Street, Manchester
(The Shop)

We had fun times and sometimes not so much fun. It didn't matter where I was, with all the celebrities that came into the store. Some were international and some were local like legends, Bernard Manning and Freddie Star, both of them always fooling around, telling jokes and making fun of everyone—they didn't need to be on stage. I loved it when the soccer players and boxers came in because of my love of both sports but when Nigel Benn, my pal, was in the shop, there was always a crowd gathered outside looking in to get a glimpse of the dark destroyer. The international stars were Marvin Hagler, Antonio Fargas who played Huggy Bear on the hit TV show *Starsky and Hutch* and the superstar, Harry Connick Jr. who always came in and ordered shirts for himself, his wife and his dad, Harry Connick Sr. Harry's dad, was the district attorney for New Orleans where Harry was brought up and learned his musical talents. His supermodel wife, Jill Goodacre, was one of Victoria Secret's Angels. They all wore my shirts with Harry always inviting us to his show. One time, when I was away, he took Lena on her own to his concert.

Once he called me to order a dozen shirts and needed them in ten days for a TV spectacular called *Christmas Eve with Harry Connick Jr*. It was being filmed a month early at The Pantages Theatre in Hollywood, California, and as it always happens with my luck, fate or whatever we decide to call it, I was going to LA a week later. I was going to stay with a girl I had met on my last trip to LA and said to Harry, I will deliver the shirts personally. He said if you do that, you must come to the show.

I arrived at LAX and Miss Beverly Hills was waiting for me, looking stunning and while we were driving to her apartment in Palos Verdes, she said that she had booked dinner tomorrow night at Spago. This is a celebrity restaurant in Beverly Hills owned by Wolfgang Puck that she knows I love. There is better food around, but I don't care, I like the same places in each city I visit, plus Spago is always full of celebs. Being cool, I said that oh, we can't do Spago tomorrow night, I have a pal in town, singing at The Pantages Theatre and I promised him we would go to the show to support him. She replied but I have booked it. Then I said that we can go another night, but this is important. She asked, who is this friend that is so important and I replied, I don't know if you have heard of him. His name is Harry Connick Jr. Of course, she had, everyone has, and she replied are you joking, I love him. I said, well, we might have to have dinner with him afterwards if you don't mind. She couldn't believe it and the next day I delivered Harry's shirts to

The Montage Hotel in Beverly Hills and that night went to The Pantages Theatre for the show.

Now to be truthful, the experience was not that great. Harry announced that I was in the audience which is always good for my ego and impresses everyone, but the show was like making a movie. The director saying, cut, Harry, let's do that again and let's try it walking on stage from the other side, sometimes four or five times before he was happy with the take. So, it all got a bit boring, taking over three hours to do a one-hour show. Harry, in between cuts, was talking to the audience telling jokes and stories but it still wasn't as good as a Harry Connick concert.

The girl, however pretty she was, didn't drink. She was in AA and obviously had a problem once which I had forgotten about. I was pleased to see her, and she was cool but a few months later, she came to Manchester to see me and then with socializing at the Hacienda and other bars and clubs, especially with my friends, it was all too much for her. I was drinking and drunk a lot of the time and with her not drinking, it didn't work out but she was a great person and it was totally my fault not understanding her illness and alcoholism in general.

Another time, I did a school fundraiser for a customer at his kid's expensive school in Greenwich, Connecticut. I had a stand at the school show, selling my English made-to-measure shirts. After about half an hour, who walks into my stand but Harry Connick Jr. and his wife, Jill. Harry saying, what are you doing here in Connecticut? This is my kid's school. I saw it in the program—Frank Rostron, London. I had to come to see if it was my pal, Frank Rostron, from Manchester. I said a friend whose kids also go to this school asked me to come and do the show. He said that I would get lots of new customers as there is nothing for the husbands to buy. Harry said to Jill, you go shopping, I will stay and help Frank sell some shirts. My friends who came to the show, all very wealthy, living in Greenwich and nearby areas, couldn't believe I had Harry Connick Jr. on my stand selling shirts and ties, saying he is our famous neighbor and not one of them knew him. Harry's sales pitch to all my friends was that his dad wouldn't go to work without wearing one of my shirts.

One of the times that wasn't so much fun in the Bridge St. shop was when I was dating a beautiful mixed-race girl called Diane. I cared about her very much and I took her everywhere with me—to Majorca, London—out for dinner with Mike and Tina Summerbee, and to all the great places I was fortunate to go to. Diane had a boyfriend who was in prison, but I was fearless and cocky, so I didn't care. I thought *by the time he comes home; we would probably be finished anyway so what did it matter*. She was very special, and we dated for a long time.

One day, a 6'3" black guy, dressed very smartly, came into my shop and asked for me. He introduced himself as Diane's brother, but I knew immediately who he was. He said that he's been away, worries about her, and heard that my car had been outside her apartment until the early hours some nights. I said, yes, it has; I thought I would front this situation up. I go to a club called The Explosion and your sister, Diane, and her friend, Jackie, go in there. We dance, drink, and sometimes, at the end of the night, I give them a lift home. I said that I do this to make sure that they get home safely because they are really nice girls and sometimes, they ask me in for a coffee. I always accept in order to sober up before my drive back to North Manchester and sometimes the three of us just talk and talk until 5 or 6 a.m. I think Jackie stays with Diane. I thought that was brilliant. Frank what a salesman you are.

He asked me to walk outside with him and he said, "I am not really Diane's brother; I am her boyfriend. My name is Victor Scott. I have just got out of prison." Then he pulls his jacket back and shows me a gun in his trouser belt. Well, I had never seen a gun before, only on TV, and at that moment I didn't act that cocky anymore. He said that I have listened to you, and I don't believe you. So, stay away from her because I don't want to have to come back to visit you. He then walked away. I thought to myself *well, my speech about taking them home and having a coffee wasn't that good after all*. Diane called asking if he had he been in. I told her the story and we agreed to take a break for a while. A few weeks later, he pulled up outside the shop in a new Jaguar. He must have done a deal and earned some money. He ordered a dozen shirts and paid cash. After that, we became reasonably good pals. Diane's name never came up again, but Victor came into the shop often, ordering shirts but he never flashed his gun again either.

I lost money on many deals usually with pals but the

couple of times that I earned some money without even trying was when I dated a girl called Christine. She was quite a serious girlfriend who lived near Oldham. So, for me to drive to her house to pick her up and at the end of the night drive her home or the next morning was too much. I used to pay for a taxi one way, either for her to come to my house and I drove her home in the morning or vice versa. Our relationship got pretty serious, and I was seeing her a few times a week and the cost of taxis added up. I went to my pal's garage and bought her a mini. It would work out cheaper than paying hundreds of pounds on taxis and she and her pals were impressed that I had bought her a car.

After a while, we broke up and, of course, I didn't ask for the car back like some cheap guys do. I have always let the girls keep the jewelry, furs, or cars that I bought them. A few months later, a letter arrived at my house with a check inside for 4,500 pounds from the Royal Insurance and I had no idea what it was for. I called them and they explained that it was full payment for the mini that had been a total write-off in an accident. I had forgotten that I had to put the insurance in my name with Christine as second driver. It was much less expensive that way. I called one of her pals and she confirmed that Christine had an accident, skidded on black ice and hit a tree but she was ok with no injuries. I thought that's not bad, I only paid 4,250 for it. So, I made profit and she drove it for nine months, plus I didn't expect to get anything back. What a touch that was.

Another time, I opened my mail and there were some papers inside and certificates—again I had no idea what they were. I called my pal, Peter Smith, who knows all about this stuff and he came to my shop and looked at them. He said that they are share certificates in a company all in your name. I told him that I had never bought any shares in my life, so he suggested taking them to a mutual friend of ours who was a stockbroker in Manchester to see if they were worth anything. Peter said that, if he asks, say that your grandmother bought them for you, and you want to cash them in. I called him and he said send them around to his office and he would take a look at them.

A couple of hours later, he called and said that you might as well keep them; they are worth nothing—only about four-five grand. Now, people spoke to me like that, thinking I had money because of my lifestyle, but believe me, four-five grand was a lot of money to me, especially in those days. This was like finding money in the street, so I said to him, sell them as they are only loose ends. He sent a load of papers for me to sign and a few days later I got a check for nearly five thousand pounds. For months afterwards, I was worrying the police, or someone, would knock on my door because of a theft or fraud of company shares and to this day, over thirty years later, I have never heard a thing or know where they came from. I had lots of touches (luck) like that but also lost money in deals straight and bent, plus loans to pals that I never got back—so it all balanced itself out.

New York

One day, an American called Paul Hanly came into my shop. I was in Majorca as usual, and Richard took care of him. He ordered a dozen shirts with his own personal touches, paid and left with instructions on where to ship them. Paul was a lawyer from New York, a clothes horse and, if not the best, certainly one of the best dressed men in New York City and in Manchester on business. He was staying at The Midland Hotel. These are the reasons why I say I am blessed, lucky or it's fate, whichever you prefer. There are hundreds of lawyers in Manchester all over town some two miles away, but the meeting Paul had that day was at a law office in the alley at the side of my shop. If Paul had been at any other lawyers in Manchester, he probably would have never seen my shop and I would probably never have met him. I would never have gone to New York for business, been married to Jane, or be living and retired here in paradise. He changed my life, and I will tell you why.

Getting that job at John Michael changed my life because I was now working in Manchester and meeting people other than from Middleton. I first met Mike Summerbee in there who set me up in business and now meeting Paul Hanly, I was going to work in New York. I was now meeting people other than from Manchester. We made his shirts and sent them to his office in New York and about three months later he was back to Manchester on business and came into my shop but this time I was there to meet him. He was a tall, impressive man who I liked immediately not knowing he was about to change my life forever and become one of my closest friends. Paul passed away suddenly at the age of seventy. I am devastated; he was my friend for forty years.

He came into the shop that day with two shirts that belonged to friends of his in New York. One belonged to Eddie Hayes, a famous lawyer, and the other one belonged to Owen Williams, a banker at Salomon Brothers. They were both made-to-measure for these guys and Paul said take the measurements from these shirts. I will pick six fabrics for each: give them the collar and cuffs you make for me. I will pay you along with six more for myself and he gave me the address for shipping and six weeks later they were sent and that was that. I thought nothing more about it except what a good sale that was from that American guy.

I went back to Majorca and when I returned a few weeks later, Richard said that he had a couple of phone calls from Eddie Hayes in New York and would I call him. Eddie said that everyone is going crazy about his shirts and loves them and to get your arse off the beach in Majorca and go to New York and sell some shirts. I called Eddie and he was great, joking and having a laugh, but seriously said that he was at a party with Paul and everyone loved their shirts and if I went to New York that I would sell a lot of shirts.

It never crossed my mind to go to New York and sell shirts. I didn't particularly fancy it, either. I called Paul, asking if it was true what Eddie Hayes was saying and Paul confirmed that everyone loved them. Besides that, Paul has eighteen partners, and he would memo them all to say I was arriving. There was no email in those days but memos; he said he could not guarantee they would order shirts but he would let them know. I now had three customers in New York and two of them I had never met but if only these three ordered shirts it would pay for my ticket to Owensboro and my hotel in New York so that was my target.

The people that I had met that Christmas in Freeport, from Owensboro, Kentucky, had insisted I visit them for a holiday as they had no one who was English in Owensboro and they wanted to show me off to their friends. I had lots of fun with them on holiday and thought it would be different. So not knowing where in America Owensboro or even Kentucky was, I called my travel agent. I asked him how much does a ticket cost to Owensboro, Kentucky, and where is it. He said, you would fly Manchester to New York then New York to Evansville, Indiana, and then on to Owensboro, Kentucky, and it would be 200 pounds. I asked him about how long the layover in New York would be. He said three hours. I said how much would it cost extra if I stayed in New York for a day; he said the same. I said what about three days; he said the same price. So, I booked it and called Paul Hanly. I said to him I am coming to New York to sell some shirts. I remember it as if it was yesterday.

Paul said that I will book you in The Hotel Elysée which is just a block from my office. Call me when you arrive. I was so nervous. I think I didn't tell Paul I was going to Kentucky afterwards but wanted them to think that I was going to New York just for them. I arrived at the hotel—a beautiful, classic, French-style hotel on East 54th Street, with an elegant restaurant and bar called The Monkey Bar. I checked in and called Paul. He said come out of the hotel, turn right, walk over the first road and then at the next road you will see my building, The Lipstick Building at 885 Third Avenue.

He said, come to Richards and O'Neil on the 44th floor and ask for me. I did what Paul instructed me to do. There was no security in those days, long before 9/11 and as I arrived at his reception, the lady there was expecting me, and she showed me to a conference room. The room had windows looking up and down Lexington (Lex) Ave. It was the first time I had been in a skyscraper and the views were spectacular. Shortly afterwards, Paul came in and said I have sent memos to all my partners. Get your patterns out, sit there, see what happens then come and see me before you leave.

I only sat there a couple of minutes before a lawyer came in called Charles 'Trip' Dorkey. He ordered six shirts, said it was good to meet you, thanked me, and said that my assistant will come in with a check. Tell her how much I owe, and she will pay. Trip has been my customer and friend for forty years now and I have seen him in Manchester and London over the years on business and pleasure. I asked him how he got the name 'Trip' as in England no one was called that. He said his name is Charles Dorkey, the third, hence the name 'trip' like triple or three so I was learning things about Americans already. Then, more and more guys came in ordering shirts, not one or two like they do in my shop but 5,6,8, and 10. It was unbelievable. Then a lady came in and said, "Frank, my husband is a lawyer in that building over there—the Citicorp building—would you have time to go and see him after you have finished here." I said, of course, I thought to myself, *I have nothing else to do.*

She called her husband saying Frank's here, Paul's shirt-maker from London (they all used to say that in the beginning, I don't think they had ever heard of Manchester) and his fabrics are fantastic. Then he spoke and she said, I will ask him, saying to me, would I have time to see his partner as well. I said, of course. When I had finished in Paul's office, I went to see him and told him I was going across the road to see two more guys and he said to call him at the end of the day. I had taken orders for about sixty shirts at Richards and O'Neil and I had only been in there for about three hours. I went to the Citicorp building and saw the two other lawyers and they ordered six shirts each. That seemed to be the norm in New York as in England that was a big order at the time. I called Paul at the end of the day, and he was pleased at how much business I had done but not surprised. We met for drinks and dinner; he gave me the plan for the next day and the day after. He told me to call Eddie Hayes in the morning as he wants more shirts and he has some people for you to see and on Thursday, you will go to Solomon Brothers to see Owen Williams and he has people for you to meet.

I was off and running and had paid for my trip ten times over already. The next morning with jet lag, I got up early, had a coffee from a kiosk on the corner of 54th and 'Lex,' and went to see Eddie Hayes about 9:30 a.m. He was brilliant. I felt that I had known him for years. He was street wise, joking, making fun; he could easily have been from the streets of Manchester or London. He ordered a dozen shirts and then made calls to several of his friends not asking but telling them that Frank's here. He will come and see you at such a time and gave me a diary of my day and where to go. These friends of his were the powerhouses of Manhattan and also friends of Paul's. The first one I went to was John Sites, the boss of Bear Stearns on Park Avenue, an investment bank.

Arriving for my first time in a New York bank, I was shown to John's office, walking across a floor with hundreds of men all in white shirts shouting down the phones and throwing paper balls and planes to each other, trying to get one an other's attention. After John ordered a dozen white shirts, he brought three more directors into his office to order shirts, saying this is Frank Rostron from London (again), he is Eddie Hayes and Paul Hanly's shirtmaker. They were impressed because they knew Hayes and Hanly were the best dressed men around. He also said it as if I was someone important. That day, I met Tom Guba who like Paul, Eddie and Trip, I still see to this day. I still make shirts for them and talk to them most weeks even after forty years. I was passed around New York for the rest of that day from friend to friend, colleague to colleague and wife to husband and the day just flew by. I couldn't imagine how many shirt orders I had taken, with no time to count them or the money.

The next day, I got a cab downtown to One New York Plaza, the home of Solomon Brothers, and went to the 42nd floor to visit my other customer who I had never met, Owen Williams. I was shown to a conference room and again crossed a trading floor with hundreds of men in white shirts and within twenty minutes I had twenty/thirty guys, all screaming, wanting to order shirts. It was unreal. That was my introduction to Wall St. where I walked up and down for the next twenty-five years. I met lots of men who made and lost fortunes on Wall Street, but I only made a fortune. I never lost one dollar even in 2008 when they had their financial crisis or after 9/11. Every trip I did from the very first one was busier each time. It was never the same as the previous trip or quieter but always busier. I had a trip booked the week after 9/11 that I didn't take but people were calling me asking where are you? I thought you were coming and three weeks later I did my trip. I had a record trip, and you wouldn't think apart from seeing the towers down or Vessey St. that anything had even happened.

Seeing all these men wearing white shirts, I thought it must be compulsory or a company uniform. Then a guy came to see me one day wearing a blue striped shirt and I said to him are you one of the bosses, he said no, why? I answered because everyone else is wearing a white shirt. He then explained that when you get up at four or five in the morning, the last thing that you want to do is match shirts with ties so it much easier to put on a white shirt with any tie and a grey or blue suit. It was so obvious, and I never thought about it. Now, I knew why they all wore white shirts. But it wasn't long before I had all the guys on Wall Street wearing pink, lilac, yellow and even orange striped, checked and solid Frank Rostron shirts and I would match all the ties up, so they didn't have to think about it.

After three crazy days in New York, I carried on with my trip to Owensboro to see my friends from Freeport and hopefully relax a little. When I arrived at the airport in Owensboro, they drove their SUV onto the tarmac to meet me and as I got off the plane, they had Bloody Marys in their hands and one for me. Then they took me straight to my hotel to change for a pool party and to get my clothes for the dinner party that they were having for me that night. They also gave me a crown that they had bought that I had to wear 24/7 whilst I was in Owensboro. They said I was the King of England, so I had to wear my crown.

We went to their home and they had about twenty people around their pool waiting to meet me, drinking and partying. And these people did love to drink. That's probably why we got on so well. I thought it was just in Freeport but no, it was at home as well. That night, the dinner party being held on my behalf was not at their home but the home of one of their friends that I had not yet met. They weren't at the pool party as they along with their staff were getting their home ready for the night's festivities. As I arrived, still wearing my crown, I am sure the couple who owned this magnificent home bowed as I was introduced to them. They said to me we appreciate you allowing us to hold your welcoming party at our house, but we know it's only because we could hold more people for a sit-down dinner than the others. I was flattered but also embarrassed.

As people arrived, there were thirty-six people for this dinner party, I stood at the entrance with my hosts shaking hands and being introduced to everyone still wearing my crown. The ladies that knew me either from Freeport or the pool earlier that day kissed me on the cheek after shaking hands. It was unbelievable and all because there has never been anyone English before in this town called Owensboro, Kentucky. The dinner was great—three dining tables in two large rooms with four staff, continually pouring drinks and serving food. Afterwards, everyone went into this massive conservatory-cum-atrium, dancing with a DJ on the decks, with the ladies taking turns dancing with The King of England, my crown not slipping once. The next night, the dinner was at their country club, with me still wearing my crown and the last night before I left for home, was at a restaurant in town. There were about twenty people both nights taking photos and making me promise that

I would come again. Whilst I was there, three or four guys ordered shirts, so I made some money and didn't spend a dollar in three days. I think the only time that has ever happened before was when I was sick in bed once and even then, I still think I spent some money.

I flew home to England. The next day, I went into work and Richard had a pile of messages for me from New York. Things like Hey, Frank, sorry I missed you when you were in NY. Please call me when you come back. I work with John at Solomon Brothers, thanks, Mark. Hi, Frank, my name is Paul and I work at Goldman Sachs and my buddy from Bear Stearns ordered some shirts from you last week. Can you call me next time you are in town, thanks, Brett. Frank, I missed you last week. Please call me when you are next here so I can order some shirts, Jim. There were about ten messages, but it had it never occurred to me to ever go back. I presumed it was just a one-off on my way to Owensboro to help pay for my trip.

We made all the shirts in about six weeks, shipped them and within a week or so I started getting more calls like Frank, I received my shirts, and they are great. Please call me next time you are in NY so I can order some more, also, I have a buddy who wants some. The ones I loved were: Hey, Frank, I loved my shirts, thanks. I have left Solomon Brothers and I am now working at Merrill Lynch. Here are my new contacts. Call me when you are in town, there's a whole new set of guys here that want to see you.

Again, I never ever thought of going back; that's how

stupid I was. But with all this pressure and the money that I could earn, six months later, I went back. I booked my trip for a week, staying at The Elysèe Hotel again, sending post cards to all my existing customers, saying that I am coming and the dates. I called all the new guys, some making appointments before I arrived at their office or at my hotel, but I was fully booked up every minute of every day and with no cell phones or emails, it was all notepad and pen. To give you an idea money-wise, I took more in that week than what we take in the shop in two months. It was unbelievable and with a lot more profit because in exporting them, I had no VAT tax to pay. That was the start of my American experience, thanks to the late, great Paul J. Hanly Jr.—my friend who walked into my shop in Manchester, both of us having no idea that it was about to change my life the minute he walked in.

The next time I went, three months later, was for ten days, then after that, I went for two weeks, and by the end it used to be three or four weeks. First to New York and then Chicago, Boston, LA, San Francisco, Palm Beach and Miami and, as I said every trip was busier than the one before without exception. The money was incredible making it possible for me to buy my building in Princess Street and new Jaguar cars, rather than pre-owned ones, as I had done before.

New York was exciting and walking the streets every day looking up at the tall buildings, I soon got to know the city, the bars and restaurants and loved its energy and the people who lived there. Paul Hanly would have a dinner party every month in a private room at one of New York's coolest Italian restaurants for his friends, usually lawyers and bankers. There was always about ten or twelve of them like Eddie Hayes, Tommy Guba and Bruce Cutler who was John Gotti's lawyer and if I was in town, I would get invited. I always sold lots of shirts, of course, but just to sit there listening to these New York guys who are the best of friends telling their stories and making jokes about each other was an experience and privilege that money cannot buy and times that I will never forget. The story about me and my shirts spread all by word of mouth and by this time I had hundreds of customers. I made shirts for some of Americas most high-profile lawyers, some of Wall Street's most successful investment bankers, famous actors, doctors and even the Governor of New York, George Pataki, who was a really special man. But there were two guys that I made lots of shirts for that I was particularly proud to know.

One day, I got a phone call from the secretary of a guy that had heard about me and she wanted to make an appointment for him. We made it for 2:00 p.m. the following day at my hotel. At 2:00 p.m. prompt, my doorbell rang, and I answered it to greet a very friendly man with a Manchester accent. I said to him, "Hello, my name's Frank Rostron," with him saying that is a familiar accent where are you from? I replied to him Manchester, England; why, where are you from and he replied Manchester, England. We laughed and bonded from that day. His name was Harold Evans, soon to be knighted by Queen Elizabeth II to become Sir Harold Evans.

I had no idea who he was when he said whereabouts in Manchester are you from and I told him Middleton. Why, where are you from? He said Newton Heath. I thought Middleton was poor and working class, but Newton Heath was even poorer and hardly anyone had a job there. He said to me what's a lad from Middleton doing in Manhattan selling made-to-measure shirts and I replied what's a lad from Newton Heath doing living in Manhattan that can afford made-to-measure shirts. We laughed again and that was the beginning of many laughs over the next several years, whilst Harry was ordering shirts. At that first meeting in my hotel room, we spent over an hour talking about our journeys from the poverty of North Manchester to the glamour of Manhattan.

He was the assistant editor of *The Manchester Evening News*. Then becoming the editor of *The Sunday Times* for over fourteen years before moving to America to become a legend in American publishing. He was the President of Random House and founded *Condé Nast Traveler* and his wife, Tina Brown, became the editor of *Vanity Fair*. Once again, I cannot stress what an accomplishment this is for a lad from North Manchester, and I thought that I had done well. We spent lots of times after that in his beautiful home on East 57th Street, reminiscing about Manchester while choosing shirt fabrics. One time, when I was there and we had lost track of time, his assistant showed the British Prime Minister, Tony Blair, into the lounge. I hurriedly packed my case and after a brief introduction, I left rather quickly.

For the people who don't know Manchester or particularly, Newton Heath, it is a very poor area with high unemployment. In fact, I know many people from Newton Heath and none of them have jobs or ever had a job. Harold said to me that his dad worked all his life as a train driver for Newton Heath Loco and I told him that I played football for Newton Heath Loco on Wednesday afternoons for my pals Stevie Bowles and members of the Quality Street Gang. The guys I know from Newton Heath are usually villains, thieves and gangsters so for a person like Harold Evans whose dad was a railway man to get out of that place and be the success he had become was unbelievable. It was also funny that with the life he had led, meeting royalty and world heads of state, he still had a north Manchester accent like me. I couldn't believe that I was meeting, making shirts and even becoming friends with all these successful people in New York. It wasn't long ago I was hanging around with kids in Middleton or villains in Manchester and now I am meeting people like Governor George Pataki, Sir Harold Evans, and Justice Anthony Kennedy.

One day, I got a letter from Justice Anthony Kennedy of The Supreme Court of The United States of America, Washington DC, saying that he wanted to order some shirts. He had heard about me from his sons whom I also made shirts for but they had never once told me or mentioned who their very famous and important father was. I didn't go to DC in those days, but he said that he often visited New York. So, we arranged to meet at my apartment on East 61st Street one Saturday. The meeting was at 11:30 a.m.; it was now about 10:00 a.m. and I am in my shorts, polo shirt and flip flops, just hanging around writing orders and counting money. I would put my suit, shirt and tie on for a new customer or even one who wasn't a close friend, but my phone rang, and it was this very important man, asking could he come earlier.

I said, of course, what time were you thinking, and he said that I'm outside your apartment now if you are free. I told him that was alright, but I've not got my suit on but shorts and flip flops. Justice Kennedy said that's fine, and I opened the door for him. I couldn't believe I'm probably seeing my latest and most important client ever, ordering shirts for the first time and I'm wearing my beach clothes. He was brilliant and a gentleman and it was a pleasure and an honor to meet him. He made me feel relaxed and comfortable serving him whilst in my Saturday casual beach outfit. I went on to make him many shirts over the following years.

I got a call one day before I ever went to any other cities from a customer called Pat McGarvey and he said, Frank, you won't believe who I am standing with—Marc Hujic. They didn't work together in New York, so I thought that's strange, but he said they are now working together in Chicago. Then one day, Marc said to Pat, I like your shirt, Pat replied, you wear great shirts also. They then found out that I made shirts for both of them. That's why they called to see if I went on business to Chicago. I said that no, I have never been to Chicago and Pat suggested come here, Marc and I will order shirts but we have lots of guys working for us at Merrill Lynch who will order from you also. Then on my next trip to New York, I took an early flight to Chicago, got a taxi from the airport to Sears Tower where their office was located, saw them plus another twenty guys and got a taxi back to the airport. I was back in my hotel, The Elysèe, by 7:00 p.m. with another pile of money and orders but more importantly new customers and a new city to go to. That's how it happened in all the other cities. A guy moved from New York and called me like Pat McGarvey did, I went, and the same thing happened going to Boston when Bobby Stevenish moved from New York.

Los Angeles, Palm Beach and Miami were never the same as New York or Chicago but I did orders and made money. However, I made it more of a holiday to see friends and relax after the hectic work schedule in New York, Chicago and later Boston. In LA, I had a few customers: two in particular were not only good friends but the sharpest dressed men in town. Don't forget, in LA and Florida, men don't dress like they do in New York and Chicago—much more casually but these two dressed up even more. I think not only because they loved clothes but also to take the piss out of the Yanks.

Both had lived in America most of their adult lives. Robert LeMoine is English and my pal from Leeds and even though Paul Schnee was born in the States, he left as a baby with his mother to Scotland. He's Scottish but lived and worked in Manchester as a young man, before moving back to America. Paul was in the car business in California selling luxury and vintage motors and Robert was in the property game. What they both had in common was that they knew how to dress. Both of them dressed like the typical Englishman in a chalked stripe suit or blazer, shirts with white collar and cuffs for cufflinks, club ties both—looking a million dollars. Whilst their American counterparts at work looked like adverts for the Gap stores. It was no wonder they left them for dead in the sales department, earning fortunes on the way and I was lucky to make shirts for both these men and also count them as close friends.

When in LA with Paul, it used to be a quiet lunch or dinner and a cocktail afterwards in The Polo Lounge at The Beverly Hills Hotel where Paul's wife was the personal assistant to the hotel director. In the hotel and bar, we always got the VIP treatment because of his wife even though the place was full of Hollywood stars, movers and shakers. With Robert, it was the opposite. Going to wild, busy restaurants, bars and clubs, girls, drugs and many times very close to fights and trouble, I cannot believe how close at times I was to getting into trouble with Robert and if I ever had, it would have been goodbye to my green card and certainly my citizenship. Again, now realizing how blessed I am.

Robert knew everyone and every place in Beverly Hills and they all knew him. He used to tip big and talk loudly but was always fun and respectful. One time, I had been to Vegas for a fight, and we always used to have three or four days in LA afterwards. It was a long way from England to Las Vegas for three or four days plus that was long enough in Vegas in those days, so we made it seven or eight days tagging on LA. Even though four or five thousand Britts would go to Vegas for a fight to watch Lennox Lewis or Frank Bruno, we always had our little crowd that stayed together—usually ten or twelve of us. This time, we are in Beverly Hills staying at The Beverly Hilton and there are fourteen of us partying and ballooning around the pool all day. But we needed restaurants at night and to try and get a table for fourteen guys anywhere is impossible, never mind Beverly Hills. So, I call my pal, Robert; he says leave it with me. He called me back later that day and gave me a list of restaurants and times that he had booked for us and the name of the manager or owner to ask for who would take care of us. Robert obviously telling our contacts how famous I was which movie directors and producers that I made shirts for and how much money we all have, probably exaggerating tenfold to impress the restaurants and make me look good.

The first night, we were booked into a hot, Italian restaurant called Mezzaluna and our contact was a guy called Ron. We arrived in three taxis and as we walked in this tall, handsome, young man approached me, introduced himself saying that he would be taking care of us. He said that Robert was a close friend of his and any friend of Robert's was a friend of mine. He had a great table for fourteen prepared with a view of the whole place and what a view it was with models, actresses and the Beverly Hills elite all dining there. Ron was brilliant in looking after us and waiting on us personally for three or more hours and believe me with fourteen English lunatics that was not an easy job. He even called a club to get us in afterwards. He was a real gentleman.

About four weeks later, I switched on my TV to watch the news and the headlines were NFL FOOTBALL LEGEND OJ SIMPSON MURDERED HIS WIFE NICOLE SIMPSON AND HER FRIEND RON GOLDMAN with photographs. Ron Goldman was our Ron Goldman from Mezzaluna. I couldn't believe it. I called Ray and the other lads in London saying remember the guy who took care of us in Mezzaluna in LA? All of them saying—of course. I said turn on your TVs and watch the news. It was unbelievable and so sad and what a nice guy he was and only twenty-six years old. The following year, another Mezzaluna waiter and aspiring actor waiting for his big break called Michael Nigg was also murdered in LA, twenty-six years old as well. I don't know if we met or saw Michael Nigg when we were in the restaurant that night, but Robert said he was certainly working there at that time.

Back in New York, I was meeting more and more people and seeing thirty or more guys every day in their office, their gym before work, their home before the gym or their home after dinner. But my favorite time was at the end of the day in my hotel room. I could have four, six or eight guys who don't know each other, all in the banking business, ordering shirts, trying to outdo each other but when they had finished, they were like old friends. We would then go to my hotel bar or a trendy one nearby that one of them recommended and drink for an hour or so. Then one by one they would leave saying thanks, Frank, see you next trip. I would end up most nights alone after having a brilliant, busy day taking in lots of money and feeling great but still alone.

More than once, this situation had happened to me after the guys had left. I would walk into the nearest restaurant where there were always a lot of hot girls looking for a vice president of any Wall Street bank to go out with. They wanted to date and hopefully marry one of these millionaires. I know a few that married one of these girls only to regret it a couple of years later when they had to move out of their Park Avenue apartment and leave it to the new wife, plus giving them a few grand a week on top.

I would be standing at the bar in one of these restaurants, looking like a million dollars, with a suntan, a chalked stripe suit, pink shirt with a blue tie with pink in the tie all matching, wearing a gold Rolex watch, and a glass of champagne in my hand. I have a smile on my face celebrating my big day and these girls would come over to you, blatant as hell, smile and say Hi, my name is Susan or Julia, what's your name. I would say, Frank, would you like a drink and then they would say, I love your accent where are you from, what are you doing in New York, do you live here and a million other questions.

I would say that I am from England, and I come to see customers on Wall Street The girl now getting more excited, seeing dollar signs in her eyes, plus an apartment on Park Avenue. What do you do that you see guys on Wall Street? Then when I tell them that I make their shirts, they have a puzzled face and say what do you mean you make their shirts. I repeat. I make their custom shirts; I am a shirtmaker. Now, they are counting in their heads how many shirts could I possibly make then how much money I could possibly have and think, wow, he looks great but no money. Then they put the drink down and say nice to meet you, Frank, and walk out. It was so obvious and embarrassing; it was a joke. I cannot believe some of my best friends in NY who work on Wall Street and went to the finest universities and earn a fortune, courted these girls and ended up marrying them.

One day, and it was only my second trip to New York, I was going to see a lawyer at 919 Lexington Avenue I am walking down a side street, rushing to my appointment, and I hear a very posh English voice calling Frankie, Frankie Rostron. I look around but I don't see anyone and hear it again Frankie, Frankie Rostron. Then a hobo stands up from a shop doorway and it's Eugene Rigg, my customer from London whose house I stayed at in Majorca with the boys when I entertained Cheyanne Pleasantfield.

I was gob smacked and couldn't believe it was Eugene. He looked just the same even though I had not seen him for over ten years, but I couldn't work out what was wrong until he got closer. He was wearing a blue blazer, grey slacks, one of my shirts with a cravat and even a pocket handkerchief but the edges of his jacket sleeves were worn and greasy as his shirt and a couple of buttons were missing from his blazer. Eugene always had beautiful white teeth and manicured nails, but his teeth were yellow and his nails dirty. I thought that perhaps he was just eccentric. I couldn't believe he had no money. He's Eugene, my rich friend from London. As I was running late, I asked him to walk with me to 919 'Lex,' and whilst walking he said, "Frankie, did you ever send those last three shirts because I never received them." I don't even remember any shirts and then he said, whilst you are in town you must go to see my lawyer, he will have a dozen shirts. I have just sued the Rockefellers and won two million dollars.

Now this all sounded strange but feasible that Eugene had become a recluse and eccentric in New York City. I didn't know. When we arrived at my appointment. I said to Eugene, wait here until I come back down, and we can carry on talking. I was shocked and had to find out what was going on. After seeing my client, forty-five minutes later, I walk into the street and cannot see him. Then, all of a sudden, he shouts, "Frankie, Frankie come over here." Now this is really funny; he is talking to another hobo who has two, giant, plastic bags full of empty bottles that he has collected out of the trash bins and who looks like a tramp not in custom clothes like Eugene even though they are grubby. He introduces us and says Frank, this is my friend, George, and George, this is my friend, Frank Rostron, from England. Frank is my shirtmaker; he makes all my custom shirts.

Well, I could have fallen over. He is introducing me to a tramp as his shirtmaker which confused me even more. I am thinking is he just a rich eccentric but, just in case, when I was coming down in the elevator, I put my cash into my inside jacket pocket and left sixty dollars in my trouser pocket. He said goodbye to George and started to walk with me back up the street asking do you still see George Best. I replied, yes, I see him sometimes and then he asks do you still see Paul McCartney. Well, I have never met Paul McCartney, so I said, no, I don't see Paul anymore. Then he says do you still see John Lennon? I was about to say John Lennon is dead when he interrupted me and said I know what you are about to say, that John's dead, but he's not. I see John and talk with him most nights in the park; he only pretended to be shot so he could live his life without being troubled all the time and be left alone but, no, John's fine now. I now know that Eugene is not fine.

As we were parting ways, he says, Frankie, could you see your way to lend me a hundred bucks. When I left England to become a tax exile here, I couldn't get my money out and it's still there. The two million dollars I am getting from the Rockafellers I haven't received, so I am little short of the old spondulicks. I pulled out my sixty dollars and said this is all I have, Eugene, as everyone pays check or credit card and I need twenty for taxis but you are welcome to this forty. Eugene replying, Thanks, Frankie, I will get it back to you soon and give you an order for a dozen shirts. He walked away and I have never seen him since.

About six months later, I bumped into a mutual friend of mine and Eugene's who used to be his accountant. I said you will not believe who I saw in New York and he said Eugene

Rigg. I said how did you know that, and he said because I saw him there as well. Then he told me the story of what had happened, starting with his wife who was an aristocrat from a very prominent English family leaving him and taking their two children. Eugene, besides being in real estate in quite a big way with offices in Knightsbridge, Kensington, and a couple of more exclusive locations in London, invested in restaurants and clubs, one being in Beauchamp Place that I went to a few times. They got into trouble, and he was pouring money into them all to keep them going and eventually went bust and fled to New York with presumably any money he could get together at the end. He lived like a normal tourist until the money ran out and ended up living on the streets with the clothes on his back, hence the blazer and shirt—tatty and worn.

A follow up on this story about Eugene in New York. A couple of years later, a friend who I did a lot of business with, in London and New York, called Douglas Davies, had a tailor's shop on the Fulham Road in London and I shared it with him. My name was on the awning—Frank Rostron Shirtmaker—and his name above the window. So, if the awning was pulled up you just saw the tailors name but if the awning was down. you could just see my name unless you were under the awning looking up. Well, one day I came into the shop and the girl who worked there said a strange man came in this week asking for you and left you this note. I opened the note and it said, "Hello, Frankie, this is Eugene Rigg. I am living at the Chelsea Hostel room 3. It would be great to see you if you have time." I was flabbergasted not only with Eugene coming into the shop but how on earth did he get back to England. He was a hobo with no money living on the streets in New York. Who sat next to him on the flight? All questions I couldn't answer went through my head then someone said the police would have picked him up as a vagrant. They would have checked him out, seeing he was an illegal immigrant by this time, giving him a shower and putting him on a plane to London, just like Miguel in Majorca did with Berit Colhead to Manchester. I did not go to see him at the hostel, and he never came back into the shop.

While I am talking about the Fulham Road shop, another funny story that you should hear is that the tailor, Douglas Davies, used to make suits for all the lords and ladies and gentry of London. With him being one of the boys, he also made suits for gangsters and drug dealers. One of his society customers was Frederick William John Augustus Hervey, 7th Marquess of Bristol—a British peer and aristocrat also known as Lord "Johnny" Bristol. Lord Bristol was a drug addict and more than once was caught with cocaine, always paying a fine and going back to his stately home, Ickworth House in Suffolk, to take more drugs. One day, two men, speaking very posh, came into the shop and said to Douglas, we work for Lord Bristol, and he asks if you could get him some cocaine. The tailor saying come back in an hour and I will get it for him. The tailor is not a drug dealer, but Johnny Bristol is a friend and one of his best customers, so off he goes not knowing that these two men were reporters from one of the biggest news publications in England, doing an undercover scoop on Lord Bristol, his drugs and lifestyle.

They had a photographer hiding across the road and when the tailor came back with the drugs, they photographed him about to walk into his shop. With the awning down you see a picture of the tailor with the words FRANK ROSTRON SHIRTMAKER immediately above his head in the Sunday newspaper. I am on the beach in Majorca knowing nothing about all this and suddenly people come showing me the paper with the headlines saying: "society tailor getting drugs for Lord Bristol" and a photo of the tailor with my name not the tailors name blazoned above his head outside the shop. I couldn't believe it but when I got back to England, we had a laugh about it, no charges were ever brought against the tailor, and it was all forgotten. Lord Bristol died a few years later of multiple organ failure due to chronic drug abuse aged forty-four.

One day, Douglas called me and said that Paul McCartney had been in contact and that his band, Wings, were about to start their world tour and needed suits and shirts. He asked would I make the shirts for him, his wife, Linda, Denny Lane and the rest of the band and he would make the suits. I said, of course, I would, and anyone would jump at the chance just to meet this music legend except the very stupid Frank Rostron who also did the same with Luciano Pavarotti in Barbados. Looking back, I cannot believe how successful I was and yet so dumb. It's unbelievable. In the Beatles days, Paul was my favorite Beatle by far but in the years since I heard and read stories about him pretending to still be the lad from Liverpool—a regular boy yet getting into his chauffeur driven Rolls-Royce and going to places a lad from the streets would never go, thus contradicting himself.

I said to Richard, my manager, that next week he was going to London to the Docklands arena where Wings were rehearsing to meet and measure up Paul McCartney, his wife, Linda, Denny Lane and the rest of the band, Wings, for shirts. He would meet Douglas at Euston station and he would drive him there. Richard couldn't believe what I was saying knowing that he had met many stars working for me, but this was on another level asking why was I not going? I don't like him, I said and gave the reasons why with Richard saying, thanks, but I think you're stupid and he was right—I was. He went the next week to London and had the experience of his life meeting this music legend, having photos taken with them all and two weeks later having to go back to give them fittings. This time not to the Docklands arena but to Paul McCartney's home, Blossom Wood Farm in East Sussex. Richard said even though he was as excited as before to meet Paul again, it was really strange this time. As they drove up his driveway, he was on his knees pulling out weeds and putting in plants and he said to Douglas to go into the house and that he would be there shortly. Richard said he sat on a sofa that looked so old it had the springs coming out of it and the place was so basic. Not the sort of thing you would expect a billionaire music legend would have in his house. Was I wrong again and did I make a mistake about Paul McCartney. I think I did once more; what a mug I was and what a great experience I missed but Richard got an experience that he will never forget.

I worked with quite a few London tailors at this time, them giving me customers for shirts and me reciprocating giving them my guys to order suits. One of them was a tailor called Edward Sexton who made clothes for the elite of London and who also made clothes for Paul McCartney. He called me one day to say that Paul McCartney's daughter, Stella, was finishing fashion college and he was going to tailor her designs. He asked if I would make the shirts for her as well, in her designs, for her college graduate catwalk show. Stella didn't have her friends from school do the catwalk modeling like the other girls did but had her celebrity model pals like Kate Moss, Yasmin Le Bon and Naomi Campbell model for her. It must have made her classmates jealous but what do you expect when you are the daughter of a Beatle. I made all her shirts, and the show was a great success doing fittings and spending time with Stella. We got on really well and ended up good pals. I liked her a lot but as a mate not a girlfriend. She was so down to earth and cool like one of the lads which is unbelievable knowing who she is and who her dad is.

When I was in London, we would go out for dinner and have a laugh just like pals would. After finishing my day at Barry Scotts shop in Neasden or running around the city all day taking shirt orders, I would go to her house in Cavendish Ave, St. Johns Wood to pick her up and head into the West End for dinner. One time, she called and said we would have to have dinner late that night as her pal, Kate Moss, was flying into London and staying with her. Usually, we would eat at seven or so after working all day and finishing at five or six. I didn't want to be hanging around with nothing to do or drinking. But this night, she said it would be nine or even ten o'clock. Well, two things: one was that was too late for me to eat—I would be starving by then—and secondly and the main thing was as anyone who knows me, I am a massive anti-smoker. I have never smoked and never dated a girl who smokes, and Kate Moss is a massive smoker. Every time you see a photo of her, she always has a cigarette in her mouth. I said you go and have dinner with Kate, and I would see her next week. Stella saying, oh, come on, wait and have dinner with us. She's my pal, I have to wait for her. Then, I told her the truth that I didn't want to have dinner with them because of Kate's smoking. Stella said she wouldn't smoke at the table, and I said I don't care she would be smoking all the rest of the time and I can't stand it. She laughed and said that I can't believe you, I don't know a guy in the world who would turn down a dinner date with Stella McCartney and Kate Moss. I said something like you know one now.

I stayed over at the London house once and it was unbelievable. The next morning as I was leaving, there were Japanese tourists standing outside having their photographs taken against the high, brick wall or the high, dark-green wooden gates which in itself doesn't sound strange, but this house has no signs or number or anything indicating that it is owned by Paul McCartney. They could have been standing outside most houses in that area; they would just have had the same photo of themselves smiling against a plain brick wall or green wooden gate. It could have even been anyone's house, anywhere in the country.

I have a great friend and client in New York who is a partner of a large law firm named Jim Badke. Jim was saying to me one day that his son was going through a difficult period at school. All he seemed to do was go home and into his bedroom and play Beatles' music and had Beatles' pictures all over his walls which Jim said was strange as he wasn't even born when the Beatles were around. I then told him that I knew Stella McCartney and that I would get a signed picture of her dad for him. Jim saying that would be fantastic if you could. The next time I saw Stella, I said I hate doing this then started telling her the story about Jim's son and would she please get me a signed photo. The next time I saw her, she gave me this great photo of her dad signed to Jason, saying: "All the best, Jason, keep rocking." I had it framed and when I went to New York took it to Jim's office. The next time that I saw Jim, he told me that after giving his son that photo, the difficulties that he was having at school changed for the better and after he left college, he became an airline pilot.

Jane Bond

When Jane finished school, she went to Bryn Mawr College in Pennsylvania and Pace University in New York. She asked her dad if she could take a gap year off, before she joined the real world, and get a job with an airline so she could travel and see the world as she had never been anywhere of note. He reluctantly agreed with a little pressure from her mum and she got a job with Continental Airlines International. She travelled to Australia, New Zealand, Italy, France, England, Spain and all the places she dreamed about as a child that she probably would never go to. Whether you believe in God or fate, and I believe in both, then no one can deny that this story was fate that we got together or God put us together. On one of her London flights from New York, she was suddenly transferred earlier that morning to a return Continental's flight to Miami. We think that because the number one on that flight was sick, she didn't go on her scheduled flight back to New York.

On that London-Miami flight that day was a certain Frank Rostron going on two weeks holiday to Miami with friends. Now, I could have flown from Manchester to Miami and met the boys there and I don't really remember why I would go all the way to London to then fly to Miami. The only thing I could think of is that I wanted to travel with the guys for a laugh and to start and finish the holiday all together. As we were climbing the steps to get on the plane, in those days there were no passenger boarding bridges, at the top was this beautiful, tall, African American flight attendant. She was looking at passenger's tickets and pointing you in the direction of your seat. Well, when it was my turn, I start to immediately chat her up and flirt. She said to me you must go to your seat as you are holding everyone up. Our seats were at the back of the plane next to the toilets—the worst and probably the cheapest seats on that flight.

After being in the air for about an hour or so, I walked down to the front, through the curtain, into first class to see the beautiful hostess that greeted us when we got on the plane. She said that you cannot come in here, it's for first class passengers only, you have a bathroom at the back of the plane. I said I don't want to use the bathroom; I want four of those small bottles of vodka for my pals as at the back they charge for them. I was only making an excuse to chat her up and show off to my pals, but she said I can't give you any vodka to which I replied, if you don't, I will sit in that chair there and not move. She replied, if you do, I will call the captain, to which I replied, what's he going to do at 38,000 feet. He's not going to be able to do anything, trust me, plus you wouldn't want that sort of commotion in here would you. With that, she gave me four miniature bottles of vodka and asked me to leave. I went back to the guys, showing off, feeling great, saying things like it was easy, I think she must fancy me. About a couple of hours later, I repeated the vodka run and with the same result—she said, you can't have any more vodka, I said, if not I will bring my pals down and we will all sit in here and you don't want that, so she gave me four more bottles. She said that is the last time, no more vodka. Me smiling at her as I leave first class. I got back to the guys still showing off with the vodka and they were suitably impressed with my chatting up skills with the girl.

Further on in the flight, I still have to get to her somehow as I fancied her like mad. I went back to first class and pulled the curtain back and she was there saying, I told you no more vodka, to which I said, I don't want any more vodka, the boys are fed up with vodka. I want some of that champagne in those half bottles you have over there. I would like four please, saying that if not you know my boys will be down here in two minutes. I'm smiling and flirting and being funny and she gives me the champagne and says now go. I go back to the guys and they are more impressed than ever with me saying stuff like she can't help herself, she's only human and these girls will do anything to please me, when really it was just to get rid of me.

Then a few minutes later and I had not stopped showing off to my pals when she appears saying keep your friend down here and don't let him come back to first class again. Otherwise, I will call the captain, to which they replied how can we stop him if you can't stop him and you are in charge of first class.

What chance do we have, and we all started laughing. Now this was my one chance to go to work on her and chat her up properly, giving her the full Frank Rostron repertoire. I asked her where she was going tonight and she replied that I don't know because I didn't fly to London with these girls so I don't know any of them and then told us the story about the plane switch earlier that day. That was my cue to make a play. That means you will have to have dinner with us then. We are staying at The Fontainebleau Hotel and having dinner at Mezzanotte, the finest Italian restaurant in Miami Beach. I said it as quickly as possible trying to impress her saying my name is Frank Rostron. Then introducing her to my pals, I asked what's your name, to which she said JANE BOND. I said, now feeling confident, well, Jane Bond, be at the Fontainbleau at eight o'clock, meet me at the bar and don't be late, otherwise you will starve to death along with this lot on the plane and miss a great night out.

We got to the hotel, checked in, and looked around the pool and beach for any action but really hoping JANE BOND would come that night. We got ready to party and I said to the boys to come down in fifteen minutes so if she does turn up, I will have a few minutes alone to get to know her. I got to the bar, ordered a drink, and before it arrived, the stunning JANE BOND walked in dressed to kill, looking nothing like today in her airline uniform but even better, if that was possible. I ordered her a drink, swapped small talk to relax us both, and within minutes the troops arrived. We had a couple of drinks and headed to Mezzanotte. This was not only the best food in town but the place to be. It was wild; the waiters singing and shouting, banging knives and forks, plates and anything else that made a noise. The customers had to talk louder, and the music had to be yanked up higher to create the greatest atmosphere of any restaurant. At the end of the night, even if people were still eating, a lot of chairs would be removed with everyone dancing in between and some girls getting onto the tables to dance. This is the place that Madonna got on a table once dancing that I mentioned earlier. Jane had the time of her life saying it was the best night she's ever had. We swapped telephone numbers—landlines as there was no cell phones in those days. As she got into a cab on Washington Ave to go back to her hotel, she said "I will call you, I promise."

Me and the boys had a mad two-weeks holiday, drinking and fooling around on the beach all day. Then out every night, bars, dinner, bars again, then clubs and girls galore. We flew home two weeks later absolutely wiped out but having the most sensational of holidays. Two or three weeks later, my manager said that there's a girl on the phone for you. I answered, "Hello, Frank speaking," and the voice on the other end saying, "Hi, Frank, this is Jane. How are you?" I had no idea who it was. I said Jane? She replied, "Jane Bond from Miami. I was the flight attendant who took you there and we had dinner on your first night." I couldn't remember the last night never mind the first but very quickly I remembered her. I said Jane where are you? She said in Philadelphia, but I am flying to London next

Thursday into Gatwick. Would you be anywhere near there that day.

I said that I needed to check my diary which I didn't keep but ruffled a few papers then saying yes, I am. What time are you there and she replied about 12:30 p.m. I said I will be around Gatwick about that time. I couldn't believe she had called me. Where are you staying and told her I would be there. I had no plans to go to London that week but really wanted to see this girl, JANE BOND, again. I arrived at the hotel where I had booked a room. Even at my most confident, I wouldn't presume that I would stay with her, plus she might be sharing a room with another girl, so just in case I booked my own. She arrived tired from the night flight but looked great. I met her in the foyer, she dropped off her bags and came to the bar; we had a drink and talked for a couple of hours. It was unbelievable; we just talked and talked, later going to our separate rooms for a sleep. I was also tired after my three-hour drive down to Gatwick Airport and we arranged to meet in the bar at 7:00 p.m.

I didn't know the Gatwick area as I only used to go into the West End of London. I had checked out a map and noticed that it was quicker to go to Brighton for dinner than drive into London. I made a few phone calls and found out about a great Italian restaurant in Brighton, so we went there had a brilliant night. After dinner, when we were walking down the beach front, I did my party piece to impress her. I ran down a line of parking meters each about five feet tall and leapfrogged over all of them until I got to about the fifth or sixth and got stuck on the top of one. Jane was chasing me laughing her head off and I couldn't go forward or back—I was stuck. So, I just slid down the side ending up on my back in the street. I just lay there drunk and helpless; she helped me get up and after I got my breath back, we went to the car and drove back to Gatwick. That was the start of a long-distance relationship between me and JANE BOND. Every time she flew to London, I went to see her. When I went to Miami, she would come to see me. I saw her when I was in New York and when she wasn't working, she flew to Manchester to stay with me. It worked out great. I saw her every few weeks even though it got a little heated with arguments at times, since us both had strong personalities—it still happens today. We carried on but after about eighteen months it was over, and I can't remember what happened. She neither called me nor did I call her. I don't know but it had run its course.

Nine years later, I am still living in Manchester but doing a lot of work in America. One day, I was walking down a side street in New York between 'Lex' and Third Avenue, rushing as usual to an appointment, carrying my bag and I hear Frankie, Frankie and running across the road was JANE BOND. She gave me a hug. I explained I was in a rush, as usual, but do you want to have dinner tonight. She said I would have to ask my boyfriend. She called him. She explained that she had bumped into me and would it be alright. He said, yes, and we met later that day for a drink then dinner. We talked for about four hours over dinner, just two old pals and had a great time. She asked about Ray and all the guys in London and Manchester, and I told her about my girlfriend who was about to give birth to my baby and all that we had been doing for the last nine years. We finished dinner, she hugged me, no kisses and we didn't even exchange telephone numbers. It was just good to see her and that was that. She was in a relationship and so was I.

Ten years later, I was working in New York with a guy who was involved in buying my business and I had a contract to stay on to show him the ropes in America. One day, he was in a shop on the corner of 61st and 'Lex' looking at watches and I was bored so I said that I would wait outside. Within five seconds of getting outside, not twenty-five or forty-five seconds, but the second I walked out, this tall, beautiful African American girl, wearing large, dark sunglasses, a hat, and a Burberry checked coat walked past. I looked as I look at most girls especially if they are pretty and as she got about twenty feet past, she turned around and said towards me, "Frankie Rostron." I couldn't hear what she was saying with the traffic and her being so far away, but I looked behind me to my left and to my right wondering who she was talking to, and she pointed saying no, you are Frankie Rostron. She walked up to me asking are you Frankie Rostron again, to which I said yes. I swear to God I had no idea who she was, and she said I am JANE BOND. I couldn't believe it. She looked better than I ever remembered to which I said Jane, you look fucking unbelievable, and she replied age has done you well as well.

The last time she saw me, ten years earlier, I had long, dark brown hair and now I had very short, cropped, salt and pepper hair. How she remembered me, I have no idea. She had seen me once in nineteen years. Also, if I had walked out of that shop five seconds later, I would never have seen my future wife.

So, going back to God and fate and how I believe how blessed I am, I shouldn't have been on that flight from London to Miami. I could have flown from Manchester and met the boys there. Jane shouldn't have been on that flight; she should have been on the London/New York flight but was transferred unexpectedly to that flight four hours earlier. What about her seeing me on the streets of Manhattan twice in nineteen years. If I took you and six of your friends or family and put you on different corner blocks in New York and said walk for a week turning left, right anywhere you wanted to go you would never see one another, yet Jane saw me twice in nineteen years—unbelievable. The last time, I looked nothing like I did ten years earlier when she last saw me. It still shocks me to this day and if meeting and being with JANE BOND was not fate or organized by God, then I don't know what is. If Paul Hanly, the lawyer from New York, had not walked into my shop in Manchester, I wouldn't have been in New York in the first place. Can you believe how scary this is.

We spoke on the street corner for a few minutes as she was in a rush this time, going to a meeting. She asked if I was still living in Manchester and I said, no, Naples, and she replied Italy? I said, no, Florida. I don't think she had ever heard of it.

Give me your number and I will call you later and we can have dinner and she declined saying you give me your number and I will call you. We had a little back and forth but she wouldn't give me her number but promising that she would call me.

All afternoon, I was worrying in case she didn't call. I didn't want to wait another ten years hoping to bump into her again but at 5:30 p.m. that afternoon as promised; she called. We didn't have dinner that night and we cannot remember why, either she had a meeting, or I had one, but we had dinner the next night and it lasted for over four hours again. We just talked about Manchester and all my friends. She asked do you still see Ray, and do you still see Barry, and are you still married. I replied, I've never been married, Jane saying I thought the last time I saw that you were married. I said no, I had a girlfriend, and we had my baby, but I was never married. After that, we had dinner every night for the remaining five days of my trip.

I am not saying it was love at first sight or anything like that, but it was certainly a different feeling than any other time in my past. She told me after we got married that she mentioned to her mum that week after three dates do you remember the guy from Manchester, England, that I used to date. Her mum said who, the shirtmaker and Jane said yes, him, well, I think I am going to marry him. Every night that week was special. We had dinner with clients and friends who were impressed with her but not as much as I was. She owned her own company in entertainment management with clients in TV, movies and the music industry. Her main clients in the music business being a band from England, with an American female lead singer called The Brand-New Heavies. They had lots of hits in the late '80s and early '90s but are still touring the world to sellout audiences today.

As I was leaving New York, I asked her to come to Naples the following weekend to see me. I really wanted to see her, and she wanted to see me, but she couldn't. She had to go to a wedding in Chicago and the following weekend she was going to England to see her band then onto Japan and couldn't come for about a month. It drove me insane. I wasn't used to that but what could I do. We spoke all the time from that day on whether she was in the US, Europe or Japan. Then came the time for her to come to Naples. I wanted to impress her with my lifestyle, my Bentley Flying Spur, my house, my friends, the bars and restaurants that I went to and beautiful Naples itself, including the white beaches, turquoise sea and The Ritz-Carlton Hotel, one of the best Ritz-Carltons in the USA, Fifth Avenue and Third Street—everywhere and everything.

I picked her up at the airport and brought her home. I had everything perfectly set, the music on low, the landscape lighting outside, the pool lights, the mood lighting in the house all perfect, in order to impress her. She said that she was tired with all the travelling and could we stay home and cook. She looked in the fridge and cupboards and still tells the story today that there was no food in the house except a tin of HP baked beans and some tinned tomatoes. I explained that I go out to eat every night. That's why I don't have any food. She said you cannot possibly go out every night for dinner, but she found out very quickly that I did. We didn't go out that night, I starved, she didn't eat but when you are in love, what can you do. I wish we could have gone out but we had a great night watching TV and the following day I took her on a grand tour around Naples. Now when I have girlfriends come to stay, I only book a two-day flight because I know I will be fed up, after one night, or we will have a fight. So, two nights is the normal and I said to Jane I was going to change her ticket later so she could stay for another few days. She said don't change my ticket. I have work on Monday. I replied so do your work later in the week but Jane insisted that it was impossible. I have meetings and a very busy week.

This was something that I wasn't used to girls saying to me, such as I can't stay longer. I had waited for over a month to see her and just had the best weekend that I can remember, wanted her to stay, and she couldn't. I drove her to the airport and usually, as soon as they step on the sidewalk, I am burning rubber while driving away but this time it was all so different. As she was walking inside the terminal, we are waving at each other and blowing kisses and I did not drive off until she was out of sight. Even then, I hung around for a few minutes; I don't know why. She didn't come back to Naples for another three weeks because of her business commitments but this time she stayed for four days and then a couple of weeks later for five days, then for a week and so forth and so forth.

By this time, I realized she was different and how special

she was and that I wanted to spend all my time with her. I think besides that, it had come to a time in my life when I was fifty-seven years old and even though I still loved going out as I still do today, I was getting tired of different girls every night and going through the motions of chatting them up and impressing them just so they would stay the night. I think the timing was perfect for both of us—again fate and God. One time, she was telling me about her roommate in New York, leaving without telling her, owing her rent, and this was the second time it had happened. She complained that she couldn't afford a Manhattan apartment on her own and that she needed a roommate. I suggested that she leave New York and come and live with me in Naples then she wouldn't have to worry about any bills or rent. She replied what about my business? I can't run it from Naples and that's something I didn't even think about. I was only thinking about Jane being here with me. I said close it down and start a business from here doing something else. Now I know deep down, at this time, she didn't love Naples; it was too quiet for her. She was a city girl and loved the energy and night life of Manhattan. This was something that Naples couldn't give her, but Naples could give her something that Manhattan couldn't—Frank Rostron. She also had the weather, the beaches and a new life with someone she loved. She said, yes, she would. I was so happy I had my girl moving to Naples but also worried that she was giving everything up in New York for me. She was leaving her business, her apartment, her friends. What if this relationship didn't work out and with my track record there was a good chance it wouldn't. Then how bad would I feel but it was too late now, I had asked her, and she had agreed.

She went back to New York and organized everything to start her new life in Florida. The big day came when she was driving her Land Rover Discovery for two days loaded up with her worldly possessions to Naples. She stopped overnight in Atlanta with her client, the lead singer of The Brand-New Heavies and left early the next morning for the second part of the journey to Naples. We kept in touch all the way by phone, Jane telling me where she was, and more important, that she was safe. The last time we spoke, I said to call me when she was about an hour away so I could be home to greet her and help her into the house with her bags and cases. I had gone out with friends for dinner and then to Blue Martini for drinks which had opened whilst she was away and was the latest hotspot in town. She called but I didn't hear it with the noise from Blue Martini music. So, when she did call, and I heard she was already at the house, I jumped into my car and drove home as quickly as I could. By the time I got there, she had unloaded her truck, and everything was in the house in its place. She still tells the story of how she drove for two and a half days to be with me, and I wasn't there to meet her. Oops, not the best of starts.

She settled into life here in the Sunshine State quickly, becoming a real estate agent with a local company called Keller Williams. She said that there is nothing else to do in Naples but be a realtor, so she worked hard selling houses, becoming the rookie of the year in her first job which I was proud of but not surprised. She moved on to bigger companies like Sotheby's still being a top salesperson and later selling the most expensive condo Naples has ever marketed, with an asking price of eighteen million dollars and Jane getting fifteen million for her client. She easily settled into the Naples social scene and met her own friends. Also, she trained for months to run in the Naples Half Marathon for charity. She had already run the New York Marathon in the past and been involved in other society events like my golf tournament to mix and meet people which she's very good at and everyone, including all my friends, loves her.

About a year later, we did our first trip back to New York to see friends, go to the theatre, and to our favorite restaurants and bars. It was winter—cold and rainy—and Jane had lived in Naples for almost twelve months by now and I know she still didn't call it home or even loved Naples as I would want; she still yearned for the energy of New York. We stayed at The New York Hilton on Avenue of the Americas. The second morning we came out onto Sixth Avenue and she clutched my arm tightly and said that she was freezing. Look at all these people, she remarked, pushing and shoving and it's so noisy. I can't wait to get home. This was only the second day of a five-day trip, and she already wanted to go back to Naples and that is when I knew that she now considered Naples her home.

When you live in New York, Manchester, or any city you take the cold weather, the traffic noise, and the maddening crowds, pushing and shoving, as the normal. That's because it is all you know but when you live in Naples, you see how much better life is and this is when I knew that Naples was now her home. Jane would do anything for me and having to meet all my friends was just one of them. From my Wall Street customers and my London aristocrats to my bank robbers and crime families, she had to meet them all and they loved her. Every time we went back to England, besides having lunch and dinner for ten or more friends at San Carlo, Yang Sing or my other favorite restaurants, we also had to visit my friends who couldn't make lunch or dinner that were in prison. This is something I have always done. They are my close friends that I care about very much. It makes them feel good to get a visit from their pal who lives in America, and I feel better for seeing them.

Jane was a little apprehensive at first as she had never been to a prison but, after a while, saw how much it meant to my friends that their pal had come to visit them along with his beautiful, American wife. She came with me to many prisons over the years in England, visiting lots of pals but after one visit to FCI Lompoc outside Santa Barbara, California, she said I love you and all your friends but that is the last time I am going on a visit. What happened was that it was 9:50 and we went through the security and the buzzer went off as Jane walked through. She was taken into a room by a female corrections officer and strip-searched—the first time that this had happened to her. It turned out that her bra had a wire running through both cups and she had to take her bra off. After the visit, go back into the room to collect it and put it back on. In the yard, it was so hot, and she couldn't take her jacket off. She was sweltering for over an hour saying afterwards when we got outside that there would be no more visits. This might be a good omen because, since that day eight years ago, not one of my friends has been locked up. So, fingers crossed and Jane keeping up her promise not to visit prisons anymore, it will stay like that.

Naples, Florida

I went to Barbados every Christmas for twenty consecutive years and one day, I had a call from an English friend, Glenn Oakley, who I knew from London but was at this time living in Tampa. We used to speak all the time about football, clothes, cars, watches and restaurants and all other stuff and Glenn asked are you going to Barbados again this year. I told him, yes, then he asked how much does it cost these days to go to Barbados at Christmas. When I told him, he couldn't believe how expensive it was and said you are joking. You could rent a mansion in Tampa for six months for that amount of money.

Now earlier that year, I had been to Tampa for a couple of days when I was in Miami to see his boss who was my client and friend and stayed at his boss's house. It was very impressive as I had never seen one of these large Floridian homes before, in a private, gated community with security guards, including swimming pool, pool house, and a glass elevator to take you upstairs if you didn't want to walk up. It took my breath away. Glenn was saying that I could rent a house like this for six months for the same price as I was paying for two or three weeks in Barbados.

At the time, I wasn't having a nervous breakdown or anything, but I was stressed out all the time in Manchester. I was thinking my staff were stealing from me and my girlfriends were messing about, I was the only one working and everyone was taking advantage of me. I am sure it was all in my head but with all the travelling to and from America, I was kicking tables and chairs, drinking too much, and just paranoid. My mind started working overtime about what Glenn had said about six months in Florida for the same price as Barbados. I thought I could base myself in Florida making the short flight to New York, Boston or Chicago to do my business, then fly back to my home in Naples, take my suit off, put my shorts and flip-flops on and relax until the next trip. Then later, with one of my staff flying back to Manchester with the money and the orders, it sounded perfect.

In the meantime, I told friends in New York about my idea and they all said great but you don't want to be in Tampa. The only two places on the west coast of Florida for you will be either Sarasota or Naples. I had not been to either of them. So, a couple of months before Christmas, I came on holiday with my girlfriend Fiona and our daughter Elle and had a week in Sarasota staying at The Ritz-Carlton and a week in Naples also staying at The Ritz-Carlton. During the day, I had agents showing me houses to rent and, in the evening, checking out all the restaurants. I liked Sarasota a lot and then it was down to Naples for a week doing the same thing—looking at homes and checking out all the restaurants. After a week, I liked Naples—both being great places and very similar in my mind. I chose Naples. Not that I knew any difference—you cannot see everything in a week—but because being a couple of hours further south, the weather would be that few degrees warmer in winter. The weather is a little warmer in winter but after now living in Naples and knowing both Sarasota and Naples, I now know that Naples is in a different class from Sarasota. So, I chose well.

I arrived alone on 5th December 2002, not knowing one person in Naples and that's what I wanted, to be alone to chill and re-charge my batteries. Then six months later, I would go back to Manchester and my business and carry on indefinitely because there was no way I could afford to retire or live in Naples. As I said, this place was perfect for me. I could have gone to Miami Beach, Ft. Lauderdale, Boca Raton or Palm Beach where I had many friends, but I didn't want to be in the overnight partying scene. I certainly didn't want to be in Miami that I knew well. If I was bored on a Tuesday night in Naples, I would stay bored but if I was in Miami and was bored on a Tuesday night, I could have gone out partying and arrived home Sunday on a stretcher—that is not what I wanted. I rented an 8000 sq. ft. house in the golf community, Pelican Marsh, five minutes from 'The Ritz' so this was now my area and still is today.

I rented a Jaguar and bought a bike even though I was only staying six months, with no intention of ever coming back. I thought six months of this will re-charge my batteries and back to Manchester I will go, selling shirts until I die because the way I spent money, I would never be able to afford to retire. I went shopping for new towels and bed sheets which was stupid as the sheets and towels in the house were luxurious. If you stay in a hotel, the sheets and towels were used by different people every day and washed but I wanted mine brand new—not caring that after six months I would be leaving them in the house. On one of these shopping days, the assistant said after I bought a ton of sheets and towels is there anything else I can get for you. Looking at the store's giant Christmas tree, beautifully decorated, I said that yes, I would like that tree wrapped and transferred to my house. I was only joking, and she laughed saying we have a young man who does our displays and he decorated that tree; he could do one for you. Without me saying a word, she gets on the tannoy, saying Rick, Rick Foreman, please come to the bed linen department. A few minutes later, this flamboyantly camp, young man comes over saying what can I do for you, dear, with the lady assistant telling him that I wanted a Christmas tree and ornaments as well and all this time I have still not said a word.

He told me to go across the road and buy a six-foot tree, it must be a real one, then let him know when it's been delivered and he would come and decorate it. In the meantime, we will now go around his store and buy ornaments. We walk into that department with a trolley and he's saying we will have four of those and six of those and two of those and eight of those and

I'm looking at the prices of these things, adding up in my head the cost of this tree and I still don't know what the tree I have yet to buy will cost or what he will charge for decorating it. As I am leaving, he shouts out and buys six hundred lights for the tree as well. I had my leg in now so there's no going back but with my mum, Lena, with Fiona and Elle, coming for two weeks at Christmas to see me, it would be nice and make my rented home look like a real family home for my daughter. I could put Elle's, Fiona's and Lena's presents under the tree and make it a real Christmas, so it didn't matter what it cost. I went across the road as I was instructed by Rick Foreman and bought the six-foot tree that was delivered the following day. I called Rick. He came that weekend to my house to decorate this giant tree and he spent the whole evening dressing it while we drank wine, talked and laughed whilst he made this tree look better than the one in his store, if that was possible. It was absolutely magnificent and that was the first of many nights drinking with Rick Foreman as he was my first friend in Naples and still is today, decorating my Christmas tree every year since.

The first few weeks before my mum, Fiona, and Elle arrived, I spent driving, biking and walking around Naples even the back streets and industrial estates, getting to know this beautiful city. I didn't know a restaurant, a bar or even the main streets. Remember, I had only been here once before, months earlier, and that week I spent looking at properties all day to rent. I enjoyed doing this and seeing all the wonderful places here in paradise. I went to The Ritz-Carlton two or three times a week for lunch at their beach restaurant, Gumbo Limbo, and put my suit on to go to the Grill Room at The Ritz every Saturday night. I was familiar with them and felt comfortable but then branched out and took risks the rest of the time. Every restaurant that I tried I liked, and I am still going to many of them today after nineteen years. I would make reservations for one at The Grill, Bleu Provence, or USS Nemo and be the only person sitting alone at a table. In the beginning, at The Ritz Grill Room, my appetizer and entrée came within minutes of each other. I had to tell them that I wanted more time in between courses and they replied that people dining alone and staying at the hotel usually want to be in and out quickly. I said not me, I want to take my time to people watch, listen to the piano player and savor the food and the evening and I still do today. I tell waiters that food can only come to quick never too slow. I am here for the evening not just the food. After that, I would be a minimum of two hours having dinner with a couple of cocktails first and then a full bottle of wine and on many occasions, Nick Dousson, the head of valet at The Ritz, wouldn't let me have my car. He insisted that the hotel car take me home and then I rode my bike or walked back the next day to collect it. I also used to do that when I went downtown for dinner—leave my car, get a taxi home, and go on my bike the next morning. I would ride fifteen miles to collect it, throw the bike in the trunk and bring it home. Plus, it was compulsory exercise that I needed after the alcohol intake the night before. It wasn't long before girls started to notice this single guy hanging around town but most of them were realtors, just trying to sell me a house. I didn't care why they spoke to me, it saved me the trouble. After that, the English accent, the black Amex card and a few dollars in my pocket did the trick.

My mum, Fiona, and Elle arrived just before Christmas, and we had a fantastic time going to The Ritz and other places for dinners and showing them around my new town and home. I didn't realize for one minute that Naples was going to be my home for the rest of my life. We went out every night like you do on holiday and swam in the pool and made lunch at home during the day. It was a sad day when they left, with Elle not really understanding why she was leaving her daddy behind. She was screaming and crying at the airport that she didn't want to leave me and pulling away from her mum with Lena and Fiona telling her that daddy will be home soon, he has work to do. I soon started living the life as a single guy again and was now looking forward to my pals Peter Smith, Martin Reynolds, and Harvey Demmy who were coming for a holiday and to stay at my new house. Even though these pals were very successful back in Manchester, we don't have homes like in Florida. All overlooking the golf course, and security gates with twenty-four-hour security guards waving and saluting you as you come home with swimming pools, very large bedrooms with sofas and tables in them, and two or three lounges that you never even use. They were impressed even though I was only renting it.

After a week of fun and games and fine dining, we went

over to Miami for the day because they had never been. With me, you see so much in a day that it feels like you have been there a week. We went to Bal Harbor shops, South Beach, the Versace mansion, News Café and all the tourist and hot spots. Harvey said to me, "Frank, could we go to the Fontainebleau Miami Beach as that where my mum and dad used to go for their holidays every year. I would love to see it." I said, of course, we can.

We drove to the hotel on Collins Ave. and valet parked and I could see how special it felt for Harvey as we walked through this glamorous hotel reception and knowing that this is where his parents, Gus and Millie, also walked and spent their holidays until they passed away. We walked through the hotel with me showing them around and pointing things out as I had stayed there many times and knew it well. We then went out to the pool area—my favorite spot at the Fontainebleau with the waterfalls coming over the rocks and the caves behind, leading to the bar for a drink. Martin goes to the bathroom and Peter walked around the pool, checking out the girls and the magnificent waterfall area. I am with Harvey ordering drinks when the barman says is your name Frank; I said yes. Harvey getting excited because the barman knows me, but I was also impressed even though I spent many holidays there, I hadn't been for over twelve years. I thought what a good memory he had. Then Harvey asked, how do you remember Frank? He said that I came a few times with the best-looking girl, with the best body that the hotel bar and pool staff have ever seen even to this day. He said that all the guys around the pool couldn't take their eyes off her. She looked that good. That was Jean Clark from Louisville, Kentucky. When Martin and Peter returned a couple of minutes later, Harvey was saying the barman remembers Frank from all those years ago and had the barman repeat his story to the boys. No wonder it had taken me over a year to get that one.

After only a few weeks, I realized how special Naples was and how different it was from my life in England. I loved it and whether it was because I was getting older and all this fell into place at the perfect time in my life again or just fate, I don't know but I was enjoying it. No road rage, no beeping horns, no one looking at you as if they wanted a fight, no drugs and no litter. It's one of the first things you noticed in Naples—how clean the streets were as well as everything else.

I also loved my television with over 500 channels—not like the four channels I had in England and Majorca. I was watching a lot of news on TV and, at that time, it was the elections that I became quietly interested in and being a Conservative in England, I was learning a little about American politics. Not a lot but enough to be dangerous. I liked George Bush and the Republican party which to me seemed to have the same values and principals as Margaret Thatcher and the Conservatives back home. I don't know why but I sent a check to The Republican Party to help with their campaign in Florida, my new home state. I got a nice letter back thanking me for my support and I don't know why but I sent a couple more checks later.

That Christmas and the following years while George W. Bush was in office, I got a Christmas card from President Bush and his wife, Laura, at The White House, wishing me and my family a very merry Christmas. One year, I got an etching of The White House signed by President Bush and after four years, I got an invitation to his inauguration to celebrate his second term as President. All these, I have framed in my home, hanging on my office wall and again I feel privileged and know that none of my pals back home in Middleton have any of these mementos.

But there was aggression and insecurity inside me that's always been there. A few times, I could have started fights with guys, just because I didn't like them or what they were doing appeared stupid and had nothing to do with me. Once, I was sitting at a bar people watching having a quiet drink and this situation happened a couple of times. Two guys were chatting away to two girls, telling them about their new boat, their new car, their tennis club, their new golf clubs and all this time the girls have to listen to this shit with an empty glass in their hand. I said to the waitress, don't ask, just place two glasses of champagne in front of those girls and when she did that they obviously asked where they were from, and the waitress pointed to me saying he bought them for you. Then the guys would want to know why I was getting their girls drinks and I said that you two, cheap fucks have stood there for an hour telling them how much money you have and how great you are and all the time they had to listen to your crap with an empty glass. I felt embarrassed for them, so I got them a drink. Why, is there a problem with that? I'm looking for trouble and they're saying, no, it's alright.

This came back in my favor more than once with a very attractive girl coming to me in a bar saying is your name Frank. A few months ago, you bought me and my girlfriend a drink when two guys were boring us to death. I gave my usual reply of really did I, now I know where all my money went. She laughed; I bought her another drink; we had dinner the next night. That weekend, she spent at Casa Rostron so the old saying: "you speculate to accumulate" certainly works.

One of the first times Jane came to Naples, we were having a cocktail in Campiello, a cool, Italian restaurant, with a friend and his wife. Jane went to the bathroom, and on her way back, a guy who was standing at the bar with three pals stepped into her path and said something to her. Jane shook her head and walked around him. When she got back, I asked who was that; she said that she didn't know. I asked what did he say, and Jane, worrying about the consequence, replied that he had said nothing. I'm then saying he must have said something, what was it, but a little firmer this time and she said that he only asked if I wanted a drink. I went over to the guys and said who wants to buy my girl a drink and looking sheepish, one says, I did. Now, I lectured him about how dangerous it is to chat girls up not knowing if they are married, engaged or even if they if have a boyfriend who might be a psychopath or a lunatic and might come and stick an axe in your head. So always watch for a while to see if the girl is with anyone or even ask the barman and don't try to be a big shot in front of your mates. You could end up spending the weekend in hospital. So, yes, she will have a drink—a glass of champagne. The barmaid, Valentine, who knew me well and was standing by listening to all this, brought me a glass of champagne to ease the tension and handed it to me. I then slowly poured it down the front of the guy's trousers, saying, thank you, and be careful next time. I went back to my guests, but this is just another instance of my old ways—jealousy, aggression and insecurity—coming back.

One time, I was dating this young, fun girl, Tiffany, who went to school at Florida Gulf Coast University and had two part-time jobs. Americans are such hard workers. I think that's why I have always loved and respected American people and their country. One job she had was at the YMCA as a gym instructor and the other one was as a waitress at Blu Sushi, a very trendy restaurant downtown that I used to go to once or twice a week. I always went on Friday nights (still a creature of habit) and this is where I met her. We became friends like I do with most barmen and waitresses and she would joke about me going in with different girls and pals. One time, she said why don't you ever ask me out, just like the beauty queen in Slack Alice and the sambuca incident did. I said whenever you want, just call me and I gave her my card and that was that.

She called the following day; we had a chat and agreed to meet outside Brio in The Waterside Shops, an upmarket shopping mall with two or three good restaurants and many fine shops. I pulled up to the valet in my car and she was there waiting and looked lovely, so sweet and nothing like how she appeared at work. There, she was one of the boys, fooling around and having a laugh in jeans or trousers but now she had this pretty dress on and looked really cute and sexy. I thought to myself, *nice one, Frankie boy*. We had a drink at Brio and she had to show her ID. She was twenty-two years old, but she looked nineteen in this dress. We went elsewhere for dinner and had a great night. A twenty-two-year-old American girl is far more intelligent, worldly and sexually advanced than an English girl of the same age. I am not saying all of them are but in general that is what I've always found starting with my first trip to California with Brian Johnson.

We dated for a year or so and went to all the hot places and had a great time; I even took her to New York, but sometimes she made me feel used. I told my married pal, Elio, about her and sex and he used to say, yes, and what's the problem. You are fifty-two and she is twenty-two; get married then you will soon stop complaining. Tiffany used to call me when she finished school and asked are you at home and most days, I used to lay around the pool as I still felt I was on holiday which really, I was. She would come to the house, walk straight through to the back, peel off her clothes, have sex with me by the pool and leave, saying she had to rush to get ready for work. Obviously, I am not complaining but I used to smile to myself afterwards and think that's usually me rushing off after sex and feeling guilty about having used a girl. But now the roles were reversed, with Tiffany doing that to me but I don't think for one minute she felt guilty.

One night, we had been out drinking and for dinner and I was really wasted. We went to a regular haunt in those days called Café Lurcat. A brilliant restaurant and bar that was open late, with a young, trendy crowd and very good music; it was a real hotspot. During the evening, Tiffany went to the bathroom, and I was there clowning around, hitting on every girl that passed me when one beautiful girl tried to pass. I was moving from side-to-side dancing and stopping her from passing. By now, it was me hitting on her; she didn't want to know but I pushed it. I started chatting to her saying where are you from and any other nonsense that came out of my drunken mouth. She replied LA. I then replied to her that I would be in LA next week which was not true—lets have dinner. I gave her my card and said to call me and let her pass. I had to rush as Tiffany would be back any second.

The next afternoon, I am home alone and suffering the worst hangover ever and my phone rings. I answer it and a voice says is that Frank, this is Trisha. I said who and she says Trisha from LA. We met last night at Lurcat and it all came flooding back to me—the beautiful Asian-looking girl I stopped at the bar. She said that she was due to go home today but she was staying one more day. What are you doing tonight? We could get together if you want. I couldn't believe my luck but as you will read, it was my bad luck. I already had plans to go for a Chinese to P.F. Chang's with my friends from London, Dave and Sue Hutton, who were visiting me and also renting a house from me, along with my next-door neighbors from that house, Paul and Sue Coashe. Tiffany was working that night so I was going alone. I told her that I am having dinner with friends but come and join us, we are having Chinese. Yes, she said, that would be great and that she loves Chinese. I said give me the address where you are staying and I will pick you up. Trisha saying, no, don't worry, give me the address of the restaurant and I will meet you there. I thought nothing of it until later and she kept texting me saying that she was on her way and again when she arrived at the restaurant. I went outside to greet her and walk her to our table to meet my friends. We all talked over dinner, Trisha saying that she was in Naples visiting her sister who was expecting a baby and that she lives in North Hollywood, California. In addition, she was a swimsuit model. She was that good-looking and leaving the next day for home.

Dave, being a world traveler, was asking her about places in Hollywood he knows well that she didn't really know. Dave saying later that he knew she didn't live in Hollywood, otherwise she would know the places he mentioned. I was only drinking sparkling water because I felt so bad from the previous night and when we finished having dinner, we left the restaurant together. We hugged and said goodnight with Trisha getting into my XKR and me saying what do you want to do now. She said it's my last night on holiday. I'm easy, whatever you want to do. Then she said what about downtown where we met last night? I said it will be dead tonight; it's Sunday and no one goes. The real reason is to keep her near my house, just in case I think there might be a chance with her later. I said that there is a sports bar not far away; the crowd is more baseball caps and T-shirts but we can get a drink and talk. She said that sounds good, let's go. The reason I said the sports bar because its halfway to my house from the Chinese, so I am heading in the right direction. The goal is to get her back to my house where the mood lights are on, music playing low, the pool and everything looking and sounding good—ready for the kill.

We had a drink at Pelican Larry's. I'm still drinking water and after about half an hour, I say I only live down the road, do you want a drink at my house. With her repeating again, it's my last night on holiday so I'm easy, whatever you want. I thought, *could this be it? She's a swim wear model and looked every inch of it. Could I possibly get a result tonight?* We drove to my house through the electric security gates, the guard waving goodnight, all very impressive and into my drive. The house lights were on outside and everything looked good and I am now feeling more confident that she might be staying the night. We walked in and she's looking around saying wow, this is beautiful. It was all set up—mood music already playing and the doors to the outside open for her to walk out. She was even more impressed with the landscape and pool lighting with the music coming from the bushes—everything was perfect. I asked her what she wanted to drink and she says whatever you are having, so I opened a bottle of champagne to have my first drink of the night. I asked her if she would mind if I changed into my shorts and polo shirt to which she said go ahead. I came back two minutes later feeling better after changing clothes that I had on for dinner into my casual clothes. I sat down next to her on the sofa, picked up my glass and toasted her saying it was great to meet you and I am glad that you came for dinner and met my friends, along with other nonsense I usually say to make a girl feel good.

I had another sip of my champagne and then that was it. The next thing I remember was waking up at 3:00 a.m. on my lounge floor. I didn't know what day it was or where I was. It took me a couple of minutes to gather my thoughts and to get my memory back to recall Trisha. I went into my bedroom thinking I must have fallen asleep and she had gone to bed but she wasn't there. I looked at my watch for the time and my watch was gone. I felt for my chain and that had gone. I started running around the house, panicking, looking for her and kept finding things missing. I went into my garage and my Jaguar was gone. I called 911 and within minutes the police arrived and I explained what had happened, the detective saying that she must have drugged you. It is the most common theft today and the least reported because usually the men are married and too embarrassed to report it to which I replied: well, I ain't married and I ain't embarrassed, so go and find her. I made a list for the police the next day of what was missing and it read like this: three Louis Vuitton suitcases, a Louis Vuitton suit carrier, a Louis Vuitton rolling case and bag to match on the top to carry on planes, a gold, Cartier Pasha grill watch, a gold Gucci chain, a white gold, Cartier Santos 100 chronograph with diamond bezel and dial, $12000 dollars in cash, 8000 pounds sterling in cash (my pal Dave Hutton had paid me the day before for the house rent) and a small safe I kept behind my trousers in my closet not locked down but it was out of sight containing lots of trinkets that I gave for presents like gold chains, diamond earrings, gold and diamond bracelets, inexpensive watches each worth between $500 and $2000 totaling probably $10-$15000 dollars plus my Jaguar XKR valued $105,000. She had walked into Aladdin's Cave and I had led her there. What a mug I am for a pretty girl. She left a couple of Louis Vuitton pieces—a suitcase and a sports bag—behind because she couldn't fit them into my two-seater car. It must have been jammed full.

The total amount of the robbery came to over $250,000 dollars, including my Jag which the police found two days later, downtown near where I met her. I thought of all the scenarios of meeting her. Firstly, she didn't want to know me in Lurcat; I pulled her, secondly, after dinner she wanted to go downtown and I talked her out of it. If we had have gone downtown and she drugged me she would have had my watch and chain only and that's it. I had little or no cash on me. How lucky was she. Then again, how unlucky was she like most criminals who get caught and end up in prison like a lot of my friends. They make one mistake and then its unlucky for them. Trisha must have been so excited when I was out cold, running around my house finding all this treasure and loading it into my car. She was a pro because she spent time wiping her fingerprints off all my doors and handles and everything she must have touched in my house because the police brushed it thoroughly for prints and found nothing. But like as I said, most criminals usually make one mistake and she did. In my lounge, where we sat and sipped the champagne, she had missed the glasses as she was too busy wiping her fingerprints away from all over the house. She had left her fingerprints and her DNA in her glass. The police bagged the glass and took it away with them.

A few months later, the detective on my case called and asked if I could come down to her office and look at some photos. Well, you know when you see the mugshot of a famous actor or rock star in the paper after they are arrested, it never looks like them. So, what chance did I have of remembering an girl from months ago. They all look like the girls who do my manicure anyway. I drove down to the police station trying to think what she looked like, trying to remember her face but I couldn't. When I arrived, they took me into this office and asked me questions then said that I must be sure it's her and not to say I think it's her or that one looks like her. They had me sign some papers and then put this book in front of me. It was nothing like what I see when watching *Law and Order* on TV. I slowly looked at all these photos of girls many of them beautiful and a couple of times nearly said that looks like her or that could be her but remembered what the detective said to me before she gave me the photos. Looking at them, there were two that I thought might be her then I studied them again and one of the two had a slightly fuller face and I remembered Trisha had a slim face so I said to the detective, that's her. I nearly said I think but didn't and the second I said that she shoved a paper in front of me and said sign here quickly, probably so I wouldn't change my mind. After I signed, the detective said that this was the girl who left her DNA in my house and had a police record in Nevada and New York State. There was an arrest warrant already out for her. But there are murderers in a big country like America on the run for years without being caught so unless we are very lucky, she could be free forever.

I had forgotten all about Trisha and the robbery. A couple of years later, I had a phone call from the detectives saying that they had caught her in Miami. She was stopped for a motor violation and the warrant popped up and then a little later, I got a call from the DA asking if I could go to her office for a meeting which I did. I had never met the DA on this case and as I arrived at the courthouse, I was shown the way to her office. I went in and was introduced to a guy that started asking me questions about the night in question with Trisha. I answered a couple of questions and then said, excuse me, who are you and looked at the women and said and who are you. I had not been prepped or advised what to say or what not to say and didn't know if I should answer these questions, tell lies or tell the truth. The women said that she was the DA on my case and the guy was Trisha's lawyer from Miami. The DA wanted to send her to prison for five years and then she gets ten-year probation as well. The DA said it was alright to answer his questions the best I could. He asked where I had met her and did we have sex and what did we do and generally the story of the evening. Then he said, if you received all your money and goods back would you want my client to go to prison or would you mind if she went free. I asked why, have you got all my stuff. He answered, no, but if I did and you got it back would you mind if she didn't go to prison. I said, no, I wouldn't. The DA explained that they wanted to make me a cash offer to save her from prison which I said that I would consider. I left the office with those two still there and went home thinking things were looking good as I wasn't insured for the robbery so any money now would be like found money after all this time. The DA called me the next day and said that they had offered me 40,000 dollars to save her from prison. I said I will think about it and get back to her which is not like me. If the forty grand had been put on the desk the day before I would have picked it up, thanked them and run out of the office. But now, I had time to think and I thought if she can find forty, she can find sixty grand to save doing five years in prison. What's another twenty grand. I called the DA and said that I would accept sixty but not forty thousand dollars so let them know. She called me the next day saying they have accepted. Greedy me, thinking perhaps I should have said eighty but it's done now and I'm happy with the sixty.

A couple of months later, I got a call from another female DA, saying she was the new DA on my case as the other one had to go on another trial. She said that she and the judge were not going to accept the sixty grand offer and are going to send her to jail as punishment as this kind of crime is growing and they have to set an example to her and other women who try this on men. I said I don't care what you and the judge say. I want my money (as before I had found it but now, I felt it had been stolen from me). The DA said the money she was giving me could be stolen from another guy, so she was stealing from Peter to pay Paul. I said how do you know that. I was fuming and said that it could be my money that she got selling my goods, so don't give me that crap. You only want a conviction on your resume. She said, anyway, it's too late; we already have a trial date and obviously I would be their witness. I said when is this trial and she said 4th April. I replied, oh dear me, I won't be in America then, I will be away. She says then we will make it for June. Again, I said, oh dear, I won't be here then either and every time you set a trial date, I will always be away. Do you understand that, miss. I will never be at your trial. I want my money to which she said then we will have a trial without you; we have enough evidence. I was angry. I had just lost sixty thousand dollars and called Trisha's lawyer in Miami and said to him that they are not letting me have my money. He said, yes, I know. They have just told me but I shouldn't be speaking with you as I am representing the person that allegedly robbed you. What I can tell you is that in American law, if the plaintiffs needs are greater than the defendant going to prison, then that takes precedent. I thanked him and put the phone down.

The next day I composed a letter that basically said, since this robbery, my mother has died and I had to go back to England for six months to sort her estate and funeral out and because of this, I lost the contract that I had with my old company that I sold. I have since married and now I have a family to support and when I sold my business with the money that I received, I invested in real estate in Florida which as you know is now worthless. I have little or no income and desperately need this money to survive. I sent this letter certified mail, one copy to the judge and one copy to the DA and got a letter back a few days later saying that they have accepted my plea and the date of her sentencing. She will be getting five years of house arrest and ten years of probation. I was happy again. On the day of sentencing, I went to court and she looked sensational even better than the night that she robbed me. Her brother was there to support her and he was the one who she said was giving her the money to pay me and he had to prove to the court that he did. The judge said to her in a very stern and threatening voice, lady, five years house arrest means five years at home. If you want to go to the supermarket; you must call your probation officer. You must ask permission and say to him how long you will be and if once you break this ruling, you will go straight to prison for five years, no questions asked. Do you understand and she said, yes, and nodded her head. I got my check for sixty thousand dollars, went straight to my bank and put it into my account. I was a little upset because she had lied to me on our date. She said that she was twenty-four years old and court records showed that she was only twenty-two.

It is unbelievable. I had never heard of this crime before

but when I told my story, it's surprising how many people would say that happened to me or that happened to a friend of mine. The funniest one was an English guy who lives here in Naples and said that happened to me twice. I said how can you let it happen to you twice? Both times, he was in Hong Kong in his hotel. He said, the first time was similar to me in that he had never heard of it and had met a good-looking girl in his hotel bar, had a few drinks and went to his room with her. The next thing he knew, he woke up on his bed hours later with his jewelry, credit cards and money gone. I asked how about the second time? He said that I thought I was being clever. I went to the bar with no jewelry, money or credit cards on me, charged the drinks to my room and I had hidden everything. I met a girl in the bar, had a few drinks and took her to my room. Same thing happened—she drugged me and ransacked my room and found everything. Some people never learn.

Even with the wealth here in Naples, everyone is so low key, you never see cars with chauffeurs as in Manchester and London where cars with their drivers are in a line, parked outside clubs and restaurants. After only a few weeks, I asked Nick, the valet at The Ritz, if any of his guys wanted to work on the weekends driving for me. He said you must be joking; it's at the weekend, they earn their big money with the Ritz clientele. A couple of weeks later, he got me a great guy called Ryan Dahm who worked in the IT department but who used to work on valet as well and he would drive me. Ryan did this for years until he left Naples for California which coincided with Jane arriving. Then, I didn't need a driver with no girls to impress anymore and Jane always drives home.

After I bought my first house in Naples, I always had two cars—a Daimler Sovereign and a Jaguar XKR convertible. Then I sold the Daimler and bought my first Bentley Flying Spur. So, a date went like this: I would ask a girl out for dinner midweek and pick them up in the XKR, usually with the top down, go to a great restaurant and take them home. There was no pressure and then thanked them for a wonderful night, saying would you like to do it again and obviously the answer would be yes. I would pick them up on Saturday night in the Bentley, with Ryan driving, and I am sitting in the back. He opens the door for the girl and again for both of us when we arrived at the restaurant. Every date loved this and was always impressed and, as I said, no one does this in Naples. But that was the idea in the first place, with me looking into their eyes and them thinking to themselves how wide do you want them, Frankie baby. Even though I was relatively poor compared to the guys here, they didn't spend their money or have fun like we do from England so I was quite successful in the dating department. Once again, this is easy when you have no competition.

One dating game that started by accident but nearly got me in trouble was with my first realtor. She was showing me houses three or four a day for about two weeks and one day the last viewing was six o'clock and we finished about seven. I was hungry and innocently asked her if she had plans for dinner and if not, would she like to join me. She was very nice and nearly my age and I felt guilty about her spending all this time showing me homes and I had not bought one yet. We went into the nearest restaurant I knew which was a very good French one and got a table. When the waitress showed us to our table, my realtor took her jacket off to reveal the most sensational body. I promise that I had not even dreamt about it with her as she was much older than my girlfriends plus it was business and I didn't even know if she was married or not.

We had dinner and talked about her business and that she was divorced and how long she had been in Naples and general chit chat. I told her that I was single and looking forward to spending more time in Naples and about my business that I was hoping to sell. She was really interesting and also the first realtor, male or female, I had ever met. It was nice to have company instead of eating alone. After we finished, we walked to her car so she could drive me back to mine that I parked in a nearby carpark where we met earlier in the day. We arrived at my car and she thanked me for dinner and we chatted for a few minutes then all of a sudden, she kissed me. I was shocked but after a bottle of red wine I enjoyed this great kiss from a very attractive older women with this sensational body. It got more passionate and there and then in her car, she had sex with me for the first time. We went out looking at houses and having dinners after that night and always had sex later but, unfortunately, I never bought a house from her. I didn't realize with being new that you really are supposed to have only one realtor. I was riding my bike around my estate one day and saw a really interesting home with a sign in the garden saying for sale. I called the realtor and asked could I view it and she said, yes, and we made an appointment for the next day.

She arrived promptly at the house and showed me around, explaining all the nice things about it but it wasn't for me. I didn't know what I really wanted at the time but this wasn't it. She asked could she show me some more houses in my price range and in my area. I said yes. She was a very classy, mature lady like most realtors in Naples are and younger than the last one. She showed me a few homes over the next few days and again one day our last viewing was late in the day and I asked her if she would like to join me for dinner. She said that she would and we had a great dinner in a nearby restaurant. I don't know if these girls were desperate to make a house sale or that if a guy bought them dinner, they thought that they had to have sex with them. Or perhaps that being single, they just wanted sex or could it be that they couldn't resist the good-looking, rich, English gentleman who is also single. But whatever the reason, after a few days, we also started sleeping together.

The magazines and newspapers in the Naples listing of homes for sale always have a photo of the realtor who is selling the property by the side of the advert. I used to be looking at houses for myself and sometimes thought she's hot or she's not bad. Then I thought I would call a really good looker and inquire about her listing even if it was out of my price range. I was looking to pay between $500,000 to $750,000 but some of these properties were two million to five million. Some of the girls I called must have had their photo taken and touched up ten years ago and looked terrible but a couple looked sensational. The good-looking ones, I would let show me houses at millions of dollars and because they had five-six bedrooms they used to say do you have a big family, Mr. Rostron. I would say no, I'm single but I will have lots of guests coming from England to visit me. They would see a single, handsome Englishman looking to pay millions for a home and think he's a catch. I would play the same game as before and after a few viewings, say can I look at that one at 6:00 p.m. as I have meetings at my bank or my lawyers. Then, after the viewing, I would say have you time for dinner or would you like to have dinner with me. These younger, good-looking ones I would date, take out for dinner and of course sleep with, even when they were not showing me houses. Then one night, it all tumbled down and came to a head when I was in a restaurant/bar with one girl and three others I was dating were also there. All were showing me properties and knew each other. It was embarrassing but something that I never thought about or thought would happen. They all saw me with her and spoke to each other and the next day, I was busted and my game was over but it was fun whilst it lasted. The kicker is that I ended up buying my house from a guy who coincidently happened to be from Manchester.

After a few weeks, I fell in love with Naples and the lifestyle here in paradise. Then within a couple of months, I started looking at properties and before my six-month lease was up, I had bought my first home in a golf community called

The Strand and my first car—a black Jaguar XJ. I went back to Manchester and couldn't wait to get back. A couple of months later, I had a business trip to New York then after flew from JFK to Naples. I spent a month here in my new house, loving it and working out how I could live here forever because a foreigner could only spend six months in any one calendar year in the USA. I had decided after six months of virtual retirement that I definitely wanted to be in Naples. I wanted to sell my business and move here but I couldn't legally so the solution would be that I would buy a place in Majorca and live six months there and six months in Naples. Not a bad life I thought to myself.

The Nightmare

By this time, Jane was living with me in Naples and honestly, it never crossed my mind to marry her. This would have settled all my immigration problems but with me being a life-long bachelor, I was never going to be married. Once, I bought her a beautiful, expensive, diamond ring, with about twenty stones in it, so it looked nothing like an engagement ring. I gave it to her saying you know that I am not the marrying kind but I care about you very much and want to be with you forever so this is a commitment ring to let you know I am committed to you. Jane tells this story about the commitment ring when I gave it to her and how she thought to herself *if he thinks this ring is going to keep me around for five or ten years then he trades me in for a younger model, he has another think coming. He's going to marry me or nothing.* I was planning how I could stay in America forever. I had a friend called Phil Butterworth, one of the boys from my Leeds days who was now living in Marbella. He also wanted to live in the States. He was coming over here buying cars and trucks, shipping them back to Spain and selling them at a profit. He was doing well but he always wanted to live permanently here in America like most of my friends. He was staying at my house and we were talking about this and he saw a couple of Quizno restaurants for sale. They are a franchise like Subway and even though I didn't want or needed to work, he did, so we decided we would buy them and he would run them and getting us both green cards to live in the States.

We went to see a lawyer here in Naples; a real flash Harry who thought he knew everything and told him about our plans. He said it would not be a problem. So, he did all the legal papers to buy the business and our personal documents to take to London to the American Embassy to apply for our green cards to run our new business and live in America. He made my appointment and Phil's a couple of weeks later. I had my appointment date, so Jane and I flew to London and stayed at the Holiday Inn off Berkeley Square for three days then we were to fly home to Naples. I went for my appointment at the US Embassy in Grosvenor Square about five minutes away, dressed smart in a suit with my briefcase holding all the documents for the purchase of the business and my green card visa application whilst Jane waited in the hotel.

I waited in the main hall for my name to be called a little nervous but, as our lawyer had assured us, it was only a formality. Then, it was announced: Frank Rostron go to office number 16, please, and my heart started pumping. I went to room 16. There I was met by this little, arrogant official who spoke to me like I was a terrorist or something. When you complete all these documents, you have to state where the money came from to buy the business and to be able to afford to live in America and for me this was not a problem. I had sold my company for a lot of money and I had the documents and bank statements to prove this. Without even looking at my purchase of the Quizno restaurants, he said that I had been entering America illegally for the last two years and he stamped my passport banning me, saying that I was no longer allowed into the States ever again. I couldn't believe what he was saying. This couldn't be right; it was like a nightmare. I asked why and he turned his back on me and walked away without answering me.

I went back to the hotel and Jane could see immediately that something had gone horribly wrong. My face was white. I felt sick because of the devastation that had happened. My homes and cars were in America, my money was there, I had no property or any personal possessions in England and had a ticket back home in two days with clothes and money for that period only. What could I do. I told her the story. We just sat on the bed and I was so numb, I couldn't even think straight for ages. I gained my composure and called the lawyer in London who I had never met that got me my last two visas: one, a regular multiple visit visa where I could stay ninety days in any one trip and my B2 business visa where I could stay up to six months in any one trip. I called him and explained what had happened and he said to come to his office and, in the meantime, he would call the embassy to see what they said. I arrived at his office and he explained what had happened. In my passport, I had two visas. When I entered the States, they stamp my passport and the agent had been entering me on my Frank Rostron Shirtmakers visa and with selling the business I shouldn't have been using that one. I said to him I had no idea which visa they were stamping for me to enter, plus I was still working for the company for another three years. I had a contract so what difference did it make. He explained that this was a very serious situation and it could be possible that I would never be allowed into America ever again. The legal process could take up to eighteen months or longer for this decision to be reversed, if ever. I didn't know what to say or do. This was the worst thing that had ever happened to me in my life. We went back to the hotel and cried. Jane was brilliant comforting me saying everything would be alright; don't worry. I know she didn't mean it but it was good to hear her say it and without her I am sure my life would be over.

I had to think straight and make plans. I called my pal, Shay McGarr, who owned a Holiday Inn near Manchester City F.C., just outside Manchester city center and told him what had happened. He said come and stay here until you sort things out and decide what you are going to do. We went to Manchester and checked into his hotel. He gave me an executive room which was good of him but it was still a Holiday Inn Hotel which is ok for a couple of days but not indefinitely. It was winter, grey, cold and rainy and typical Manchester weather. We had clothes for three days and that was it. So, Jane flew back to Naples and spent a couple of days organizing everything for me: paying my bills, putting everything on auto pay so I didn't have to worry. She packed suitcases with summer and winter clothes for both of us and flew back to Manchester. I have no idea how I would have survived all this without her being with me and in my life at this time. She was another blessing from God. We called the lawyer in London every single day but got the same answer—it could be a year or two or never that this problem is sorted out.

After a few weeks of Manchester weather even though seeing all my friends was great, I said to Jane come on let's go on holiday, so I planned places that I had never been to. The first trip was to Cape Town, South Africa, staying at a One & Only Hotel, Cape Town. A brilliant hotel but I only chose it because it had a Gordon Ramsey and a No Bu restaurant in the hotel which were both fantastic. We went to all the tourist spots like V & A Waterfront, with all the great shops and restaurants and I made Jane come with me to the stadium that was being built for the 2010 Football World Cup. We got there and saw large signs saying, "no entry" and "danger" and "under construction" but I said to her we must go in and get a photo so we were able to sneak in like kids hiding behind bulldozers and wagons. We got into the center of the stadium before security and construction workers saw us and chased us out blowing whistles and shouting. We were running and laughing all the way until we were out of sight but I got to see the stadium. We got a hotel driver that took us to the wine regions like Stellenbosch and Constantia and we loved it all.

We relaxed and forgot as much as we could about my problems back home even though we still called the lawyer every day. He assured us that, if there was any change, he would call us at once.

With this lawyer being in London and specializing in visas, he knew the US Embassy and many of the officials well, going to their Christmas parties and socializing with them after work. He told us that the guy who I had my meeting with didn't have the authority to do what he did. He didn't have the status to do this without permission but it still didn't do me any good. We returned after a great holiday to Manchester, stayed for a few more weeks, going out with all my pals again, having fun but we are still living in a hotel room. We had to go out every day and night otherwise we would go crazy in the hotel room and the weather was terrible. One of the plusses was that my pal, Shay, had an executive box at Manchester City so we went to all the matches having lunch or dinner in the box before the match with Jane becoming a big City fan.

On our next trip, we went to Dubai staying at The Royal Mirage, another of the One & Only Hotels & Resorts and another sensational hotel. We went shopping every day, then to the beach, eating, drinking and having fun, trying to forget my nightmare. But it was always there in the back of my mind. The longer it went on, the more I thought that I would never be allowed to go back to America but always praying and hoping. Dubai was very good and another experience for us but it had no soul like Barbados or the Caribbean. Everything was fake—the beaches, the buildings; it reminded me of a cross between Las Vegas and Disneyland. Back to Manchester and to real life after another great holiday, we started to plan our next trip which was to island of Mauritius in the Indian Ocean. I had never been and neither had Jane so we had fun and it passed the time in our hotel room, looking at brochures for hotels, restaurants and flight deals for the holiday in Mauritius. I was also thinking about the next year or so as the lawyer kept saying that this process could take a year or more. Even though my pal, Shay, was really good and said we could stay at his hotel as long as we wanted, Manchester was cold, wet and grey and I remembered why I wanted to live in Naples in the first place—the sun.

I said to Jane, we could go and live in Majorca and base ourselves there. At least, we could walk and bike ride in the sunshine and walk the beach and swim. If we rented a house, we could stay at home sometimes and not have to go out every night like in Manchester. I called my friends, Claude and Sally, in Majorca and told them of my plans and would they start looking for a place for us to live for a year or so when we got back from our next holiday in Mauritius. We had another great holiday on this paradise island staying at the sensational Shangri-La Le Touessrok with a butler for our suite twenty-four hours a day, white sandy beaches and clear blue sea. It was unbelievable luxury and even though living this life of first-class travelling and privilege, the stress was getting to us both and we couldn't wait to get to Majorca and start to live a normal life together.

We were still calling the lawyer every few days with him repeating the same old message. But then, he suggested that we should get married. In case all else fails, we could go this route later. I spoke to one of my best pals, Mark Warren, who if he didn't have something, he knew someone who did. I asked Mark if anyone had any nice diamonds? He replied I have three. He said I took them as security on a loan and the guy has not paid me back. He gave them to me and I took them to a friend in Hatton Garden, London, called Malcolm Freeman to have them checked and valued. Malcolm gave me the all clear and I chose the largest of the three, of course, a four carat, round, beautiful stone that at the price Mark gave it to me, I could have sold it to Malcolm wholesale and made a profit so I got a good deal. I gave the stone with a design to another pal of mine, a jeweler called Laurence Levey who made the shank with four diamonds two down each side. It was exactly as a picture that I gave him and then Laurence gave that to us as our wedding present which was another great gesture from a good friend.

That Saturday night I took Jane to The Lowry Hotel for dinner as it was her birthday and I ordered a bottle of Dom Perignon to drink. Now she knows we never drank champagne with food as its too gassy and not class. I always told her only drug dealers and armed robbers do that to show off so she asked besides her birthday what are we celebrating. I gave her a birthday card which she was about to put in her bag and I said, no, open it here. She says, no, I will open it back at the hotel. I insisted, no, open it now, please, and she read the words "Happy Birthday, darling, I love you . . . and will you marry me . . . PLEASE." I went into my suit jacket pocket and pulled out the ring I had made and gave it to her. She was shocked and little did she know so was I but she accepted and gave me a kiss and a big hug. I realized over the last few months living in a hotel room with her and all the travelling she had to do, going to and from America, sorting out all my problems and business stuff that I could never have done it without her. I was in love with her and was going to spend the rest of my life with this special girl. I would have married her in the next year or so anyway but with the lawyer saying to get married all that I did was bring it forward. I still joke to this day that I only married her for a green card.

The Wedding

Jane now took over the show taking me to different hotels, looking at rooms and menus for the wedding, and all the stuff that I had no idea about. But girls plan this from when they are young so she knew exactly what she wanted. We decided to have our wedding at The Lowry Hotel in Manchester where I proposed to her over dinner. What a great job she did; sixty close friends, all couples, except my single pals, about ten of them sitting on a guy's only table. Except after about half an hour, my single girl pal, Gemma Hopkins, joined the boys as she said it was more fun than sitting with her mum and dad, Christine and Derek, who also have a home in Naples that we see all the time.

Forty years earlier, I had a friend called Warren Shaffer who was a photographer and we used to hang out and go to Abersoch in Wales together. I always joked with him that if I ever got married that he would be my photographer and I had not forgotten. I had not seen Warren for probably over thirty years and that was at one of my friend's weddings where Warren was taking the photos. I called his house and his wife answered the phone, me asking if this was the photographer Warren Shaffer's home. She said, yes, then I said could I speak with him, please? She asked who I was and I replied, Frank Rostron. I could hear her saying, Warren, Frank Rostron is on the phone. He came to the phone and said after all these years, Frankie, I can't believe it. Where are you, what are you doing, and a million questions in two minutes.

I said, Warren, do you remember I always said that if I ever got married that you would be my photographer? Well, I'm getting married. I want you to be my man and photograph my big day. We went to his house in Whitefield north Manchester the following night and it was great to see my old friend and meet his family. To plan and discuss my wedding, he particularly said for me not to drink alcohol that day, before the photographs, as alcohol distorts your face and the photos would turn out much better if I didn't have a drink. I said you are joking. On this day, I would be so nervous, I would have to drink more than normal but I did as Warren asked and I think my first drink was near the end of the night. In all, I think I only had two glasses of wine and a glass of champagne and I certainly didn't have any of the cocaine that Jamie bought for the boys that night. Warren knew the Lowry Hotel well, having done lots of weddings there before and what a great job he did with everyone loving our wedding book which comes out every time we have house guests.

My neighbor and best friend in Naples, Elio D'Amico, agreed to be my best man and flew to Manchester with his wife, Anna, for my wedding. Another old pal, Barry Tildsley, organized the day for me, including the wedding cake and a Master of Ceremonies to announce the guests and to host the evening. The dining chairs were covered in pale blue with large, blue bows on the back along with the cake also in pale blue, the colors of my beloved Manchester City. Even though I say it myself and Jane says it often, it really was a great wedding. My dear friends, Ann and Cedric Jeffay, made the day extra special with Ann dressing and helping Jane to get ready and Cedric walking her down the aisle as Jane's dad had passed away when she was a young girl. The Master of Ceremonies said it was the best wedding he had ever done being so informal and fun. He said it was like a great party rather than a wedding.

During the evening, some of my pals stood up and said a few words and told a story or two about me to the other guests. Cliff Brierley told the story of taking me to AA and my pal, Ray Ranson, the former Manchester City star, talked about the time he first went to Majorca with me. Ray said that he was twenty-one years old and at the time, he was captain of England under twenty-ones and a regular Man City first team player, with a glittering football career ahead of him. He said then after the holiday with me, his career went downhill fast but he had a fantastic social life. Of course, that was not completely true. Ray had a brilliant football career for Manchester City, Birmingham City, and Newcastle United playing over 440 league matches and representing England at U21 eleven times. But, of course, he had a great social life with me going to Majorca many times which included lots of stories I cannot tell as he is married so I cannot put them in the book.

During the evening, the hotels food and beverage manager came over to me to say the boys table had ordered a case of champagne and was it alright. I was paying for all the drinks on this day and night but I told him not only was I not paying for their champagne but unless he listened to me carefully the hotel wouldn't be getting paid either. The guy's table, all my very best friends, are a mixture of gangsters, thieves and rogues who I could trust with my life and my money but no one else could. I explained to the manager that if they give you a credit card for the champagne check the ID for the person who gives it to you because it will not match the card. Also call the card company first for authorization and even after these checks you still won't get paid. If they give you cash have the cash checked because it will not be real so again you will not be paid. Do you understand. So don't come tomorrow asking me for the money; you have been warned. He looked at me as if I was joking and walked away. The boys got their champagne and brought a bottle to Jane and I never heard if the hotel got paid but, if I was a gambling man, I would put money on that they didn't or at least American Express or Visa didn't.

Before the dinner started, the Master of Ceremonies asked for quiet whilst I gave Jane the wedding present that I had bought for her which was a Cartier watch. But for fun we also gift wrapped another present which was a Manchester City shirt. So, he gave me the present which I then passed to Jane to open. When she opened it out came a Man City jersey and everyone laughed with the Master of Ceremonies saying that was only one of my jokes and here was the real gift. As she was opening it, she said I wonder what it is, with Ray Ranson shouting out, it's the away strip again with everyone laughing. But then laughter turned to cheering as Jane opened this red and gold Cartier box, showing everyone her new watch. The day and night went perfectly with the band playing and everyone dancing to the sounds of the Blues Brothers music.

A few weeks earlier, we had been at San Carlo, the best Italian restaurant in Manchester, owned by one of my oldest friends, Carlo Distefano, and frequented by soccer stars, TV and film stars every time they are in Manchester. The walls are covered with photos of them with Carlo or one of his managers and every night there are paparazzi outside taking photos of the stars going in and out.

On this night, we are having a drink at the bar, waiting to sit down and Jane jumped and spun around. Behind her were two guys looking like poster boys for a prison gym. They had shaved heads, their arms covered in tattoos, white T-shirts and muscles on top of muscles with one apologizing immediately for his friend. Apparently, Jane had her dress label sticking out of the back of her dress and this guy's friend had just tucked it back in not knowing that is not the thing to do. I don't know what would have happened if this guy hadn't apologized immediately because even if I had one of my tough mates with me, I still wouldn't have fancied a row with these two. That's what would have had to happen because of what he did. This guy kept on saying that he was sorry and could he buy us drinks but we said, no thanks and went to our booth. The next week we were having dinner again in San Carlo and a guy came up to our table saying that he was sorry for his friend. I had forgotten all about the dress label incident. It was the same guy again saying he was sorry and embarrassed about what his mate did last week. He genuinely meant it and I appreciated his apology and couldn't believe such a tough gangster-looking guy could be so nice and respectful.

Usually when situations like this have happened in the past, the other person has found out who I am or more like who I know and my connections around the town and in the country. They usually want to apologize or make friends before it goes too far like Selwyn said to my girlfriend's new boyfriend after I beat him up badly in Brambles years earlier. This guy whose name was Jamie had no idea who I was or who I knew. He really was embarrassed. That goes to show what a good person he is and how you can never judge a book by its cover. Later that night, after dinner at San Carlo, we went to a club and were having a drink when the manager came over with an ice bucket with a bottle of Krug champagne. He said, Frank, someone sent this over for you. I asked who and he nodded in the direction of Jamie, the guy from San Carlo who stood alone with his own bottle of Krug. I went over and thanked him and said it was unnecessary. He had apologized and that was enough but he insisted. I asked who he was with and he said that he was alone so I asked him to join us, which he did and after that Jamie became one of my new best friends. He had no idea my name was Frank Rostron or that I even made shirts or that I had a shop in town which made it even more impressive.

After about fifteen minutes, he asked me without speaking but just by touching the side of his nose and a nod in the direction of the toilets which I had seen hundreds of times before. I have even done it myself many times if I wanted a line of coke. Now I had not had any for years and especially since I had been with Jane but I followed him to the toilet and he walked straight into a cubicle gesturing me to follow him in. Now two or more people going into a cubicle together had stopped a long time ago with it being so obvious what you are doing and especially with a toilet attendant in there. I looked at the attendant and he says if you are with Jamie, it's alright so in I went. This Jamie guy was impressing me more by the minute and I was still wondering who the hell he was.

He opened a bag and made four lines and I had two of the best I have ever had. I went back to join Jane and my friends and I was flying—a big smile on my face, non-stop talking and wanting to go dancing, Jane didn't know what had happened but she knew something had because of my new strange behavior and fooling around with my new best pal who suggested we go to another club around the corner. We finished our drinks and left for this club that didn't really open until 2:00 a.m. when most other places were closing. We walked there and the lines to get in were massive at both sides of the entrance. Jane was scared stiff as the crowd looked intimidating to say the least and mostly black so I don't know why Jane was intimidated.

She now tells the story of why she was upset. Because we had been to dinner and we were dressed up, it seemed all these people were dressed to rave and take drugs. Jamie walked straight to the doormen who immediately lifted the ropes to let us in, leaving two hundred revelers standing in the cold outside. I thought *who is this guy?* It's the treatment I always got in Manchester but I had been away a couple of years and clubs and their doormen had changed. We went in and the music was great. I started dancing on the spot as Jamie orders champagne and the waiter takes us to a VIP room with no one in but us. I said Jamie, I want to be out there with the crowd not in here on our own. I think Jane felt safer in the VIP but I was buzzing and wanted to dance. During the night, I saw many old friends from my Hacienda days who were still raving and they came up hugging and surrounding me, with me introducing them to Jane and the rest of my party then offering me coke and pills but me refusing as I had Jamie with me. That night, lots of people came up to Jamie, kissing him or hugging him that reminded me of the movie *The Godfather*. Especially a lot of Chinese people, so I asked Jamie who they were and he just said that he likes Chinese working for him, whatever that entailed.

After that night, Jamie came out with us a lot being our guest sometimes but he was always a gentleman and obviously well-connected with plenty of money. One time, City was playing United at Old Trafford and Jamie, being a City fan, said he would get the tickets for the match. We met in town and it was getting late so I said that Jamie, we must go. He said not to worry, he had it sorted and we left twenty minutes before the kickoff. Jamie drove us in his car at speed down Deansgate towards Old Trafford, ending up in a cul-de-sac one minute from the ground, parking on someone's front lawn. A guy comes to the bedroom window shouting, what do you think you are doing? With Jamie saying, its only me and the guy saying, sorry, Jamie, didn't see it was you. I asked him who that was and he said my tenant. I own that house and a few more in the area and all the time I'm thinking *who is this Jamie, and what does he do for a living*. I would never ask him what he does for a living as it's something you never do. If the person doesn't have a nine to five job or work in a shop or an office but has unlimited money you know it must be something illegal. I asked the staff in San Carlo where I met him and they didn't know either, just saying that he is their best customer, coming in three or four times a week, eating lobster, drinking champagne and spending thousands of pounds in the restaurant. So, I left it at that.

The weeks running up to our wedding, we spent a lot of fun time with him and we both liked him a lot but I couldn't invite him because I hardly knew him. The venue was already booked and planned plus everyone there were friends of mine for over thirty or forty years and I had only known him for a couple of months. I had no idea how he would come dressed as every time I saw him, he was in jeans and a white T-shirt proudly showing off his tattoos and not one of my sixty guests even on the boys table would be able to show one. But I asked him if he wanted to come to the evening party after the main event of the wedding service and dinner was over. He said that he would be honored to be there so both Jane and I were happy.

He had met, over the few weeks that we knew him, the single guys that were coming to the wedding and said that he would bring as my present a dozen small bags of coke, a gram in each for the boys. That would cost around six hundred pounds so that was a nice present that the boys appreciated. They waited all day and night for Jamie to arrive, excited to know that they had a present coming with me telling them to behave or they wouldn't be getting it. I also said that when he does arrive to go to the bathroom one at a time as I don't want my guests knowing or wondering what the hell is going on with you all disappearing at the same time. I might as well have talked to a brick wall and should have known better. The minute Jamie walked into the room, they all dived on him welcoming him like a famous rock star dragging him outside for their gifts leaving their table conspicuously empty for at least an hour.

They all came back one at a time with a big smile on their faces grinning like hyenas, with one of the London lads dancing by himself facing the wall and door frame for the rest of the evening. Jane and I left for bed about 1:00 a.m., tired after the day and the previous days, going to our suite in the hotel, but left everyone else still dancing and parting until much later.

When we went down for breakfast, the first person that we saw was Laurence Levey, my pal who made Jane's engagement ring. He had a bandage over his eye. I asked what happened and he said he had been in hospital all night and just got back to the hotel after having stitches above his eye and his head. Apparently one of the boys was chatting up Billy McPhee's girlfriend and Billy, walking past this room, saw this, picked up a brass statue and threw it at him. He missed the guy but hit Laurence who was sitting next to him. The statue hit Laurence on the head splitting it open with blood everywhere. The police were called, Laurence went to the hospital, Billy had gone home and that was that—a typical end to a Manchester party whilst the bride and groom slept peacefully, missing all the action.

The next day we went back to the Holiday Inn to plan our move to Majorca but in the meantime carrying on the same in Manchester until it was time to leave for Spain. Hopefully, it would be soon and in a few weeks. But we couldn't go until Claude and Sally had found a suitable property for us. Next, we had a trip to Southern Ireland for the wedding of Shay and Anna, our hosts from the Holiday Inn and all the single guys, my friends from our wedding, were also there so it was a blast.

Once again, Jane and I are the party poopers, going to bed tired about 1:30 a.m., leaving everyone, including Shay's mum who was in her '80s and the rest, dancing in the hotel bar as if they were twenty-one years old. As we were walking out of the bar, my pal, Billy McPhee, of the brass statue and Laurence Levey fame, shouted to Jane what room are you in and I will give you a shout for breakfast in the morning. Before I could say, don't give it to him, she shouted back 128? I said no, no baby, you shouldn't have given it to him. Jane asking why not? When I got my bill the next morning, with over 2000 pounds worth of champagne and booze on it, she realized just why not. I told the hotel that I was in bed when all this stuff was signed for and it wasn't my signature on the receipts anyway even though it was charged to my room. They could see clearly from when I checked in that it wasn't my signature and so another hotel didn't get paid for the champagne. I have seen this trick with my friends done many times over the years but Jane hadn't. She knows now and is learning fast.

The Nightmare is Over

We flew back to Manchester after the wedding in Ireland and a couple of days later, Jane got an email from the lawyer in London, asking to call which I did immediately. He said where in the world are you and I told him we are in Manchester and he asked how soon could I be in London as the US Embassy wants to interview me. I said that I could be there in the morning as early as they wanted me. So, he said alright, I will tell them and get back to you. I was so excited and also nervous because I knew if I could get in front of someone of authority and explain to them about the visas, it would all be ok. I was still working for my old company and it was a big mistake with no intention or I had no need to enter the USA illegally having two visa's and that they would understand. We sat in our hotel room waiting for him to call back. It seemed like an eternity and about an hour later he called saying that I didn't need to go to London and the order banning me from the USA had been overturned.

I could go back but not for a week or so because it takes that long to sort out the paperwork on their side for immigration and customs but in the meantime to book our flights. I first had to get a regular ESTA visa online until a plan was made for me to stay there. We hugged and cried for ages. We couldn't believe that this nightmare was nearly over; we didn't leave the room all day we were so overwhelmed with joy. We went online to get my ESTA visa, filling all the questions in carefully but at the end, it said "refused." I couldn't believe it. I was devastated and called the lawyer explaining what had happened. He said he would call the Embassy to see what they have to say. He came back to us and said the Embassy had told him that I didn't need an ESTA visa as I have a US visa that didn't expire for another two years. Giving the exact dates and that it was in my previous passport that had expired and even though your passport expires the visa doesn't. I thought *that is unbelievable. The US Embassy is telling me details about a visa I have that I didn't even know about.*

When Lena died, I found my old driving license along with other papers and the letter I wrote when I was eight years old, saying I was going to be a footballer and buy my mum a house. Well, also in her box was my old, expired passport. She had saved it for all those years. Good old Lena saved me again even whilst she is in Heaven. The box with the passport was in my home office in Naples, so Jane would have to fly back to Naples and send it to me by FedEx before I could buy my ticket back to the States. It just seemed obstacle after obstacle but I didn't mind because I could now see the light at the end of the tunnel. So, she flew home the following day to find my passport. She called me from the house and said she had been up all night looking for my passport and that she had found Lena's box in my office with my old driving license but there was no passport. She said that she had searched the house all night but couldn't find it until she fell asleep.

I could have sworn that's where I had seen it but if not, it must be in my safe. I gave her the combination and said to call me when she had it in her hands. I remember it like it was yesterday. I was in a carpark behind Piccadilly gardens in the center of Manchester and sat waiting for her call to say she had my old passport in her hand. She called twenty minutes later saying she had tried every combination I gave her and the safe wouldn't open. I screamed into the phone; you can't be doing it right. Did you wait for the clicks and all the instructions I gave. She said, yes, of course, and she tried it again with me listening through the phone from a car park in Manchester and her in Naples, Florida. I thought that I was going to die from the stress of it all—so near yet so far away. She tried it several times with me listening but with no luck. Then I put the phone down on her. I couldn't take anymore.

The next morning, she called me early to say that she had the passport with the visa in. I couldn't believe it. I said what happened and she told me the story that only Jane Bond could have done. I don't know another girl who would or could have done this. She had no idea where I bought the safe. It was a five-foot-high gun safe converted inside for my needs. I had bought it from a local store called Bass Pro Shops in Florida but she didn't know that. Embossed on the side of the safe was the manufacturer in St. Louis, Missouri, so she called them direct to explain the problem. They said the engineer was out of the office but would call her later. He called later that day and she explained her husband was in England and gave her the code but she could not open the safe, giving the engineer the code. He asked if you pressed the hash button after the code. She said, no, he didn't give me that so he said try it again, pressing the hash button after your code. She did that and it opened immediately.

I had not been in the safe for over six months and you press the buttons automatically without thinking and I had forgotten that after the code, you had to press the hash button. But she had the passport and had done a brilliant job. It was now Saturday and FedEx was closed until Monday so she went in first thing on Monday morning and sent the passport to me, Frank Rostron (Guest) at The Holiday Inn, Oldham Rd., Newton Heath, Manchester. I couldn't book my flight until I physically had the passport in my hand with the visa inside and I sat in the hotel reception all day Tuesday and nothing arrived. I sat in the reception again Wednesday and at about noon a FedEx van pulled up with the courier and a couple of parcels. I ran up to him and said do you have a package for Frank Rostron. He looked and, with the receptionist saying it's alright, passed me the envelope with my passport. I couldn't believe it; I ripped it open and just stared at the visa. It had all been so unreal and a complete nightmare but it still wasn't over until I walked into my house in Naples.

I went that day and bought a return ticket from Manchester to Ft. Myers, Florida, changing planes at Chicago, knowing quite well that I wouldn't be using the return part for a long time, if ever. I didn't care; I just wanted to go home. Speaking with Jane before I left, she told me to call her the minute I get through immigration at Chicago. All the time, from checking in at Manchester airport, going into the business class lounge, and waiting to board for the eight hours flight to Chicago, I was so nervous. I couldn't eat or drink. I felt so bad and it got worse as we got nearer to Chicago and as the plane landed, I felt terrible. I had bad vibes about everything and I thought that I was going to be sick, walking down the corridors towards the agent to inspect my passport.

It was my turn. I handed him both of my passports. He looked at me then looked at his screen, looked at me again then looked at his screen again. I wanted to die; I felt so bad. Then he said, in such a harsh rude manner, what are you doing here, where are you going and I told him for a holiday to Naples, Florida. I didn't even say to my house, although he must know everything about me. He said are you seeing customers whilst you are here. I couldn't believe what I was hearing. I replied, no, I don't have any customers. I am retired. He says again, are you seeing any shirt customers whilst you are here? Again, I say no. He said so if I search your cases will I find any shirt patterns or samples? I said, of course not. I thought, *what information do they have on you in their computers?* It's scary. He said how long will you be here and I said that I wanted to be home by such a date as I have a big soccer match that I want to go to. He stamped my passport for two days after that date and that I must leave the country by then. I had a six-months visa, saying I can stay for six months and he should have stamped my passport leaving six months from my date of entry but he didn't—only until my supposed soccer match six weeks later.

I went to collect my cases in the customs hall and was still shaking and worried even though I had nothing in my cases to worry about. I walked straight through without any problems handing my customs declaration form to an agent there and put my cases on the carousel for my next flight to Ft. Myers. I carried on walking not looking behind me still thinking that I am going to get a hand on my shoulder any minute, saying, excuse me, sir, come this way but it didn't happen. I was outside on American soil for the first time in six months and still trembling as I called Jane and she said are you through? I said yes. She screamed with happiness but I remarked how intimidating and rude the agent at immigration was and what a hard time he gave me. I was still so upset and angry but she said not to worry, you are in America and you will soon be in Naples, so hurry up. I don't know why because she was right but I still felt sick and even flying first class from Chicago to Ft. Myers, I still couldn't drink or eat anything because my stomach was aching and I still thought I was going to throw up at any minute.

We had been referred to a law firm in New York that

specializes in visas and problems like I had just experienced. We had been speaking with them about what happens when I get back into the country. There was a legal procedure to follow and we couldn't say that we were married as I entered the country as it would look like we got married just for the purpose of staying here. We also had to wait I think thirty-five days before they could send my passport and immigration form to them for an indefinite extension saying we are applying for a green card. Then I couldn't leave the country which I didn't want to anyway until the day I got my green card. So, everything was being done officially and legally. As the days went by and my papers were going through, I felt better but still didn't feel 100%. My new lawyers in New York assured me everything was going to be ok but I had heard that from lawyers before and had a nightmare experience but I believed and trusted these people.

It was great to be home and we soon settled back into our old routine, seeing friends, walking the beach, and going out for dinner. I organized a wedding party for Jane, with a sit-down dinner for about forty-four of our closest friends, around the pool at my house. We had live music and caterers serving great food and a bar with Raphael, a friend and barman from The Ritz-Carlton, making the drinks and pouring the wine. My other pal, Rick Foreman, making the center pieces for all the tables like only he can do. He made flower arrangements with candles, bows and confetti sprinkled everywhere. It was really beautiful and felt like a wedding. I put disposable cameras on every table for guests to take pictures of everyone dancing and partying until late at night. It really was like our second wedding but for our American friends that couldn't attend the English one and that we had not seen for over six months.

Paradise

We were now home in paradise for good and living a great life together. Jane had started work as a realtor and I was retired with a few properties and my life was good and I felt so blessed. Every morning, I had a routine as I always have had. I would go for coffee at 7:30 a.m., meet the guys, some retired and would stay late, others still working and would leave at around nine o'clock. We would chat about girls, football, basketball, new restaurants, anything that guys gossip about. Then after, I would go on my walk. That would usually be for an hour then sometimes go grocery shopping or other jobs that Jane had for me. Then go home for lunch unless I had lunch at a restaurant with pals or house guests.

One morning, I was driving in my XKR convertible to coffee. It was 7:30 a.m., a beautiful blue sky, the sun was shining brightly and I am stationary in a traffic jam on Immokalee Road near where I live. I am looking around, thinking how lucky I am. I am retired, I have beautiful home, a beautiful wife, great cars, enough money to go out for dinner tonight with anyone who asks without worrying. I am healthy, go on great holidays and life couldn't be any better. I have all this after coming from poverty and a council house when I look to my left and there towering above me is a new church that's only been open a few months. It's a pure white, New England design with a seventy-five-foot steeple.

I remembered something a friend from Manchester, Stuart Marks, had said to me a couple of years earlier in Barbados. At the beginning of that week, Stuart's dad, Victor, called my shop, saying Frank are you going to Barbados this week. I replied, yes, why and he asked if I would take Stuart's prayer books as he has forgotten them. I said, of course, I would and about an hour later, Victor's chauffeur pulled up outside my shop in his Rolls-Royce and brought in a package wrapped in brown paper tied with string. I flew to Barbados on Friday morning and when I arrived at my hotel called Stuart and arranged to deliver them to him which I did later that day. I said to Stuart you are only here for two weeks could you not have managed without them for a couple of weeks to which Stuart replied something that I will never forget. He said, "Frank, I have a beautiful wife and family and we are all healthy. I have a very successful business and I have wonderful life and I am very blessed and if a man cannot spend one hour a week to say thank you for his blessings, then there is something wrong with him." What Stuart said to me that day always stayed in my mind and when I was sat in that traffic jam at 7:30 a.m., with the sun beating down on me, looking around, thinking how lucky I am, I remembered his words. I knew I had to go to that church on Sunday morning to say thank you for my blessings.

I had never been to church, only for weddings and funerals and I didn't enjoy any of them. That was because it was either a friend getting married that I wasn't happy about because I thought all guys should stay single and have a life like mine. Or a friend who had passed away and I was upset and sad. But always, when I was in a church something spiritual happened that I cannot explain and I always had an experience that I also cannot explain. There was no way I could leave a church and within minutes start swearing and cursing or trash talking as I do generally in my life. This experience lasted a long time before it wore off. I got home from coffee that morning and said to Jane that we are going to church on Sunday to which she replied I'm not going to church, I pray privately. She said I went to church every week of my life with my mom and dad and my sisters. We had to but now I go when I want. I will go with you on special days like Christmas and Easter and other important holidays which she does.

Sunday arrived and I was excited but a little nervous and I went to The First Congregational Church of Naples for the very first time. As I was walking in, there was a line of about six people waiting to talk and shake the hand of the pastor. With me not knowing the protocol and with being really nervous, I brushed past them all into the sanctuary and took a seat at the back. They looked at me as if I had just jumped the turnstile at a football match without paying. I again had this spiritual experience during the whole service. It felt good but strange and all I did was pray saying, thank you, thank you, thank you for everything in my life. I couldn't believe just how many things I had to say thank you for. From my mum, Lena, who loved me from the minute I was born to Jane being in my life today and the dinner I had in a great restaurant the night before and everything in between. I could have been there all day saying thank you.

After the service, even though I was at the back, there was already a line walking out, shaking the hand of Pastor Les Wicker and his wife, Phyllis, and thanking him for a great service. There was no room to push past like an hour ago so I waited my turn and as I approached to shake his hand, I couldn't find any words to say and broke down. I rushed out crying my eyes out. I jumped into my car and drove home, sobbing and crying all the way and then sat in my garage for over half an hour until I regained enough control to go in and face Jane. As I walked in, she was in the kitchen and said how was church? With that, I ran into our bedroom and locked the door which we never do and broke down again, falling to the floor. I was crying uncontrollably with Jane knocking on the door asking if I am alright with me saying, yes, I will be out shortly but I was there sobbing and crying for over an hour before I was in control enough to talk to her.

What happened that day I don't know or cannot explain but the spiritual experience I had was overwhelming and even now, some days, I still have a tear in my eyes during the service. Ever since that day, I go to church every Sunday to say thank you for all my blessings that I don't deserve and ask for forgiveness for all the crimes that I have committed in my life and the way that I have lived it. If we are travelling and away from Naples, I always try to find the nearest church, whatever denomination it is, and go in to say thank you and ask for forgiveness. I will always remember Stuarts words "if a man cannot find one hour a week to say thank you for all his blessings, there is something wrong with him."

On one of my last business trips to New York, I was with a friend in a client's car. He said we are going to miss you, Frank, and all the fun we have when you are in town. We will have to tell our wives that you are having a golf tournament and come to Naples and play golf for the weekend. In fact, we don't have to even play. We can leave our clubs in lock-up at JFK and just come and have fun in the sun. The next night, another client said the same thing so I said that last night, Tony said you could come and play golf for the weekend in Naples. We could get together and have a reunion there in the sun. He said what a great idea; my two partners would want to come as well. At the end of the trip, about a dozen or more customers had verbally signed up for a weekend in paradise to play golf. A couple went even further saying we could play for money, all contributing and instead of the winner takes all, give it to charity. After church that Sunday, I asked Pastor Les if the church had a charity. I explained about my wealthy clients from New York coming to see me for the weekend and playing golf and giving the prize money to charity. Pastor Les said that we do, it's called Miracle Limbs Courage in Motion and they support amputees. Well, with my dad and sister being amputees that no one in New York or Naples knew about, you couldn't write this script. Pastor Les then saying I will play as well plus a few of the church congregation love golf and they will play and from that day the FRANK ROSTRON GOLF INVITATIONAL was born.

    I had a girlfriend, Porsha Salvino, who said why don't you invite Donald Trump to play in your tournament, he loves golf. This was a couple of years before he became The President but I said, I don't know him, how would I get Trump to play. She then said my best friend from school, Keith Schiller, who I speak to all the time, works for him. He's the head of his security and travels the world with him. She said give me your invitation and brochure and Keith will get it to him. I thought *The Ritz-Carlton, Bentley Motors and now Donald Trump. Dare I dream that big or am I reaching too far?* I gave Porsha everything in an envelope and fingers crossed waited and hoped for the best. Two weeks later, I got a brilliant letter from The Trump Organization, 725 Fifth Avenue, New York, NY 10022 saying:

> Dear Mr. Rostron,
>
>   Mr. Trump received your invitation to attend The Frank Rostron Golf Invitational on October 25th-26th through Mr. Keith Schiller. While we truly appreciate you bringing this to our attention,

Mr. Trump usually does not attend events not hosted at one of his clubs and unfortunately has a prior commitment during that time. We thank you for reaching out and wish you the best of luck with this invitational.

Best,

Chelsea Frommer, PA to Mr. Trump

I was told that if I held my tournament at one of Donald's golf clubs that he would definitely attend and play. I was planning on doing that another year when we made the event even bigger but the first couple of years, I thought it needed to be in Naples because of the guys who lived here and the travelling even though it was only to the other coast. But I imagined in a couple of years, The Frank Rostron Golf Invitational being sponsored by Rolls-Royce Motor Cars and played at The Trump International Golf Club in Palm Beach, then having my celebrity auction and dinner at The Mar-a-Largo Club that evening. Then, I would have known that I had made it but unfortunately, Donald decided to become The President and I got arthritis in my hands. Alas, Frank and Donald were never destined to become an item.

I had no idea what I was doing but we started telling people about it and strangers were calling me asking if they could they play. Pastor Les announced the event in church as it was for the church charity, Miracle Limbs Courage in Motion. I got three friends to be on my committee: a lawyer, a banker, and Pastor Les himself and we were off. The three committee members were mad golfers so their friends wanted to play plus friends of friends and before long we had over 100 golfers and 180 people for the evening dinner and auction. The committee told me what was needed and ideas for the event but I had my own spin on it. With me not playing golf, it was just going to be a party and social event. For everyone else, it was a golf tournament for charity. I decided to make it a weekend golf event but everything had to be bigger and better than all the other charity golf events in Naples and there are over a hundred of them. The program was twice the size of the others—the size of a glossy magazine—and when the others had a first prize of dinner for four somewhere, I had a Bentley Flying Spur for a hole in one. I also had an Infinity SUV for another hole in one courtesy of my local car dealership. I had spent over a million dollars with them since I arrived in Naples so I think that they felt obligated and that was just for starters.

We needed auction prizes and one committee member said that there is a company that sells you auction prizes and you pay after the auction and if they don't sell then you return them like on consignment. We got their brochure and ordered a dozen or so great prizes just to impress everyone like a Tom Brady signed jersey, a week in Aspen skiing or a house in Hawaii—all good stuff like that. I didn't know until later when my friend, Gary Metzner, from Sotheby's in Chicago, who kindly did my auction for me, said that people, if they find out that the prizes are on consignment, they don't like it. This is because they bid top dollar thinking every penny is going to the charity not to some company in New York and a small fraction of what they spent going to the charity itself. This was my first venture into this charity stuff so I didn't know and had to learn fast but of course he was 100% correct. It was too late now for this year but after that we had every single auction prize donated, no more consignment ever again.

I am the best salesman around as most of you know so I went to work on my friends and contacts not only getting golfers to play but sponsorships from friends and clients on Wall St. They were advertising in my program, giving prizes for the auction, gifts for the players, gift bags and, of course, luxury cars for my hole-in-one prizes. I had to get a golf club at which to play this tournament and even though it's not the best in Naples, I chose The Ritz-Carlton Tiburon Golf Club because of the prestigious name. I thought it would be more impressive when I'm selling the event around the States and even in England and I remembered what I was told as a young man that "you have to put a show on the road." The Ritz-Carlton and Bentley Motors—it doesn't get a lot more impressive than that. We had the evening dinner and celebrity auction at The Ritz and I got a special rate for anyone who stayed the night or weekend. That first year, a couple of guys from out of town said that their wives wanted to come not to play golf but for the weekend in Naples and the evening dinner. I didn't know what to say because I thought this was going to be a men's only event but when I told my committee they said to encourage women to come. This was because they are great for the dinner auction, they start bidding and get their husbands at it and buy more stuff, so women it was. I was learning fast.

That first weekend, the guys from out of town wanted to know what we were doing on Friday night. I had not even thought about it. The golf was on Saturday and the dinner and auction were on Saturday night but I hadn't planned anything for Friday. But, of course, they are flying into Naples from different parts of the States and even a few pals came from England so they expected to see me, plus have a jolly up in Naples on the Friday before the big event the next day. The first year, I think there was about twenty guys from out of town and about eight wives so Jane said you take the boys out for dinner and I will take the girls out and meet you later somewhere and again another night on the FRANK ROSTRON GOLF INVITATIONAL calendar was born.

I took the guys to Barbatella, a restaurant that had sponsored me and Jane did the same with the girls to another sponsor, Osteria Tulia. The Blue Martini gave us the VIP room for the night so that's where we all met later, drinking and dancing until the early hours. How I got to the course at 7:00 a.m. to start organizing the day along with the guys to play golf, nobody knows but we did. The next day, golfers from Naples were asking the guys from out of town what they did last night and they told them what an unbelievable night they had and where they had been. All the Naples guys saying to me that they want to be at the Friday night party next year, with me saying, sorry, it is just for the out-of-town players. On the last year that we did the event, I think there were over fifty guys and thirty-five wives and girlfriends for the Friday night dinners and the Blue Martini party.

The event became well-known for the great golf locations, the evening dinner auction and party but also for the luxury cars and the celebrities that I got to come. The gift bags that every player received was an idea that I got from the Oscars in Hollywood. Everyone that plays gets a goody bag with sponsors giving us gifts to put inside. We had Tommy Bahama sports watches, bottles of Macallan whisky, packs of golf balls, Bentley pens and Bentley baseball caps and gift certificates from different businesses. Each goody bag contained over 500 hundred dollars value in gifts. Not bad seeing that the whole event only cost 300 dollars to play, including the evening dinner and auction. Yet, I still raised over 100,000 dollars net profit for the charity.

I got friends from England like ex-Manchester United legend, Paddy Crerand, get me a Wayne Rooney signed Manchester United shirt, plus a pair of his boots signed. Chubby Chandler, my old pal from Manchester, getting me sensational golf stuff like a Masters flag signed by the winner, Danny Willett, who Chubby managed and the soccer agent, Michael Morris, getting me a Ryan Giggs signed Manchester United shirt. George Graham, the Arsenal legend, getting me Arsenal signed shirts and another English pal, Gary Shaw, got me Usain Bolt signed running spikes, as at the time he was working with him in Jamaica. I had Rodney Marsh, ex-QPR and Manchester City star, sign half a dozen City shirts that I had already sold to City fans in England with a photo of him signing the shirt to them. Rodney came to all my golf events and was a big hit amongst the guys particularly the English ones.

An old friend from England and a brilliant artist called Malcolm Young who now lives in New York gave me three of his paintings and this went on and on. So, after the first year, we didn't need any consignment prizes. We had lots of great suggestions for raising money and one of my favorites was a dining tree where we got a Christmas tree and put over a hundred and fifty envelopes on it, hanging like ornaments. In each envelope was a dining certificate from a local restaurant the minimum in each envelope was fifty dollars but most of them were 100 to 300 dollars and an envelope only cost fifty dollars so you couldn't lose. There was a small chance of you getting your money back but most of them you doubled or even trebled the cost of your ticket and it was all going to charity. People were buying half a dozen at a time and in the end, I had to say two maximum to give others a chance. Another one was a pal from Naples, Bryan Rodriques, who had just started a luxury car hire company and offered me a Ferrari to raffle for a day's free hire. I had Jane and a pal set up a table selling raffle tickets at the green where the Bentley Flying Spur was on show for ten dollars a ticket. Just to impress the girls, plus a chance of having a Ferrari for the day, the guys were buying 10 or 20 at a time. They raised over six grand at their table.

One of my English pals let me auction his Spanish villa for a week. We sold that every year and another friend gave two gift certificates valued at 2500 dollars each to spend at any of his menswear stores. One of the more expensive gifts for the main auction was a piece of beautiful diamond jewelry donated by Todd Schusterman who owns The Diamond District here in Naples. Mark Slotnick, a good friend from New York who came every year to support me, always bought the piece of diamond jewelry. He said it saved him going Christmas shopping at Tiffany & Co. for his wife. Another local jeweler gave us a Bentley Breitling watch because of our partnership with Bentley Motors valued at many thousands of dollars. So, we had the greatest of silent and live auctions prizes which everyone loved, making it a Naples charity golf event to put in your calendar and not to be missed.

The next two years we played and held the event at different golf clubs. First after The Ritz was at the Bonita Bay Golf Club. It had a beautiful course, with a great clubhouse and restaurant in Bonita Springs. The third one which was probably the best of all was at The Naples Grande Golf Club that owned a hotel on the beach as well. We all stayed there that weekend and held the evening dinner and auction at the hotel. This year, I changed things around a little making Make-A-Wish my charity receiving the money and my main sponsor being Rolls-Royce Motors. They gave me a Rolls-Royce Wraith as my hole in one prize and at the desk where everyone signed in and registered, I had a line of Rolls-Royce models: The Phantom, The Ghost,

The Wraith and The Dawn—to say it was impressive was an understatement.

The Sheriff of Lee County, Mike Scott, wrote a letter with a photograph of himself which took a full page in the program and I quote:

> "On behalf of the men and women of the Lee County Sheriff's office, I congratulate and thank you for supporting Make-A-Wish. Your generosity and compassion for those facing significant challenges makes me even more proud to be of service to such a wonderful constituency in Southwest Florida. Special thanks to our friend and Honorary Lee County Deputy, Frank Rostron, for his unwavering commitment to this noble cause."

I was honored and flattered that the sheriff would say those kind words about me but no one knew I was an honorary deputy sheriff, especially my old pals from the Quality Street Gang back home in Manchester. They said jokingly, particularly Ricky Gore, what did you do for that? Are you a fucking grass or something. A grass for those who do not know English slang is a police informer. I replied, if I was, you would all be in the nick (prison) and they laughed.

I did the golf tournament for three years and it was like running a busy company. I worked most days for nine months putting this event together. Sometimes, most nights going to restaurants begging for certificates for my dining tree and goody bags, plus getting advertisements for the program. It didn't stop. To be truthful, I wasn't getting any help from my committee but I loved it and it's what I am good at, plus it was for charity. I was retired, living here in paradise and didn't have a lot to do anyway so it worked out perfectly and what started as an excuse for a few pals from New York to come and see me ended up as a very successful Naples charity golf tournament.

It ended in the fourth year, although I was disappointed as it was getting easier, because people were now coming to me to play and to sponsor the event and advertise. Also, I was not getting any help from my committee, I got arthritis really bad in my hands and couldn't even muster the enthusiasm to go out and sell the event. I was in so much pain and it got so bad and my hands were so swollen that Jane had to put my socks on and off, put on and take off my shirts, and fasten my shoelaces. I was in pain day and night so there was no way I could run this business for nine months which is what it really had become.

I went to the doctors who gave me arthritis pills with side effects that were worse than my arthritis itself—like you can get heart disease, heart attacks, strokes or even cancer. It was frightening. Friends suggested many things like CBD pills and oil and others recommended acupuncture so at the same time as I stopped taking the doctors pills, I started with both of these recommendations. Within a few weeks, my hands started to improve, the swelling went down, with less pain. I started to feel normal and after about three months of acupuncture and taking CBD pills, my Chinese doctor went on holiday to Europe for six weeks and I didn't hear from them again. They used to call me the day before my appointment to remind me but with my hands getting better plus the 150 dollars a session it cost me, I didn't go back to the acupuncture doctor. I've kept on my CBD pills and today my hands are great except for a little early damage on a couple of fingers. I can't clench my fists tight together but my fighting days are well behind me so it's not a big deal.

So now, I am back to being retired here in paradise, back into my old routine of going to coffee every morning but now, not at Starbucks but at Seed to Table near my house. It is an unbelievable venue that officially is a massive grocery store but people go for lunch and dinner and at night there are DJs and live music. People are dancing and the four bars are packed with drinkers and people are still doing their shopping with trolleys in amongst all this until late at night. It really is a special place and after my coffee I do my walk for an hour and still do the jobs Jane gives me to do. Then I go home for lunch and in the in the afternoon I make my phone calls, do my emails or just relax by the pool, watch soccer or make dinner for Jane when she gets home.

Compared to the life that I have lived, this is now in slowdown mode and I love it. I still enjoy and look forward to having guests but it's not like the old days, staying at the house for two or three weeks and out partying every night. Jane will not have that anymore and I understand it's now her home as well. She works every day and most weekends and she doesn't want to come home to a house full of people and have to entertain them so now they must stay in hotels. They can stay at the house for a weekend or two or three days at the most which I encourage and even though Jane stays home most nights because of work, if I have pals in town, that's my excuse to go out with them. We drink, have dinner, and reminisce about the old days but without getting into any trouble. I still do a few deals to earn a few quid and to keep my mind occupied like rent, buying or selling a property, buy and sell a few watches and I still have friends who want shirts made. So, I am not completely finished yet. Until that day arrives, I will enjoy every minute here in paradise but never forgetting where I came from and how blessed my life has been.

Lightning Source UK Ltd.
Milton Keynes UK
UKHW021226080722
405575UK00007B/1477